D1448853

# A TIME TO SEARCH

Henry Ehrlich

# A TIME
# TO
# SEARCH

PADDINGTON
PRESS LTD
NEW YORK & LONDON

Library of Congress Cataloging in Publication Data

Main entry under title:
A Time to search.

1. Adoption—United States—Case studies.
2. Secrecy (Law)—United States. I. Ehrlich,
Henry, 1949-
HV875.T55   929'.1   77-6314
ISBN 0-448-22241-8

Printed in the United States
Designed by Patricia Pillay


**IN THE UNITED STATES**
PADDINGTON PRESS LTD.
Distributed by
GROSSET & DUNLAP

**IN THE UNITED KINGDOM**
PADDINGTON PRESS LTD.

**IN CANADA**
Distributed by
RANDOM HOUSE OF CANADA LTD.

**IN AUSTRALIA**
Distributed by
ANGUS & ROBERTSON PTY. LTD.

**IN SOUTHERN AFRICA**
Distributed by
ERNEST STANTON (PUBLISHERS) (PTY.) LTD.

*For my parents*
*Norma and Eugene Ehrlich*

All of the stories in this book are true. The names
(including those in newspaper reports), places, and
dates have been changed in order to protect the
privacy of the individuals and families concerned.

# Acknowledgments

I would like to thank Emma May Vilardi, genealogist, historian, and research coordinator for the Adoptees' Liberty Movement Association in the western United States, for her generosity with her invaluable time and expertise. Without Emma Vilardi's efforts, thousands of adoptees would have no access to proven search techniques. Further thanks to Emma and Anthony Vilardi for being such gracious hosts during my research in Nevada.

Many people deserve credit for special contributions to my research: Belle Blanchard and Jonathon Lazear for introducing me to Florence Fisher; ALMA organizers Sarah Howe, Mary Anna de Parq, and Mary Jo Rillera for their assistance on the West Coast. For discussing various aspects of adoption with me, I would like to thank David Leavitt, attorney; Lenore Campbell, head of the Los Angeles County Department of Adoptions; Annette Baran, social worker; Dr. Joseph Davis of the Committee on Adoption and Attendant Care, American Academy of Pediatrics; and Randy Fasnacht, formerly of the New York Foundling Hospital.

Appreciation also goes to Chris and Phil Clark and Merry Conway for their hospitality; Nicolette Gramatikos for stationery supplies and moral support; Susan Baxter and Stanley Eigenfeld for keeping me fed and in good humor; Karen Thomas for her company; and my neighbors, the Hansens, for their company and innumerable cups of coffee.

Thanks to Antony White and Janet and John Marqusee for their enthusiasm and support in this project and to editors Catherine Carpenter and Diane Flanel.

Finally, thanks to the many adoptees, natural parents, and adoptive parents who shared their experiences with me.

H.E.

# Contents

# Preface

Since the 1920s those who have been adopted in most parts of the western world have been prevented by law from learning the names of their natural parents. In a sense they do not know who they are. Because all of us are innately curious about our origins, statutory restrictions on access to personal history deny a basic human right. It is time for the law to recognize that grown adoptees are not exceptions. With all of humanity they share the need for roots, for heritage.

The adoptees who tell their stories in this book have had widely different experiences in growing up adopted. Their motivations for searching for their natural parents are correspondingly different. These stories have been selected among thousands of available histories because they represent particular facets of a larger issue. Adopted children, like all other children, carry within themselves genetic characteristics and early childhood experiences that cannot help but affect them as they mature. Some adoptees can only reach an understanding of themselves by searching for and meeting their natural parents—by filling in the gaps in their personal histories. Others have a more practical need to fulfill, such as the verification of a hereditary disease.

I went to work in July 1975 for the New York headquarters of the Adoptees' Liberty Movement Association (ALMA), founded in 1971 by Florence Fisher. In early 1973 this dedicated woman wrote *The Search for Anna Fisher*, the story of her twenty-one-year search for her natural parents. I am not an adoptee and was totally unfamiliar with adoption as a public or personal issue until I began to work for ALMA. I soon learned through my work that the adoptee in our society faces a life filled with special problems. As part of my duties I answered letters from adoptees and natural parents all over the country, and I became aware that most of the problems faced by adult adoptees stem from the present state of adoption laws—a strange mixture of Victorian charity and social theory.

I also learned that the need to complete a self-image by discovering the truth about the past is not confined to any one social or economic class, nor does a desire to know one's natural parents have anything to do with childhood happiness or unhappiness. This desire is simply a human need more evident in some individuals than others. Yet adoptees are the only group prevented by law from satisfying this need. The records of their births and adoptions are sealed.

The problems faced by adoptees are unique, but, as the stories in this book show, they are not the only parties to adoption who stand to gain from open records. Sealed records affect millions of people. There are approximately 2,500,000 adoptees in the United States alone, and there are at least four times as many natural parents and adoptive parents, half-sisters and half-brothers.

The secrecy and the finality of adoption affect adoptive and natural parents as well as adoptees themselves. Adoptive parents, no matter how much they love their children, cannot supply them with the missing information. Natural parents are almost always plagued by doubts over the fate of the child they gave up, even though they relinquished the child willingly and with clear conscience. For natural parents, a reunion with their grown children can bring relief from years of quiet suffering.

Through litigation in the federal courts of the United States, ALMA and other groups are seeking to overturn state laws that prevent adoptees from learning the full circumstances of their adoptions. Some steps have been taken toward reform of state laws by legislators and judges. Various plans involving intermediaries have been put forward. It is my conviction that the problems of people like those who tell their stories here will not be solved until adult adoptees are given full access to their own records.

It is time for the rest of us, who take our individual histories for granted, to support those to whom full knowledge is denied. I hope my book helps by showing that, for many, there is indeed a time to search.

# Introduction

The practice of sealing birth records began in the United States, but in 1956 an English court wrote: "In general, it is the policy of the law to make the veil between past and present lives of adopted persons as opaque and impenetrable as possible, like the veil which God has placed between the living and the dead." Such a legal attitude effectively summarizes the source of the innumerable obstacles placed in the path of today's adoptee who searches for his past, his heritage, his identity.

Yet the search for one's natural parents is not a recent phenomenon. Ancient civilizations had extensive, complex adoption laws that hint at the need of some adoptees to find their roots. In the Code of Hammurabi, dating back to the eighteenth century BC, we read that if an adoptee denied that his adoptive parents were his real parents, his tongue was cut out. If an adoptee "searched out, looked upon his father's house and tried to enter it, hating his adoptive father," he lost his eyes. Under certain circumstances, however, an adoptee who showed an extraordinary longing for his natural parents would be permitted to rejoin them.

History, religion, and mythology are rich in stories of adoptees. Romulus, the legendary founder of Rome in 753 BC, was raised by wolves along with his twin brother Remus. Moses was abandoned by his mother because she did not want him brought up as a slave. The tragedy of Oedipus resulted from his ignorance of his background. He unwittingly killed his father and married his mother. Incest taboos being what they are, he probably would not have married his mother if he had known who she was, and he would have been spared the punishment of blindness and exile.

In ancient Rome the distinction was made between full adoption and conditional adoption. *Adoptio plena*—full adoption—could proceed only after the adoptee's natural father was dead. Isn't this implicit recognition of the ties that bind children to their natural parents?

Social order in the civilizations of Babylonia and Rome depended heavily on the custom of ancestor worship. Certain rites had to be performed, prayers said, and graves kept. Businesses and trades needed heirs to carry on. Adoption, then, was a system of providing for continuity when couples could have no children of their own.

After the fall of Rome, this complex aspect of Justinian law disappeared. It was not until the nineteenth century that a social order formed that was stable and complex enough to provide a system of inheritance based on anything but blood relationship. Before new adoption statutes were passed, children were placed, not as adoptees, but as apprentices in the shops of craftsmen, permanent house guests in the homes of the wealthy, and servants in the homes of merchants.

Modern adoption laws first appeared in the Napoleonic Code and Germanic law. The English and the Swiss were the last nations in Europe to allow adoption. The first adoption law in England was not enacted until 1926, a year after the enactment of a law that permitted inheritance by non-relatives. Adoption was accepted slowly in England and throughout Europe. Many saw adoption as an "out" for immoral women who wanted to escape the consequences of their acts. Others thought adoption a misguided attempt to imitate nature. Reformers thought the middle classes were after cheap domestic help. As a result, when adoption legislation was passed, adoption procedures reflected the suspicions of the various opponents and provided for strict control of the ages of adoptive parents, consent of the natural parents, and assurance of inheritance. In addition, the adoptee was related only to the parents, not to brothers and sisters.

In the United States the growing need for labor led to early acceptance of adoption. The first state to enact adoption legislation was Mississippi, in 1846. As white settlements expanded westward, an extra pair of hands could always produce more than an extra mouth could consume. Less attention was paid to class origins in the United States. The relation between indentured servitude and adoption was hard to shake, lasting until the twentieth century.

Church-related charities established the first adoption agencies in the United States. Their interest in serving members of their own sects made it almost impossible for a couple of no particular religious background to adopt a child. Those with unconventional religions faced the same problem. This pattern has survived the creation of public agencies.

Public non-sectarian agencies did not gain a strong foothold for a long time. Politicians in the United States were not eager to expand government into areas in which private institutions were already functioning. They were supported in their resistance by those who felt the taxpayer should not play a part in relieving immoral women of their responsibilities. Adoption was not a large-scale solution to problems of child welfare. Children who did not meet rigid criteria were not adopted; they were put into institutions or foster homes.

What were the goals of these exclusive adoption agencies? The evidence suggests that they wanted to supply childless couples with the kind of children they imagined they might have had themselves. A catalog published in 1923 by The Willows Nursery, a private, non-sectarian institution in Kansas City, Missouri, self-proclaimed purveyor of "Superior Babies for Adoption," gives vivid expression to the spirit of adoption as it has been practiced widely. Founded in 1905, The Willows placed approximately 35,000 children and sheltered women from all over the United States and abroad before it closed sixty-four years later:

It is known by those who have knowledge of their parentage that many among The Willows' babies are fit to grace any home in this country that is open to a child. Investigators have found that there are thousands of childless homes that would welcome a child if they knew it was of good health, intelligence and moral fibre.

The catalog goes on to boast of "an exceptionally high grade of babies for adoption":

They are practically all "Accidents of Fate," being children of unfortunate parentage. Since such babies must be for adoption, The Willows is proud of the opportunity of placing them in homes. Taken as a class, they are recognized as being far brighter than the average child offered for adoption. They are more affectionate, have better dispositions and temperaments and have clearer heads and brighter intellects. The risks usual with adoption are decreased, and their attendant consequences diminished.

These babes, although by man's customs and laws deprived of a mother's love and a father's guidance, are nevertheless some of Nature's choicest products. Nature, in her universal law of reproduction, does not require man's obedience to his matrimonial custom to produce a desirable specimen of the race. These children, born as they usually are from clean American stock, mostly from the rural districts of the Central West, although more or less from all over the United States, make far more creditable members of a family than the legitimate child born in the poverty and vice of a congested city.

If the character of a child is influenced by its heredity, can there be found for adoption a better child than the offspring of young, healthy Americans of good education and refined home influences? The parents of these babies are largely from well-to-do families, for The Willows, having no charity support, must of necessity charge well for the class of service it renders.

Among the babies that have been placed in the past are the offspring of school teachers, college instructors, music teachers, Sunday School teachers, orchestra and concert players, high school, college and university graduates, ministers, lawyers, physicians, real estate operators, brokers, reporters, wholesale and retail merchants, manufacturers and bankers, as well as farmers. A complete list would include practically all the better vocations, both commercial and professional.

It is our experience, gained from intimate knowledge of practically forty-five hundred cases, that the mothers of these babies are good girls. To some, in the safety of their matrimonial ties, it may seem paradoxical to call these unfortunates "good girls." But they are in the majority of cases simple, unsophisticated young girls, lacking knowledge of their sexual self, who either through love or ignorance make their first misstep. Being uneducated in these matters the result is inevitable. Too late they realize their mistake, and the security of The Willows is the only course left to protect themselves and their unborn babe from a life of shame and disgrace.

The catalog has something to say about every issue that might be raised by prospective parents: "Given an average child and having placed it at birth under proper surroundings, practically anything may be done with it." Only 10 percent of "its future would be due to heredity." If less desirable children, "the offspring of depravity," can do well in adoptive homes, these pedigreed children have unlimited potential.

There is even a section that shows that the "chosen baby" story is not entirely apocryphal. "It is important for you to come, see and choose one for yourself. . . . Each baby is different. It has its own personality and it will perhaps be this 'something a little different' which will decide you in taking some particular child."

Using a careful mix of specious science and sociology, the authors of the catalog manage to pander to every desire of the affluent couple who perhaps lack the one thing that money can't buy anywhere else—a child who will fit comfortably into their image of themselves as a family. The pages are adorned with photographs of Willows' products, captioned with such phrases as "pet of the flock," "a home maker," "a heart breaker," "the flower of the nation," "an empire builder," "a future president."

No doubt The Willows was sales-oriented, seeking potential customers who shared Willows' values. But their spiritual heirs can still be found today, perhaps most obviously among those who pay large sums to lawyers who compile catalogs showing photographs of handsome college students willing to procreate for a price.

The Willows characterized itself as a business, so the sales approach is at least understandable if not acceptable by modern standards, but the most prestigious sectarian adoption agencies relied on snob appeal as well, restricting their clientele to members of the Junior League and other organizations associated with high social standing in the community. These criteria were very much in force when the movement for sealed records began in the mid-twenties at the behest of the agencies. The undemocratic tradition of sealed adoption records was the invention of this special interest group.

Since World War II standards of adoptability have broadened. Not only is there a shortage of healthy white infants, but there are too many non-white, non-infant, and handicapped children to ignore. It is now generally acknowledged that adoption is more agreeable than institutionalization for all children. But only in the public sector is there enough flexibility to handle massive new problems of child welfare.

The State of California, for example, did not establish any public agencies until 1949, when the supply of white, healthy infants exceeded the capacity of private agencies to handle them. But the Los Angeles County Department of Adoptions has since grown into the world's largest such agency, with other California municipal adoption agencies growing commensurately. It has been these public organizations which have led the way in providing homes for needy children.

Sealed adoption records have impeded the correction of abuses by all kinds of adoption agencies, social workers, lawyers, and other independent adoption agents. If law and social pressure had not prevented adoptees from investigating the circumstances of their own adoptions, the inadequacies of the system and the people who operate within it might have come to light long ago, and the publicity might have led to reform. Indeed, this secrecy doesn't guard anyone's rights as much as it hides the caprices of a generally uninformed class of people.

In the International Child Welfare Review of March 1976, Mrs. Hilary A. Halpin, Secretary General of the National Children Adoption Association in London, wrote, "In the early years, agencies were run by voluntary workers, enthusiastic, dedicated, and in almost every case, totally unqualified." The description is apt. Unfortunately, the zeal of amateurs didn't die with the paying of salaries. By the time England got its first modern adoption law in 1926, the pattern of adoption in the United States had been firmly established. Agencies were staffed by professional workers who were enthusiastic, dedicated—and unqualified.

Annette Baran, a Los Angeles social worker who spent nearly twenty years working for adoption agencies, has become a prominent critic of adoption practices and an advocate of open records. With Arthur Sorosky and Reuben Pannor, she writes on adoption as part of the Adoption Research Project. At the Annual Conference of the American Orthopsychiatric Association in 1974, Annette Baran described her profession:

> We adoption workers were a rare breed. Our practice was more fulfilling and more happiness-getting than any other. What social worker hasn't felt omnipotent and benevolent and ecstatic when she has called a family and announced she has their baby for them? What adoption social worker hasn't basked in the grateful hallelujahs heaped upon her by the beatific parents during those visits of the supervisory year? She personally has brought fulfillment to their barren lives. Other social workers deal with family breakdown, mental illness, old age problems, child abuse, unemployment, poverty, etc. Adoption workers hand out happiness. No wonder I stayed with it.
>
> Of course, working with the terrified, tearful pregnant girl wasn't fun, but we helped her understand that out of love she would relinquish her child, we safely put her in the protective confines of a maternity home, we assured her that she could resolve her ambivalence and could go back to her usual existence (with contraception), and life would be beautiful again, neatly solving her problem and making her emotionally virginal again.

It became apparent to Annette Baran, as she gathered experience, that there was a great deal wrong with agency practice. The agency head bragged that their agency was the best, because only 3 percent of their natural mothers kept their children. Other social workers would agonize over their mistakes after failing to persuade a mother to relinquish her child. They encouraged adoptive parents to bring their children in when there were any questions about their origins, but they made it clear that the information divulged would be inconsequential.

When adopted adults came back to seek real information, we saw this as sick and obsessed and we spent the time quizzing them about why they had a need to know. We sat there in possession of their record, their identity, and we grudgingly offered them bits and pieces that we decided they could and should have.

Over the past fifteen years I have seen many birth parents who should never have relinquished their children and would not have if they had really been given the right to decide, and not made to feel guilty if they kept, and I have to admit that I was probably instrumental in perpetuating this practice for a long time.

I sat behind the desk facing adoptees scores of times during the past years, and I honestly admit that I cringe now as I recall my attitude and my behavior with them. That they remained polite and controlled is an indication of how pitifully eager they were for even the little I told them. I know now because of the many adoptees I have spoken with during my research. They have described their intense anger at that woman, me, who had the power to keep their records from them. The stranger, me, sitting there deciding what facts of their lives she would permit them to know.

Annette Baran finally left the adoption field after the Supreme Court overturned anti-abortion legislation in the United States. Reasoning that with abortion legal, abortion counseling should have a place in adoption practice, she organized a conference to discuss how to accommodate this new alternative.

"The agencies came to fight," according to Mrs. Baran. "They argued that abortion was psychologically terrible for the natural mother, *worse than adoption*." If abortion is psychologically worse than adoption for the natural mother, then obviously there are consequences for a mother who relinquishes her child after all. The social workers were at last acknowledging that it isn't possible to become "emotionally virginal."

Adoption workers often have what one writer has called a "pseudo-professional conscience." Dorothy Hutchinson, in an article entitled "Competence and Conscience in Homefinding," published in 1958 and reprinted in *Readings in Adoption* (Philosophical Library, 1963), coined the term to describe "a conscience that has absorbed indiscriminately the culture, the standards, the values deeply imbedded in years of social work practice in general, and of adoption practice in particular." The "pseudo-professional conscience" seeks procedures that can be applied as uniformly in all phases of adoption work—homefinding, counseling of the natural mother, and so on—as a surgeon's techniques are applied in removing an appendix or tonsils.

Hutchinson goes on to describe the case of a childless woman who had a hysterectomy and went into a brief depression at the prospect of never giving birth. She took a part-time job in a nursery school and, after becoming accustomed to children, applied to adopt a child. She was turned down. Her admission of her single brief depression was enough to disqualify her.

In these times of shortage of healthy white infants for adoption, people are sometimes disqualified because they are too fat for the social worker's taste or because the prospective adoptive mother wants to continue working. At the same time another woman whose bridge-playing amounts to a full-time occupation will be accepted.

Some social workers quit the adoption field soon after they enter it. A Detroit woman quit after a stint of adoption work while still a student. She couldn't turn down weeping childless couples, but at the same time she couldn't persuade natural mothers to give up their children. As Annette Baran said, "Adoption agencies are geared to adoption." If workers can't produce, they are useless.

Many younger social workers are carrying on a kind of quiet revolt in dealing with adoptees who have launched their searches. They recognize the dubious assumptions on which adoption practices are founded and feel uncomfortable in being forced to apologize to grown adoptees for their predecessors' mistakes. While most agencies authorize the release of "non-identifying" information, the definition of this term is vague. With diligence and experience, a searcher can use non-identifying information to find his natural parents. Persistence can lead even a wary social worker to divulge important information inadvertently, and repeated interviews may convince a less rigid social worker to give much more than guidelines allow.

A worker in one agency told a searcher: "Here in front of me is your file. It is open. It has all the information you could possibly want or need to find your natural parents. I am going to the men's room and will be gone for ten minutes. You are not to touch this file." Of course the adoptee went through the file, and in a short time had a joyous reunion with his natural parents and their relatives. Obviously the "pseudo-professional conscience" has the power to help as well as hurt, but the negative examples far outnumber the positive ones.

While some social workers, as in the case above, can improvise when faced with a new problem, the "pseudo-professional conscience," by using rigid ideas in previously unheard-of situations, makes judgments that are bizarre and sometimes dangerous.

For example, in 1947 a woman gave birth to a daughter in New Orleans and nine days later gave her up for adoption. In the early 1950s, this natural mother began to suffer from hardening of the skin. After many years of steadily worsening health, the condition was diagnosed as scleroderma, a cancer-like disease. In order to give her daughter, by then in her late twenties, the benefit of a full medical history, the natural mother contacted the adoption agency in New Orleans and turned over her medical records. After some time had gone by, she sought assurance that her daughter had been given this information. The social worker said that she had called the adoptive parents instead. They decided to put the records in their safe deposit box to be opened upon their deaths. When does the adoptee pass infancy and become a party to her own adoption?

Many of the stories in this book adequately describe the pain which can be inflicted on adoptees by social workers who seem to enjoy their own power. But adoptive parents can also suffer because of the actions of social workers.

An adoptive mother said that her daughter's natural mother changed her mind five times in the five days after giving birth. The problem was that the natural mother considered herself married, but the baby's father had decided to move back in with his legal wife. On the fifth day, the social worker called. She was jubilant. The mother had finally made up her mind to give up her baby.

Should the adoptive mother have had to suffer the pain this knowledge caused her? She writes:

> I almost wanted to say, "No, I don't want the baby, give her back," but of course I didn't because that would make me crazy, wouldn't it? And they wouldn't give her back. They would have given her to someone else. If this sounds as if I don't love my child or didn't want her, nothing could be further from the truth. But why did such pain have to be a part of my good fortune in getting a baby? In this particular case, perhaps the mother should have kept the child. But, in all cases, why can't the natural mother be given more consideration and her rights be respected to a greater extent? She should be honored instead of castigated.

In theory adoption is associated with renewal. A young mother gives up her child and goes on to build a "new life." An adoptee is issued a new birth certificate. Ironically, in justifying adoption, many people resort to images of death. As adoption has been practiced in the United States, nothing is so final as the formal signing of papers and the receipt of the baby. Whatever life the adoptee may have had before this process was completed is assumed to have never occurred.

Some adoptive parents have resorted to fabricating stories of the natural parents' deaths to silence their children's questions. The stories vary according to the era in which the adoptee was born. If the adoptee was born during a war, the story might be that the father died in combat and the mother died of heartbreak. Automobile crashes were frequently cited until air travel became common. These stories could be useful if the adoptive parents were particularly concerned over illegitimacy, since they could say that the couple was married before death. Occasionally such stories are embellished. The automobile crashed while the natural father was speeding his wife to the hospital for delivery. Or the child was found nursing from the dead mother. In one case an adoptee was told that her natural mother died in childbirth of kidney failure. She grew up in mortal fear of a similar fate if she had children of her own.

People who are told stories like these are scarred. Regardless of what they may feel about their natural parents—sympathy, love, gratitude—their own satisfaction with life is tempered with sorrow. Was the accidental death associated in any way with their birth? It is hard to avoid feelings of guilt.

Social workers sometimes use the symbolism of death in dealing with natural mothers as well. Mothers who give up their children today are often advised to relieve their anxieties by undergoing a program of ritual mourning, or to think of their babies as having been aborted, thus accomplishing symbolically what they would not do in fact—kill their children.

It must be made clear that the call for open records is not by any means a condemnation of adoption. Many critics of the adoptees' movement continually bring up stories of child abuse and abandonment in making their arguments. They try to portray proponents of open records as opponents of adoption and, by extension, as unconcerned with child welfare. They ignore the fact that adoption has never been a solution to the problem of huge numbers of unwanted children. Standards of adoptability are set by those who want to adopt, not by the needs of the greatest numbers of available children.

Modern adoption still retains many of the tenets of ancient practices. Writing in *Case and Comment*, March-April 1976, C. Lester Gaylord points out the similarities:

When a childless couple adopts a child now, is there no consideration in the law of providing a way to perpetuate the family line? When the authorities, ecclesiastical and secular, insist on a similarity of religion between the adoptive parents and the adopted child, is there nothing in that suggestive of the "ancient duty of perpetuating domestic worship"? When we require that the child and the adoptive parents be of the same race, nationality, and physical characteristics because it is in the "best interests" of the child to blend as much as possible into the adopting family, is there no residual there of the ancient rationale that nature is imitated when the child resembles the parents?

If modern adoption procedures inadvertently parody those of ancient civilizations, isn't it time we recognized—as Hammurabi did—that adoptees are inclined to wonder about their origins? There is no greater constant than the search for identity by adoptees and non-adoptees alike. Sealed records are a recent invention. Before 1924 the records were open. Only 3 percent of adoptees took advantage of them then. In Scotland and Finland, the only European countries where records have never been sealed, the percentage is the same. The fact that 97 percent do not bother should not be used to prevent the minority from satisfying their deeply felt needs. It should be reassuring that individual needs have survived fifty years of pressure to conform. If we prize conscience, memory, and history, we should welcome a revival of a basic freedom. This freedom is not new or novel. The prohibition against finding the truth is an aberration.

# Finding Talent's Source
## —— Mimi ——

*Where does talent come from? What does it mean to have an "ear for music" or an "eye for color"? How much are our abilities the result of exposure to special fields and encouragement in them by parents and teachers and how much is due to heredity? In speaking with many adoptees, I have been impressed by how much ability emerges unexpectedly. Artistic talents in particular, by their nature demanding devotion and often obsession, can sometimes be a source of anxiety for adoptees and adoptive parents alike.*

*For some adoptive parents, a child's willingness to spend long hours practicing a skill that has emerged independently of any example at home serves as a continual and sometimes uncomfortable reminder that the child was born with traits that were not provided in the home. Even though adoptive parents usually take pride in and encourage such talent, adoptees themselves can feel uncomfortable about their innate abilities. They often wonder what other characteristics will emerge from their genes.*

*Mimi Kirkland is a commercial artist. Her talent became evident at a very early age, and it was always a source of curiosity for her. Eventually she developed a health problem that caused her to begin a search for her natural parents. But in clearing up her medical mystery, she also found the source of her talent.*

My adoptive parents have always impressed upon me the fact that I was special. They never pretended I was not adopted. In fact they made adoption seem so wonderful that I have always adopted things. As a child I adopted my goldfish and turtles and took them to bed with me. The poor things were always dying, so my parents figured they had better get me a dog. Pooch lived to be twenty years old. He was a substitute for the brother or sister I never got for Christmas.

I had an advantage over other children at Christmas, because all the presents under the tree were always for me. Then I began to realize that for games like "Monopoly" you really had to have other kids to play with. You couldn't do it by yourself. I used to hear brothers and sisters playing in the neighborhood. I was the only kid in my parents' house and had to spend a lot of time by myself.

Although I was a tomboy and wanted a brother, I would have settled for a sister. In the Catholic elementary school I went to, there were two little Polish girls who didn't speak English. Their names were Martha and Stella and they were new in the diocese. They were twins and, when I met them, they were either in kindergarten or first grade.

I decided to adopt them. I don't know how we communicated, but I got them off the school bus and had them walk home with me. Their mother became hysterical when they did not come home. She called up the school, but since she couldn't speak English there was a problem. The nuns didn't know where Martha and Stella were.

When we got home, my mother said, "Aren't these two cute little girls? Who are they?"

"These are my two sisters, Martha and Stella. I already adopted them. I took them off the bus."

My mother turned green. "Oh my God. Where do they live?"

The girls couldn't say. They just stood there.

"Mommy, I want to adopt them."

"You can't just go and adopt people."

"Mommy, you told me you *can* just go and adopt them. You pick the ones you want and take them home."

By this time she wasn't paying much attention to my logic. I guess I taught my mother that time not to make things too simple when explaining to children.

My mother said to Martha and Stella, "Please, little girls, speak

English!" Not a word.

She finally called the convent, and the nuns knew what was going on because the twins' mother was on the other telephone line.

We got them back in one piece. Mother tried to explain to a woman who could not speak English that her adopted daughter wanted to adopt other children. Then she told me that the twins had their own mommy, and you only adopt children who don't have mommies.

"Don't I have a mommy?"

"Yes and she loved you, but she couldn't keep you."

Martha and Stella's mother could keep them. I asked my mother if she couldn't go back to the place where she got me and get a brother for me. Then she explained that she was too old to adopt another child.

My mother was getting close to the upper age limit for adoptive parents when I was adopted. Her age is related to an incident in my early childhood. I was about a year old when I swallowed a piece of carrot that had fallen to the floor. It went down the wrong way and became lodged in my lung. A surgeon had to be flown in from the West Coast to remove it, using a newly developed technique.

My mother worried for a long time afterwards that the accident reflected her shortcomings as a mother. As a child I saw how much it troubled her. Knowing how religious she was, I thought she felt that God hadn't wanted her to be a mother and that, by adopting me, she had gone against God's will. After that, my parents never did adopt a brother or sister for me. They had passed the adoption agencies' upper age limit by the time things settled down to normal after my emergency surgery.

My mother used to tell me I was the prettiest baby ever. She implied that I had been chosen from a roomful of babies. She wanted me to think I was special. Outside our house I let people know just how special I felt. I said I was better than anybody else. I was never mean about it, but when the subject came up, I said, "I'm better because I was picked and you were had."

The fantasies began when I began to see movies. I put myself into every movie I saw. One day I saw *Gone with the Wind*. I was the daughter of some rich man with a plantation in the South.

A rich woman gave me up. If I went back to the South, I would own a plantation full of horses. When I saw Cary Grant or Gary Cooper in a movie, I would fantasize about them. I never understood the time periods of the movies. I saw a movie about Queen Elizabeth. I was the daughter of the Queen and Errol Flynn. He looks like me, I thought, and the Queen had a baby she never told anyone about. I couldn't understand the passing of time, the centuries gone by. Anything I saw on television seemed desirable.

Gradually the idea of adoption became more important and complicated for me. My mother had waited three years to get me, and that wait had made a deep impression on her. What she had to go through to adopt me could never be the same as natural motherhood. No matter what the social workers say, adoption procedures affect the mother. And they affect the way a child is raised.

When I was about ten, my mother lectured me on honesty. To explain why I could not lie, she told me that a social worker had come to the house to check on me when I was ten months old. At one point the social worker asked, "Is she potty-trained?" I was still in diapers. My mother was concerned that she was doing something wrong because I was not potty-trained. She thought they might take me away because of that. She almost said yes, but then decided to tell the truth.

"Oh good," the social worker responded.

"Is that good?"

"Of course," said the social worker. "There's no way for her to be potty-trained at ten months old. A lot of women say 'Yes' because they think it's expected of them."

They were testing my mother's honesty.

My mother was never made to feel comfortable with her situation. As I later found out, this was not the only ridiculous thing social workers did in dealing with her.

My teachers used to say from the beginning what a gifted artist I was, but I never really knew what they were talking about. It became especially important as I formed career ambitions. I didn't know where I got my talent.

As a teenager I became aware of an upsurge in ethnic pride. My friends were wearing badges that read, "Kiss me, I'm Italian" and "Kiss me, I'm Polish." What was I?

When I was sixteen I made my first attempt to find out. I asked my mother. She said that all she knew was a name. Luckily it wasn't very common. The social worker at the agency had asked my parents at the time of my adoption what they wanted to know about my background. My mother had answered that they didn't want to know much. They wanted to make me theirs to the greatest degree possible.

I talked my problem over with my boyfriend. He said, "Why don't you go there and ask?" He knew how to get to the agency, so we cut school, caught the subway train, and walked to the office. I went in to talk with the social worker while he waited out in the hall.

The social worker told me I was too young to find out.

I returned when I was eighteen and again when I was twenty-one, each time with a different boyfriend. The last time I went, I was a full-fledged adult, I thought, but finally they told me I could never know what was in my records.

By then I had been away from home a long time. I had been to college. I had traveled by myself to Europe and all over the United States. I wear a necklace with a roadrunner pendant because I have itchy feet. I'm only four-feet-ten-inches tall, but I am healthy and vigorous enough to do anything I want to do.

In 1972 I took sick. Three or four times a day I would get a horrible pain around my head and down my spine. Then everything in front of me would begin to blink like a strobe light. Finally I would pass out.

For a condition like that you think of all kinds of doctors, and I tried them all. They X-rayed my head to see if I had a sinus problem. They checked my inner ears. They shook me in a machine until I felt like a milkshake. They did spinal taps. All negative.

Who would think of going to an allergist? I didn't have rashes and I didn't sneeze. I didn't even have clogged sinuses. But I went to an allergist. He did scratch tests and one of them exploded. He gave me a shot. After a series of shots, things gradually returned to normal.

The doctor told me I had a bacterial respiratory allergy; I was allergic to the bacteria in my own lungs. He also told me the condition was hereditary.

Now, after all the years of fantasizing and wondering about where I had got my talent, which might have been explained through environment and schooling, I had something medical to wonder about.

I began to look in telephone books for the name my mother had told me was my natural mother's name and my birth name. I started with the New York City books and the only family with that name I found was in Brooklyn where I had been born.

I worked for a time at a telephone answering service, where there were lots of telephone directories. I went through all of New York, New Jersey, Connecticut, and eastern Pennsylvania. I wrote to friends all around the country, and they looked in telephone books. I was in Florida for a while and checked out phone books there. Still, the family in Brooklyn was the only time I hit paydirt.

I asked a friend to call the telephone number listed for them. He had a made-up story about doing a research paper on ethnic origins for his course at Queens College. When a woman answered the telephone, he asked her about the name. She told him it was her husband's name and that he had died six months before. My friend asked the nationality of the husband, trying all the while to get more information about the family, especially whether they had any daughters who might be old enough to be my mother. She kept saying she didn't know what my friend meant about "nationality." "Was he Russian or German?" my friend asked. At last he hung up.

"Mimi, if that man was your grandfather, then you must be black."

I broke up. My hair's too straight for that.

One day I happened to meet a social worker who dealt with the agency where I was adopted. I told her about my medical mystery. I had heard how difficult it was to get information and wondered whether she could tell me how to go about it. She was sympathetic and invited me to have lunch with her a few days later.

I had met her first on a Tuesday. That Friday, over a pastrami sandwich, I received all the information I needed. Fifty-seven pages straight from the records. I was in a state of shock. I had been prepared to search for years.

I paid to have most of it copied and took it home where I could study it. I couldn't understand the entire process. The adoption agency had gathered all this information and then had done everything it could to make sure no one would ever read it again.

But I had all the information I needed about my background. My natural father's mother was Russian and an orthodox Jew. She objected to the marriage of her son to a Pennsylvania Dutch girl. Her other son had recently eloped with an Italian girl. Heights and weights were supplied. There was the name of a great aunt's village near Kiev. But, for all their thoroughness, the social workers had listed my natural mother's hair color as blond. I later discovered she had only dyed it to cheer herself up.

There was a section in my records on my adoptive home. They told what kind of house we had and how my father was going to pay for it. In one part that was supposed to be technical, they described me as a "rosy-cheeked, chubby child who wandered around the floor like a fat mechanical mouse."

They described what my mother did when I spat up food or when I cried. They said they thought my mother was well adjusted and that I was happy. All their remarks seemed derived from observation and from what my mother told them. They were not out to help my mother learn how to be a good mother.

One thing they had right: "We feel the mother is over-protective and this will not pass in time."

My mother and I talk about everything. She is the first to be shocked by what I do and the first to get over it. When I had motorcycles, she used to put sheets over them in the garage so she didn't have to see them. One day she bought a pair of crutches and put them by my motorcycle. She made me promise not to sky-dive until after she dies.

I was satisfied with what I had learned about myself. I felt as if I had eaten a huge meal. I was stuffed. Meeting the people in those papers didn't mean anything at all. I got the papers in May and didn't tell my parents about them for some time. Then one day I was talking with my mother.

"Mimi, I wish you would start going to church again."

"I don't want to go to church."

"It isn't the way it used to be. They have a nun who sings folk songs."

We argued back and forth. I guess I wanted it to come out.

"I'm not going to go to church. I'm not Catholic. I'm Jewish."

That did it. My mother was upset. My father too. They said they were worried for my sake, not for theirs. If I went to meet those people and was turned away, it would hurt me. I showed them all the papers.

I still did nothing to contact my natural parents. I went to the library and studied whatever I could find about Kiev. Then I began to wonder whether I had any half-sisters or brothers. I felt like an only child again.

My friends began to egg me on. Many of them had helped me, and I felt I was letting them down by not going further. I felt especially close to the girls who were with me when I met the woman who got the papers for me. One of them was adopted through a lawyer, not an agency, so she had seen her family records. They were too sordid to motivate her to go on. Her mother was an alcoholic who had given up seven of her ten children, some of whom had had rickets and tuberculosis.

Finally I took a step. Most of the information was too old to be of any use. But my grandfather, my natural mother's father, still lived in western Pennsylvania at the same address at which he had lived in 1948. He was eighty-nine years old when I called him. I pretended to be an old friend of his daughter.

He told me all about my natural mother. The one thing I had not expected to hear was that she had married the same man who was listed as my father. He told me where they lived in California. He couldn't give me their telephone number, because it was unlisted and they had neglected to give it to him. I never got to see him. He died soon after my call.

If I had had the phone number, I probably would have called. But I was afraid. I kept the papers in my dresser drawer. I kept telling my parents I didn't want anything to change for us.

Then I took sick for a few weeks. I had high fevers. My mother says now that I was delirious. I kept repeating, "I want to go. I want to go."

When I recovered, Daddy came into my room. He asked whether I wanted to meet my natural parents. I felt uncomfortable and said I did not.

"You're not going to be satisfied until you've met them."

I tried to tell him it didn't mean that much, but he kept on telling me that I would not be satisfied until I met them. Finally I said quietly, "Yeah. I guess I ought to meet them."

He smiled and said, "Good. Your plane leaves at nine o'clock tonight." He handed me my round-trip ticket to Los Angeles. I couldn't believe it. I kissed him and began to pack. He told me to take some proof, but I didn't listen. Mommy was crying.

That was the way to do it. I didn't have time to think.


My plane was a night coach. I didn't know what to do with myself. I kept going to the bathroom and washing. The plane arrived at one in the morning, Los Angeles time.

On the map, the town where my natural parents lived looked very close, maybe a taxi ride away. It wasn't. I was too late to catch a bus. I decided to find a ride, as I had done many times before. I know all the tricks of the trade.

I looked around for a prospect, someone who had collected his luggage and looked halfway decent. I went up to him with my suitcase and my map and asked him how far away the town was. He said it was a two-hour ride.

"Where do you think I should stand to thumb a ride?"

He made a face. "You can't hitch a ride. It's the middle of the night. You'll get mugged, raped, and assaulted."

"I do it all the time. Any old truck driver will pick me up."

I knew he would give me a ride or worry himself half to death.

"I can't stand it. I'll take you there."

He was a mathematics teacher in a high school. He drove a van, and he was supposed to be going in the opposite direction.

I told him what I was doing in California. He became interested and seemed to share my excitement. When we arrived in the town, he asked directions, and we found ourselves at the curb alongside the lawn in front of the house. We just stood there on the grass, stretching our legs.

"Aren't you going to ring the bell?"

"It's been twenty-six years. It's going to be bad enough without waking them up at three-thirty in the morning."

"Then we'll have to wait."

I put my foot down. "You've done enough already. I'm not going to let you wait with me. Go home and go to bed."

"I'm not going to drop you here by yourself. There are gangs around here. This is California. It's worse than New York." That was the first time I'd ever heard that.

We got into the van, and he said he would take me to a motel. That gave me something else to think about. "I know what he has in mind," I thought.

He drove to a motel, checked me in and then said goodby. I was pleasantly surprised.

"There's one more thing. I want you to send me a postcard and tell me how it comes out."

We still write to one another.

I went to my room, but I couldn't sleep. I called my parents in New York. Mother was anxious about how it had gone, but nothing had happened yet. She told me to try to sleep.

I was like a jack-in-the-box. Every time I settled down I would jump up. I took a bath and washed my hair. Then I started to dress. I had brought along all kinds of clothes so I would be prepared for any kind of weather. I tried everything on and finally decided to wear jeans instead of a dress. There were four pairs of jeans to choose from.

I took a shower and washed my hair again. I didn't know what to do with myself. I just thought, "I have to be really clean."

Finally I chose a pair of jeans and a cotton top. It looked windy so I put on a red jacket. I didn't want to come on like I wasn't me. I put on my best earrings and all my rings, and I started out.

That morning we had arrived from a different direction than the one I had to take. I ended up on a highway parallel to the street where my natural parents lived. Separating me from their street was a high chain-link fence with barbed wire strung across the top. Those fences are hard to climb over. I went up and down the street, looking for a place to get through. To find the start of the fence would have taken a long time. Finally I found a place where grapes were growing up the fence. I managed to get to the top and fell over, catching my leg on the barbed wire.

There I was, hanging upside down with blood gushing out of my leg, grapes smashed in my face and leaves stuck to me. A woman came up to me, screaming in Spanish. I thought she was angry. Then I heard words like "pain, hurt, I'm sorry." I knew she was upset.

She finally got me down. I was covered with dirt and grapejuice. Blood was running down my leg, and my motel was two and one-half miles away.

But there was the house, with the house number in big bold numerals. I stood there. I didn't want to go back and I didn't want to go in.

All of a sudden a woman walked out of the house, carrying garbage. She was standing in the driveway, looking at me. All I could think of was, "What the hell! She might just as well see me the way I am—incompetent."

I walked up to her and said, "Are you Ellen?"

"Yes."

"Could I talk to you for a second?"

"Sure."

Then she saw the cut and began to make a fuss. I said I didn't want to talk about my leg. She invited me in for a drink.

Then she said, "I bet you're a relative." I was stunned.

"You think so?"

"We've been expecting you."

"I don't think so."

"Aunt Lucy called me the other day about you."

"I'm not that person. I'm from New York."

She led me inside, sat me down, and poured me a soft drink.

"Exactly what is it? Is there something wrong with the family in Pennsylvania? Has someone died?"

Again I told her I was from New York. "I wanted to talk with you. You see, I was born in 1948."

She cried out and threw her arms up in the air. She started kissing me all over my face and crying at the same time.

"My baby. My baby. God sent me back my baby." Ellen kept on crying for almost an hour.

A boy and girl walked in. They had been outside. The boy didn't really look like me, but for some reason I felt I was looking into a mirror. The girl was much younger, but she was tall and lanky for her age. She had blond hair. She saw Ellen crying. She started to cry too.

Ellen turned to them and said, "This is the sister I told you about." She had told them about me a year before. Sam just said, "Oh, super!"

Ellen started hugging me again. She started saying things like "How did you ever find me? I cried every time you had a birthday."

I thought something was going to happen to her because she just kept on crying. Her whole body was shaking. It started to make me shake. My brother went out the front door and ran up and down, shouting, "Oh boy, my sister's here."

Then Ellen called Claude, my natural father, who was at work. She told his answering service that there was an emergency at home. Claude worked for an architect and was out in the field when she called. The answering service asked her to leave the exact message, but she wouldn't do it. She told them to try and contact him on his walkie-talkie.

Finally he called the house, and I listened on the extension. His voice was so coarse he scared me. "This better be an emergency, Ellen. If the shower curtain fell down again, that isn't an emergency. If you can't plug the toaster in, that isn't an emergency. All these emergencies you think are emergencies aren't emergencies. This better be a good one."

Ellen screamed at him, "Your daughter is here, right in the kitchen."

"So what? She was there when I left this morning too."

I went to her and prodded her. I indicated that she should say which daughter she was talking about.

Her voice became very soft. "It's your daughter from New York."

He paused and said, "Does she have any proof?"

That was the same thing my father had thought of. I don't know why men always think in terms of proof.

Ellen said, "I'm sure." Claude said he would be right home.

The car screeched into the driveway. The door swung open and banged against the wall. I thought he would be mad after the sound of his voice and the tires and the force of the door, but he came racing in. He took one look at me and said, "Oh my God."

Then he said a name over and over again—Irene. It was his mother's name. Apparently, I look just like her. He just kept saying it and sank back in a chair. I didn't say anything because I was so scared. Ellen was still crying. Sam came in and Claude sent him for a glass of whisky.

Claude and I didn't talk much for the two days I was there. I think he didn't know what to talk about. I told Ellen I didn't think he liked me.

"He's crazy about you. At night he goes into your room and stares at you while you sleep. He's used to having a nine-year-old for a daughter, but not a grown woman."

Ellen was very open. She asked about my boyfriends in great detail, but I didn't think of her as my Mom. Claude didn't talk openly. We talked about art until we had nothing else to say on that subject. I asked him about the navy and he talked about that. The whole thing was ridiculous. I knew all about his navy life. I had memorized the name of his ship and his serial number when I studied the adoption papers.

When I'm at my parents' home in New York, I run around in my underwear. The man who raised me is my Dad. Out in California, I felt funny in a bikini. The first time I took a shower there, I came out of the bathroom with one towel around my body and another around my head. The only parts of me that showed were my shoulders and legs from the knees down, but when he saw me he turned away. He was embarrassed.

With the kids it was entirely different. Suzanne took me around the neighborhood and introduced me to everyone as her grown-up sister from New York. In school she told her teacher and all her friends that she had a brand new grown-up sister. "She's twenty-six and she's real neat."

The teacher said, "She's probably not your sister. She's your cousin." When Suzanne insisted I was her sister, the teacher sent a note home: "It's not so much that we don't want her to tell fibs. It's that she really believes it. It must be a problem that her fantasies are becoming real."

Ellen had to write back and say, "Sorry, but it's real."

Suzanne followed me everywhere. She stared at me.

Suzanne's adopted too.

At one point she and Sam had an argument. Sam said, "She is *my* sister."

Suzanne said, "She's *my* sister too."

"She's *not* your sister. You're *my* sister. You're adopted and you're *my* sister. But you're not *her* sister."

"I am too."

"How do you figure that? She and I have the same blood, and you and I have the same name. What do you two have in common?"

"We're both adopted. We were both picked. You were just hatched." She stuck her tongue out. From the expression on Sam's face, I could tell he was thinking hard. Just for good measure, she added, "If they had known what they were getting, they wouldn't have taken you."

While I was visiting in California that first time, my torn blue jeans disappeared. I had had four pairs, and suddenly there were only three. I figured Ellen had done something with them, but when I was getting ready to leave, the blue jeans reappeared. A patch had been sewn over the tear. The sewing was crude. Sam had measured the tear, gone into town on his bike, bought a patch, and sewn it on. I still have those jeans.

When I was getting ready to leave California, they took me to a Chinese restaurant. Sam was quiet all through dinner. In the car he gave me a necklace that I wore until it changed color. At the airport he suddenly ran after me as I was going up the ramp. "Don't leave. It took you all that time to come to us. Don't leave." Sobbing away, he threw his arms around me. It's a real disadvantage looking as young as I do. On the plane people were nodding with understanding and making comments about young love. I had to have a drink.

I know Sam is their child, but I almost feel he should be living with us. My parents are in New York, but my brother is in the wrong place. Suzanne is so ingrained in my heart, so loving, that I only think of her as being adopted when I tell this story. She writes me all the time. She draws pictures and sends them to me. They aren't great, but she is a terrific athlete and dancer and gymnast. She really latched onto me. One day in California Sam yelled at her, "For heaven's sake, let her take a bath by herself."

Now my mother sends Ellen locks of my hair she cut when I was little. She has sent one of my first shoes and the first picture I drew at school. It is a spaceship. Sam's first picture is also a spaceship.

Mother and Ellen are both Catholics. They write every week. Mother is so pleased I will have a family after she dies. Ellen has always been open with her entire family about me, and they have come from all over to meet me. Claude's family isn't that close.

I think Claude and Ellen did the right thing when they gave me up. Claude had just left the navy. He had no job. His brother had eloped with an Italian girl. I get the feeling he thinks I'm blaming him, but I don't. I haven't gotten to know him well enough to come out and say it.

He has said to me, "These things happen. And it's not that we didn't like you. You were a beautiful baby." I get the feeling he doesn't want me to hate him. I don't hate him at all. I could probably get to like him a lot. He's the one I seem to inherit everything from, including my talent and my allergy. We like to eat the same things. He eats peppers for breakfast, just as I do. He recently bought Sam a minibike, but Sam doesn't even want it.

# When Records Lie
## —— Bill ——

*One of the most important things an adoptee can do to advance his search is to enlist the support of his adoptive parents. Adoptees have discovered widespread corruption in systems for recording births, and it often proves impossible for them to uncover the truth without the help of someone who can remember specific facts about their past. An adoptee who feels he should wait for his adoptive parents to die before he begins to look for his natural parents may be burying any chance for a successful search.*

*Bill Michaels is an important banker in his late forties. He developed habits of self-reliance early in life. He has been a scholastic athlete, a manual laborer, a soldier, a student, and a father. He didn't learn he was adopted until he was a grown man, and he then waited twenty years before any real curiosity about his roots began to emerge. When he finally began his search he was handicapped by the fact that his parents once had a lawyer create a false birth certificate. Without the help of his adoptive mother, he would have been locked into this falsehood forever.*

I learned I was adopted in May of 1957. My wife told me. I was twenty-eight years old and had just finished my master's thesis. I had been in the army, played lacrosse and football, and wrestled in high school. I had worked on the railroad as a teenager, but until that point I had no idea I was adopted. Things that had happened when I was a kid suddenly began to make some sense, but I had never paid any attention to them when they were going on. My wife had known for months, but she hadn't wanted to disturb me while I was working on my thesis. She heard it from her mother who had heard it from people in the neighborhood.

My adoption had never been discussed in our house. My father died when I was a senior in high school. My mother didn't find out that I knew until 1963. She is a nervous person and very easily upset, so I never brought it up. That year an uncle died and both of us received copies of the will. One section began "To my adopted nephew, I leave. . . . " My mother almost had a nervous breakdown. I told her it didn't matter to me, that I had known for years. She began asking me when I had found out and accused me of treating her differently once I knew. I played a game with her. I said I would never tell her when I heard about the adoption because it would enable her to pinpoint when I "started treating her differently."

I said, "I love you. I've always loved you and always treated you the same." She's eighty-eight now, extremely sharp, healthy and independent. Nothing's changed between us now that I've found my natural mother. Yet Mother still claims it has.

According to my birth certificate, she was thirty-seven when I was born and my father was forty-five. She admits she lied about her age and that she was older than that. She says she has lied about her age so often that she doesn't remember it herself.

Because of my parents' ages and medical difficulties, I developed the habit of independence early in life. Before she married, my mother worked as a cryptographer in the foreign exchange department of a bank, coding and decoding currency transactions. After she married, she developed a number of illnesses I suspect were mostly nervous in origin, because she has lived to such a ripe old age in good health.

My dad was a super guy. He had a heart attack when I was ten and had to stop working. He became a great companion, although we couldn't participate in many activities together. I was a good athlete in school: varsity lacrosse and football, captain of the wrestling team. Father came to all the games and meets. Four or five of us never had to ride the team bus because he would take us in his car.

They hired a Scottish girl to take care of me when I was little.

She looked after me as if I were her own child, even passed me off as her own when she took me out. This began to disturb my parents, and they were getting ready to let her go when she found a husband. After that there was a series of girls, none for any great length of time, and, when my parents were getting well into their fifties, I could look after myself. They went out frequently and I stayed home to make airplane models by myself. I didn't mind being alone.

In 1941, when I was still at P.S. 222 in Brooklyn, my wealthy uncle decided I should go to Poly Prep, a first-rate private school. Poly had a good athletic program and appealed to me for that reason alone. I entered a wrestling tournament without any training and won. I joined the other teams when the coaches saw my ability and invited me to try out.

My parents had a cabin on a lake in upstate New York. There were lots of other kids around, and we did everything without supervision by adults. It was like a camp without counselors. We swam and hiked and camped out. None of the parents ever bothered us.

When some of us decided we didn't have enough money, we would caddy at a local golf club. The work didn't pay well and was dull. I heard there were lots of jobs on the railroad, because the war—World War II—had taken most of the men away. To get railroad work you needed working papers if you were under age, and to get working papers you needed a birth certificate.

When I asked for a birth certificate, the roof almost blew off the house. My parents offered me a big allowance instead. I wanted to work, so I took a farm job with some of the others. Not only did that pay a mere $10 for six fourteen-hour days, but I discovered that I had an allergy to corn and some other things. I puffed up and sneezed so badly I couldn't function. At last my parents decided I could have a birth certificate, so they paid a lawyer and he got it for me. He claimed that my birth had not been recorded, because it had been at home and the doctor who had delivered me was now dead. As evidence that I existed, he gave census certificates and papers from the Board of Education listing my birth as May 3, 1929, in Brooklyn. I got my working papers.

The pay on the railroad was great. If you worked weekends and holidays, you got double time. If they called you out at night because there were trees on the line or broken rails, you got triple time. So I said I would work anytime they needed me. I took off Mondays and Tuesdays because then I only got regular pay. One week I took home $115, which was great in those days.

It got me in good shape for fall sports too, lifting ties and tamping the track beds. Football was pretty tame by comparison. A railroad section gang consists of the dregs of the barrel, and during the war it was worse than ever. I would get into two or three fights every summer. Most of the men were alcoholics. Once a state trooper came and dragged a guy away. I don't know what he had done. It wasn't a very nice bunch and you had to take care of yourself.

My dad died when I was seventeen. I was wrestling in the junior championships and he was watching from the stands when he had a heart attack. Some friends took him away. I didn't know about it until I arrived home at 1:00 AM and the lights were on.

My mother had a nervous breakdown and went to the hospital for months. I went to live with neighbors. I had my father's car, and I have to admit I had some great times. I did some dumb things and made some mistakes, but I survived. By the time my mother returned I was pretty self-reliant.

I graduated from high school in 1947. Only my mother and a neighbor, a nurse, were at the ceremony. My uncle said I should go to college. I spent four years at college in upstate New York and scraped through. I went to graduate school to find out what I should have learned in college. I took a job in a bank to support myself.

The army drafted me for the Korean War. They put me in an infantry unit and immediately stuck us on an airplane and flew us to the West Coast where we got on a troop ship. We hadn't even had basic training yet.

We didn't know where we were going, and someone started a rumor that we were headed straight for Korea. They issued full uniforms and helmets. We were dying. Then they dumped us at Pearl Harbor and gave us our seventeen weeks of basic.

The war was raging. We had a crazy lieutenant-colonel, a ranger with seven Purple Heart decorations, who went to the commander of the Pacific and said, "General Moran, I volunteer my whole battalion for duty in Korea." They turned him down, but most of us went as individuals. Seventeen of us were left behind to go to school, and I was chosen for cryptography. I'm glad my adoptive mother and I have some abilities in common. We seventeen were put in a signal corps unit and I needed a security clearance.

For some reason, and it might have been my birth certificate, it took the Federal Bureau of Investigation two years to give me a clearance. It came through the day I got on the ship to go home.

I spent two years in Hawaii. In the beginning there was nothing for me to do except tend bar in a serviceman's club in downtown Honolulu. The guy who ran it before I arrived was robbing it blind. I was working on my master's degree in business administration, so someone suggested to the colonel in charge that, since they needed a new manager and since I had business training, they should try me out. I got an extra ninety bucks a month. Because I changed the accounting system, in two weeks the club was showing a profit. They said as long as I made a profit I would never go to Korea, so month after month I made money. We did land-office business.

During this time my mother met a young woman at church and they became friends. She asked the girl if she had been on the church basketball team that I coached before I went into the service. She said she hadn't. They talked all the way home.

My mother's very pushy. She said, "You'd like my son. He's in the army. You ought to write to him." Mother kept after her until she wrote. After a year away, I came home on leave for ten days and went out with her every day. I was a few years older and had been in a class with her older sister once.

I was discharged the following December, engaged in January, married in February. One day after we were married, my mother-in-law said to my wife, "Did you know Bill was adopted?" She's not sure how the word got out but it was probably neighborhood gossip for a long time. Since we only lived six houses apart as children, it could have happened any time.

I had a nine-to-five bank job, and after work I would go to the library at New York University to work on my thesis until ten. I lived in Long Island, and by the time I got home it was nearly midnight. My wife figured that, with that kind of strain, she wouldn't bring up something as important as my adoption.

On the day the thesis was done, a friend and I carted our five copies of our theses to the dean, who was our adviser, and then went to New Jersey to get smashed.

When I got home, my wife said, "I've wanted to talk to you about something for a long time, but I didn't want to upset you. Did you know you were adopted?"

I said, "No, how about that?" It didn't bother me, but little things from the past began to occur to me. I remembered a Christmas party at my uncle's home. Someone asked, "Where is your mother?" I pointed. They said, "No, your other mother." I went to my mother and asked, "Where's my other mother?" She said, "Oh, she's in heaven." That was the end of it. I forgot about it.

I had had two good friends in my neighborhood when I was a kid—Betty and Dave. Betty's grandmother was a registered nurse about the same age as my mother. Betty had heard somewhere along the line that I was adopted and had told Dave. They said things I didn't understand. They seemed to be laughing together all the time. Betty's grandmother was the only person who came to my high school graduation with my mother.

It occurred to me that my birth might have had something to do with my uncle. He had been so good to me all my life when there were no real ties. He had been married before, and it seemed there might be some connection with him or with his first wife.

That was about the extent of my fantasy. It seemed likely there was a family skeleton in a closet and, in fact, the fantasy was strengthened before it was dispelled.

In 1974 I went for a physical examination. The doctor asked if there was a history of heart trouble in my family. I answered quite matter-of-factly, "Yeah, my father died from a heart attack." I added that my mother was still living and was a healthy woman.

Then I thought to myself, "This is stupid. I'm telling this to the doctor and these are not my natural parents." Whatever I told him could only mislead him.

I decided to find out about my beginnings, but I didn't know how to go about it. The first thought I had was to find a lawyer who knew the right official and that would be it. I asked a friend who knew his way around the Brooklyn Surrogate's Court. He went down there, and I took him to lunch a few days later. He told me, "There's no way. I can't find out anything. I'd like to help you, but I can't even pay anyone off."

I let it ride for a year. Then, in August 1975, I saw a program on television about adoption searches. Since this had been in the back of my mind for so long, I decided to investigate. So I went to the ALMA office, which is near the bank where I work, and joined. The search consultant there told me to try and get information from my mother. He stressed this over and over again. But I didn't want to upset my mother and I did a lot of scrounging on my own. I picked up scraps of information and thought I was on to something.

Once I went to the Surrogate's Court in Brooklyn and talked to some of the people there. One fellow told me which office I wanted. He gave me the name of a clerk in that office.

I walked in and told the clerk, "I just came from Bob Carlisle's office and he said you could help me." He assumed that the first clerk had given an authorization, and he said, "Sure, whatever you want."

He went to an index of every adoption in Brooklyn in 1929. I wasn't there. In 1930 I wasn't there . . . '31, '32, '33. My heart began to pound. I kept thinking, they've got it right there. I'm going to find out.

He said there was nothing. He invited me to look for myself. I pored through the whole thing. I thanked him and left. I was crushed and felt discouraged. The first thing I could think of was going through the same thing in Queens and Manhattan, but I knew that I had been lucky to receive such treatment. I knew that it wasn't legal for me to go into the records the way I had. They thought I had permission. It wouldn't be as easy in the other boroughs.

I thought that the lawyer who had arranged my false birth certificate might have had something to do with my adoption. I located him. I reasoned that since I was a grown man he could level with me. We met in his office. He was all but retired and he needed a young associate to be present. He couldn't hear very well.

When I explained what I wanted, he got angry. "My daughter has adopted children," he said. "She's telling them everything and I don't think it's right. I'm not going to help you and I think you've got one hell of a nerve trying to find out. Don't you appreciate what your parents did for you?" He walked out. It turned out he had nothing to do with it, but he wouldn't even admit that. He merely arranged my birth certificate.

Then I remembered a name of a doctor—Kline. My mother had mentioned him years before. He was her gynecologist. I went to the New York Historical Society. There were only three doctors of that name practicing in Brooklyn in 1929, and only one was a gynecologist and obstetrician. He had to be my man. He practiced in six hospitals, one of which was in the Long Island town where I live. Another was the hospital in Brooklyn where my son was born.

There were several coincidences. My uncle had lived in the same town where I live, which meant he was near one hospital where Dr. Kline practiced, and when he lived in Brooklyn before moving to Long Island, his house was two doors away from Dr. Kline's house.

The whole thing began to fall into place. They had an adoption business. They were all involved in it. They would take the pregnant woman out to Long Island and she would have the baby. Dr. Kline practiced there. The adoption would be arranged in Brooklyn. No one would be the wiser.

I went to my mother and said, "I know all about it. I've got a pretty good picture. I know all about Dr. Kline."

At that point she began to take me seriously. "How do you know about him?"

"You mentioned him years ago and his name stuck. I know which hospitals he practiced in." Then I added, "I've gone through all the records in Brooklyn and I know I wasn't adopted there."

This really registered with her. She knew very well I wasn't adopted in Brooklyn; she knew it all. Yet she claimed, "I can't remember. It was so long ago."

I said, "If you had a baby in a hospital fifty years ago, you'd remember what hospital it was. Adopting a child is no different. You'd remember where it happened. If you told me you simply don't want me to know, I could accept that, but don't tell me you don't remember. You're too sharp for that. You're not senile."

She said, "I can't remember." She paused, "But if I do, I'll tell you." That was the big break. She finally conceded that she knew I meant business.

I went on. "I'm going to find out, no matter what. It's going to take a lot of weekends. A lot of weekends when I'm going to be doing research. You're going to be visiting my house and I'm not going to be there. You can end that if you remember something that will mean I won't have to go hunting anymore."

I didn't mean it as a ploy, just a simple statement of the facts. But not long afterwards she called up and said, "I think I remember something." She could see that I had been away on several weekends and that I had a certain amount of information. This wasn't something that would just go away. It would get worse for her the longer I worked on it.

I asked her how they got to where they picked me up. "Did you drive or take a train?"

She answered, "I just remembered as you said that. We took a train, first to Manhattan and then over to Jersey City."

That opened it all up. When Dr. Kline had told her she couldn't have any children, she was already past forty. He suggested adoption. He said he knew a place where she could adopt—a Salvation Army home in New Jersey. She discussed it with my father and he approved. She discussed it with a neighbor, her best friend, and this friend went along to pick me up. She was a nurse, and she was the grandmother of my friend Betty, the same woman who accompanied my mother to my high school graduation.

It took her about two hours to give me four basic bits of information. I was born in Jersey City in a Salvation Army hospital called, as she remembered, Door to Hope. My natural mother's name, she said, was Adele Mosley.

She thought the girl's father was a minister, because there was a minister around at the time of the surrender. The minister spoke of returning to Clifton. She couldn't be sure of anything because my father had signed all the papers, but the story was that my natural father was sent to Europe after I was born and that they were a very wealthy family. My natural mother was sixteen, according to the information my parents were given, and my natural father was nineteen.

She told me this on Thursday night, April 22, 1976. I took the next day off from work to go to Jersey City. I looked in a 1975 telephone book and got the address of the Salvation Army in Jersey City. When I got to Jersey City, I asked a policeman where 422 Bell Avenue was. He gave me directions. I was all charged up. I knew I had something substantial now. It was a long walk, but I didn't mind. As I walked down Bell Avenue it felt familiar, as if I'd been there before. But at 422 there was a new building under construction. That brought me down.

I'm a tenacious type, however, and I had made up my mind I would find my natural parents. I've always been like that. When I was a senior in high school, I had to wrestle a junior from Columbia University. This was after World War II and the fellow had been a fighter pilot. There was more separating us than just a few years. He was a mature man. He came out and beat the daylights out of me for two periods. The coach said to me between the second and third periods, "Don't let him pin you. We need the points."

I got so mad that I told him, "I'm going to beat the son of a bitch." I pinned him with four seconds left. I was beaten four times by a blind wrestler, couldn't beat him to save my life, but the Columbia fellow had beaten him twice in championship matches. Once I make up my mind I'm going to do something, I do it, and that's how it was with the search.

As I prepared to return to New York, I thought, "There was a hospital there, and now there isn't." The current phone books showed that it wasn't there, but I had looked at an old one. I called the Salvation Army and asked what had happened to the hospital.

"Oh, you mean the Door of Hope," the clerk said. This was a slightly different name than Door to Hope, the one my mother remembered. Still, it wasn't bad for an eighty-eight-year-old woman who used to claim she couldn't remember anything about it. "We tore that down a year ago."

"Well, there were people there and records. What happened to them?"

"They were moved to the Eastern District Office in New York."

I went to the Eastern District headquarters and told them that I was born at the Door of Hope on May 3, 1929, and that I wanted my mother's medical records. I gave them the name Adele Mosley. He went to the files and returned. "We have no Adele, but we do have an Ada Moseley." My mother was wrong again. He spelled Moseley with an extra "e." He gave me a Clifton address. He showed me a second card, a blue card with the name Randolph Moseley. I thought it must be my natural father. But the birthdate was May 23, 1929.

"What's this?"

"That's her son," he said. "She had a son on that date."

"Well, I'm her son," I said, "And I was born on May 3, 1929." Then it dawned on me. They had changed the date. They had changed the state. I could have searched for a hundred years but, without my mother's help, I would never have found anything. For all her illnesses over the years, she had survived with her memory intact. No matter how my mother worries, I can only love her more for having done this. Anyone who feels he is sparing his adoptive parents pain by waiting until they die before he searches is hurting himself.

I called my mother and told her, "It's a great gift. Only you could have done this." Still she worried.

After finding out the name was Ada Moseley, I couldn't do much because it was the weekend. But recalling my mother's comment that Ada Moseley's father was supposed to be a minister, I looked at a Clifton phone book at Grand Central Station. There were eight Moseleys, and one of them jumped off the page at me. Reverend Gerald Moseley. I figured that had to be my grandfather, or perhaps an uncle who had followed my grandfather into the ministry.

I must have sat for an hour trying to screw up my courage to call him, but I finally dialed his number. He answered, "This is Reverend Moseley." I knew from the sound of his voice that he was black. He was a gentleman about it when he heard the disappointment in my voice. I said I was looking for an Ada Moseley who had lived in Clifton in the twenties. I made eight calls to Moseleys in Clifton. They were all black and all related to one another.

I went over to the library and started looking through the Polk Directories* starting with 1928. They didn't have 1929, the year I was born. I found a Moseley family at 35 Devon Avenue which jibed with the information I had been given by the Salvation Army. In 1930 there was a different address. The Moseleys moved around quite a bit.

Then in one directory I found the entry "Francine Moseley, widow of Ralph Moseley." I felt this was a good clue. I planned to call the cemeteries in Clifton, asking if any of them had records of a Ralph Moseley who had died in 1935. Once I did that, I could check obituaries and find out where the survivors lived.

At Cedar Lawn, the first one I called, the secretary said that they didn't have Ralph Moseley, but they did have a Francine Moseley. She gave me the date of death and everything else they had in the files. It turned out that Ralph Moseley hadn't died, but had left his wife. The researcher for the Polk Directory had found Francine living alone and assumed that she must have been widowed, but her husband lived nearby for many years.

I arranged to take Tuesday off from work. I went to Clifton and found Francine Moseley's obituary. It listed an Ada Dern as a survivor. I went to the phone books and looked up all the Derns. There were two. The first was E. Dern. I called her and said, "I'm trying to find out all I can about a woman named Ada Dern."

She said casually, "Oh yes, she lives out on the Jersey shore." Then she caught herself. "Who is this?"

"I'm an old friend. I used to know her back in the late twenties."

"Oh."

"May I have her phone number?" She gave it to me.

---

*The Polk Directories make it possible to trace the movements of people within a city of the United States. They can also help to determine if or when a person has left the city. These directories have been invaluable search tools for adoptees looking for their parents.

I was calling from the library. There were people running up and down the stairs behind me. It wasn't even a booth. I didn't have the right change, and the librarian hesitated to give it to me because she needed it for the copying machine the library maintained. Finally she relented.

I called and asked for Ada Dern. She came to the phone. I identified myself as Randolph Moseley. I asked if her maiden name was Ada Moseley and she said it was. I asked if she had lived at 35 Devon Avenue in Clifton. She had.

"Did you spend some time in Jersey City in 1929?"

"Yes, I did."

"I think we have something in common."

"What do you mean?"

"I'd like to get together with you."

I could tell she knew exactly who I was. I knew she was married. I didn't want to embarrass her. I didn't know if she was widowed or if she had a family.

Finally I said, "I can't meet you today or the day after. Can I call you Saturday?"

"Fine."

We left it at that. I knew she was my mother, and she had to be sure I was her son. It was forty-seven years after the fact. Who knew what to expect? I went back to work, but I was on pins and needles. I had to drive upstate in New York to meet my daughter, who was planning to transfer to a different college. She didn't know about this. None of my kids did. I had made a deal with my mother that she would remain my kids' only grandmother while she stayed alive.

I called from the Albany airport after I put my daughter on the plane.

Ada was disappointed that I wasn't going to be there that day. She had misunderstood my plans.

"Is your husband alive?" I asked.

"Yes."

"Can you talk freely?" I was still concerned that I might be an upsetting influence. In fact she had told her husband about me before they married, and he had never mentioned it since.

I told her I would like to visit as soon as possible and she agreed.

When I arrived home I told my wife about it. I wanted to go the next day. I called Ada and she said, "Fine, we'd love to have you." Her husband got on the phone. I was apprehensive but he was totally at ease. He gave me directions.

The next morning I got up very early. It was May 2, the day before the birthday I had always celebrated. The following Sunday was Mother's Day, so I took a card with me. Eight days had elapsed since my mother had given me the crucial information.

A heavy layer of fog covered the highway, so I drove with the headlights on. When the fog cleared about halfway, I forgot about the headlights and continued to drive. I couldn't figure out why people were getting out of my way, but they kept pulling over to let me through.

Cecil was outside to greet me. He isn't my father, but I couldn't want a finer man for a father. Before he retired he had been a foreman at a utility company. He's a big tough guy.

"Come on in," he said.

Ada was in the kitchen and we just hugged one another for a while. She cried a little. I cried a little. Cecil cried a little. Not much. We all felt very comfortable. Then we sat around and talked. I showed pictures of my wife and kids.

They had never had any children of their own. She told me about herself. She was one of fifteen children and, though her family had always been poor, they were always very close. They are still constantly getting together, the ones who are still alive.

She called two of her sisters and put me on the phone. I said my name was Randolph Moseley. They both told me that Ada had borne great heartache over the years. She constantly worried and wondered about me.

At the time she had become pregnant, Ada had been working in a silk mill for three years. She was fourteen. Her father and most of the rest of the family worked there too. She had no education. She met a man who was twenty-one and she became pregnant. Her father was very upset and very strict. She had wanted to get away, but she didn't feel she could make her own way.

When she got pregnant, her father forced her to go to the

Salvation Army, where she worked scrubbing floors and making beds to pay for her keep. She remained there after the birth to pay for her medical bills.

When she returned home she was still only fifteen. She became so despondent that she drank a bottle of iodine to kill herself. She hardly understood what had happened to her.

She didn't work, but remained at home doing very little for two years. Then she went back to work in the mill. She met the guy who had gotten her pregnant. He didn't know about me and she didn't tell him. He asked her to marry him. She refused and never saw him again.

Then she married Cecil. She's a very religious woman and has prayed for me for fifty years, and now her prayers have been answered.

Ada remembered my natural father's name, but she couldn't recall how it was spelled. So even the Salvation Army fabricated stories about the children they found homes for. They told my adoptive mother that my natural parents had been wealthy, influential people and it simply wasn't true.

I'm trying to find my father now. He will think it's sort of peculiar to have a grown man suddenly present himself as his son, when he never even knew he had made Ada pregnant. More than anything I would like to find some brothers and sisters. Ada is a wonderfully warm person, but she never had any other children.

I also have to look out for my own family and for my mother to whom I owe everything. She's very stubborn. She maintains her own apartment, but she contends that if she can't take care of herself I'll put her in a nursing home. Over and over I promise that I won't.

The funny thing is that for all her fears she won't have anything to do with her sister, her only blood relative. They haven't spoken in twenty years. She tells me not to let her sister come to her funeral. They had an argument about my wedding present. Her sister said she would get me something that would be worth $50. She gave me a savings bond that cost $37.50. My mother said, "You didn't spend $50." My aunt said it would be worth $50 some day. That was it.

I think it's ironic that my mother worried for all those years about the strength of my feelings for her as an adopted son when she had this serious conflict with her own sister, a blood relative. Since my reunion with my natural mother, my adoptive mother and I are closer than ever. The energy she expended in holding on to her secrets now goes into enjoying family life.

*Bill Michaels has now located his natural father. The revelation of the existence of a son was a shock and Bill's father has not accepted any relationship. He refuses to talk or to answer Bill's letters.*

# In Search of a Twin
## —— Lisa ——

*People who control the records that adoptees need to complete their searches have for the most part been unstinting in refusing to give up vital information. They often ignore the fact that a medical mystery has provided the impetus for a search and that such a mystery may be the cause of serious worries and insecurities in the adoptee's life.*

*Lisa Donatello began her search when she was married at age seventeen, shortly after verifying a suspicion that she was adopted. She has always had a strange scar on her hip, and it has always been a source of wonder to her. In conducting her search, Lisa discovered that her natural mother was one of a pair of identical twins. With the help of Emma Vilardi, the ALMA search consultant, Lisa has concluded that she may have been attached at birth to an identical twin, and that an operation took place to separate them. This would explain the scar. She also now has reason to believe there may have been a third child in the womb—a brother—yet no one will confirm or deny either possibility in convincing form. The hospital where she spent the first months of her life will not part with Lisa's own medical history. All refusals to cooperate on the part of hospital workers have been characterized by uncommon zeal. Lisa's records are guarded closely, not by clear-headed professionals, but by people who seem determined never to make an exception to any rule unless it suits them.*

One day when I was twelve I came home from school late. Like any other kid might have done, I went to a friend's house first. My mother wouldn't let me in the house. She was inside screaming and ranting and raving. She finally let me in and started hitting me. That's when she told me I was nothing but trouble, that she didn't want me, that it was all my father's idea, that she should never have let him talk her into it.

At that point I didn't know I was adopted, although I suspected it. I thought she meant that he talked her into getting pregnant. They married late in life. She was thirty-eight and he was older. He wanted children, and after my mother had a series of miscarriages, he was ready to adopt. My mother insisted that they get a girl; she wanted someone to take care of her in her old age. She was born in Sicily and has strong Sicilian ideas about what a daughter is supposed to do for her mother. They were offered a boy by the adoption agency and they refused him, at her insistence.

All children go through a phase when they think they're adopted, then they get over it. I never got over it. The older I got, the more differences between me and my relatives became evident. We looked very much alike. That's one area where the agency succeeded. The baby pictures of me and one of my cousins look like twins. But my father's five brothers had mostly girls and they all talked the same, their likes and dislikes were the same, their tastes in clothing were similar. I was always different. If they all liked a dress, I hated it.

When I was eight, my father took me to the movies. The picture was about an adopted girl who looked for her natural parents and found that they were both alcoholics. After that she appreciated her adoptive family and felt sorry that she had ever gone looking. When we got home, my mother was out on the stoop. My father said to me, "What would you do if we told you you were adopted? Would you want to look for your real mother?"

If he wanted to tell me, he never got the chance. My mother yelled at him, "Why don't you shut up?" From that moment on I think I knew, but no one confirmed it for me until I was seventeen.

Maybe it was my fault, but I wanted nothing to do with my parents' families. I didn't want to look like everyone else. I had to be different. My mother always played it up: "Why can't you be like your cousin and wear sweaters to school? Why can't you do the dishes like your cousin? Why can't you be like this one? Why can't you be like that one?"

Not me. I was always a rebel. I fought her tooth and nail. She hated me and I hated her. If she wanted me not to do something, I'd go right ahead and do it simply because she didn't want me to.

I started smoking at thirteen. I'd come home and leave my cigarettes on top of my bed so that she would see them. She would crush them and throw them away and I'd go out and buy another pack. She'd punish me and I couldn't care less. At fifteen she gave me permission to smoke and I stopped.

When I reached the sixth grade I was very unhappy in school. If you were bright you got plenty of attention, and if you were slow you got extra help, but if you were average you were on your own, so I decided to transfer to a new Catholic school. It only went up to fifth grade the first year, but I decided to lose a year and go there. I did well and maintained a high average.

My father was an upholsterer. He was also from a Sicilian family but, unlike my mother, he was born in the United States. He's always been great to me, but he had all the old-fashioned ideas. I could only date Italian boys, for example. For twenty-eight years I thought I was Italian. Still, my only complaint is that he didn't have the strength to tell me I was adopted.

Because I didn't know for sure that they adopted me, I didn't spend any time thinking about it. My mother kept me busy fighting and I looked for ways to get away from her.

I met my husband-to-be when I was sixteen. He was in the service at the time. While he was at sea, his mother would call me up on weekends and invite me over. She was so sweet to me. She introduced me to people as her "second daughter." She always called me "honey." She told me it made her feel that her son was closer to her if I was around, so I would take a bus to Mineola, another bus to the Bronx, and then a train to where they lived.

Then, when Martin was home and we were getting ready to announce our engagement, I told her, "Mama, we're getting engaged."

She said, "What do you mean? You're not good enough for my son."

I was flabbergasted. I never thought she didn't like me. After a big fight, I yelled, "If he's so precious, why don't you shove him back where he came from, 'cause you'll never let him go."

Martin got up from the table and said to his mother, "If my future wife isn't good enough for you, then you're not good enough for me. I'm marrying her." Then he picked up his duffel bag and off we went to my house where we spent the rest of the weekend.

She called to apologize. "Wait two more years," she said, "until he gets out of the service. I'll give you a big wedding. I'll invite three hundred people at some fancy place."

I said, "I don't want a fancy wedding. I don't care who you invite. As a matter of fact we're eloping." That went over like a lead balloon.

I'd spent a year with this woman, taking buses and that disgusting train, and now I wasn't good enough for her son.

Then she said, "It isn't only you. I would say the same thing to anyone who wanted to marry my daughter too. If his pockets were lined with gold, I'd say he wasn't good enough."

"Then you have a very deep problem," I said. Maybe she was worried about our ages. We both needed permission to marry. He was only twenty at the time. Looking back on it, I wouldn't want my own children to marry as young as that.

But my problems with getting married were only beginning.

I wanted my cousin, the only one I still have any kind feelings about, to be my maid of honor. She had a very rough life. Her father took off with another woman when she was very young. We were always the same size so my mother sent all my old clothes to her, and her grandfather resented it. He resented the fact that I was an only child and always had everything.

I heard him pass a remark that I was no good. He implied that my mother was a tramp and, since I came from the same stock, I was too. I was shocked because that was the first reference anyone had ever made to my natural mother.

Sicilians don't like other Italians. My adoptive family is Sicilian but my husband's family is Neapolitan. One weekend I stayed at their house to meet his family. My father-in-law had some of his *paisani* in the house for coffee on Sunday morning. I was in bed next to the kitchen and they were speaking Italian. I had never let on that I understood the language. My father-in-law said, "She seems like a nice girl, except that she's a Sicilian." His *paisano* said, "Maybe she won't be a bad one."

I lay there thinking, "Boy are they stupid. What am I marrying?"

The Sicilians are supposed to be Mafiosi. I guess they thought that if I didn't get along with Martin I would cut his throat.

To get married in the Catholic church, I had to present my birth certificate. I came home and asked my mother for it. She said she didn't have it.

"Where is it? You have to have my birth certificate."

"Oh no. Your godmother has it."

I thought that was very strange. "What's she doing with it?"

I could see her struggling. "We didn't have any place to keep it so we gave it to her to hold." I knew they had a safe deposit box. I couldn't believe they had nowhere to keep it.

I said, "I'll tell you what. Since you don't have my birth certificate, why don't you give me my adoption papers?" I was calling her bluff. She went to talk with my father. I ran upstairs to my room. Within five minutes, my father came up and walked into my room and handed me my adoption papers.

I couldn't believe it. I had asked for them but couldn't believe that they were right there. After all the years of secrecy, all the efforts they made to keep it from me, suddenly I had proof I was adopted. At that moment I hated the world. I hated him. I hated her. I hated my relatives because now I knew I was the family joke. They all knew something that I didn't know, something that was important to me.

It was three weeks before my wedding. All my relatives were calling. This one couldn't bring her daughter. Why didn't I invite cousin Vito? I had to go over seating arrangements. Then, for extra measure, I looked in *The New York Times* and saw a notice that Martin's ship would be leaving on the day of the reception, and the place we hired would just be reopening after their vacation on that day. So I had no place for a reception.

I called him up in Jacksonville and told him I couldn't marry him. I didn't know who I was. Maybe his mother was right. Maybe I wasn't good enough for him. Until I learned who I was, I couldn't marry him.

He came through. He said, "I don't care who your mother and

father are. I know you, the woman I'm going to marry, and I'm not taking no for an answer." I let it go at that.

We got married. I loved Martin, but at least part of the reason I was so anxious to get married was to escape my mother's clutches. That backfired. When his ship left, instead of getting my own apartment, I ended up back with her. So I started my search while he was at sea.

I knew that I was born at St. Bartholomew's Hospital in Burton, Pennsylvania. I wrote to them saying that I knew I was adopted and that I wanted information. They wouldn't send me any. The Sisters of St. Bartholomew ran the hospital and they had taken vows of confidentiality. I then wrote to the Bureau of Vital Statistics in Harrisburg and asked for my birth certificate. I didn't know anything about search techniques then, so I used my adoptive name, Lisa Moro, instead of my birth name, Lisa Pankovic. They sent back the amended version with my adoptive parents listed as my parents.

So then I started looking in phone directories for the name Pankovic and calling everyone with that name.

Shortly thereafter, I picked up the *Times* again. I read that there had been a fire on my husband's ship. Seven men from the New York area were killed, but no names were listed. That put an end to my search for a while. I called Washington, I called the naval base at Newport News, I called the Brooklyn Navy Yard, trying to find out about my husband. Nobody had any answers. At the Brooklyn Navy Yard they told me that the ship would be pulling into a base in Greece for temporary repairs, so I started making arrangements to fly to Greece. The provost marshal at Brooklyn Navy Yard talked me out of it. They would surely know how he was before I could get to Greece.

Then I got a call from my husband. He said that they would be going to Virginia for repairs and I should meet him there. I was so happy to be with him that I forgot about the search. I was in a different state and away from my mother for the first time. During those months I became pregnant and had a miscarriage.

When Martin sailed again I returned to New York and started searching again, this time using my birth name. But all I got was an amended birth certificate and a pamphlet on adoption from the hospital with a letter from the Mother Superior saying, "My child, I pray that you will get over this feeling."

It took me many years before I got any information. I would see cars on the highway with Pennsylvania license plates and speed up to see if the driver looked like me. God forbid I should ever have found someone who did. I don't know what I would have done—maybe pulled them over and questioned them.

It became an obsession and it almost wrecked my marriage. I couldn't function for more than a year. I became very depressed. I had two children by this time. My doctor put me on oral contraceptives and that was part of the problem. I would get sick after taking them and she increased the dosage.

I lost interest in my home, my husband, my children. I went into therapy, going to three therapists without liking or trusting any of them. I felt sorry for myself.

All the time I would think about my natural mother. I would have dialogues in my head with her. "Why did you do this? Why did you put me in this situation?" I hated her, blaming her for my problems with my adoptive mother. Why had she punished me? She should have placed me with a younger woman, one who could understand me and my problems.

We didn't have very much in those days. Martin worked two jobs, so he was out at night a good deal of the time. I worked and the rest of the time I was stuck home with my babies. At the same time we had very little privacy. My adoptive parents worked below us and they were constantly in my apartment. I had no outlet for my frustrations. I started drinking and going out. I could never make up my mind what to wear and ended up in tears at my own indecision. When the man came around at work to take lunch orders I would start to cry because I couldn't make up my mind.

My husband is not the type of man to yell, and he kept his feelings bottled up for a long time. My mother, my natural mother, was constantly on my mind. I had to tell her what she had done. I swallowed a bottle of aspirins one day and got sick.

A girlfriend was the one who convinced me that the birth control pills were part of the problem. We had known each other for twelve years and she could see the changes in me. She said, "Those damned pills are destroying you."

I've always been a shy person, especially when it comes to eating in front of other people, in front of strangers. I never went to restaurants by myself. My girlfriend pointed out that I had begun to think nothing of walking into bars by myself and ordering drinks.

She convinced my husband, and the two of them persuaded my doctor to take me off the pills because they affected me mentally. I began to think how I was destroying the only person who had been kind to me, the only person who really accepted me. Martin had begun to talk about divorce. I pulled myself out of it.

When my son was in the second grade, they hit on the subject of family trees. He came home from school one day very excited. He's a bright child. He said, "Mommy, Mommy, guess what? We started talking about family trees and someday when I'm older I'll be able to trace ours."

The only thing that ran through my mind was "What's he going to trace?" What would I say to him? My husband came home and I was in tears.

"The only family he'll be able to trace is yours. What about me?"

"We're going to find out," he said.

We drove to St. Bartholomew's. We arrived at 7:00 PM and asked for the Mother Superior. She was getting ready for bed and couldn't see us. I told the nun at the desk that I had come from New York and would return the next day. They called the Mother Superior back and she informed us that she would not be able to see us the following day either. I said that was too bad, but I would sit there all day long if I had to. At that point they knew what they were dealing with and she agreed to see me.

She was vague. Her vow of confidentiality came up about fifty times. She couldn't understand why I had to know. No one ever comes searching, she told me. There must be something wrong with me. Why couldn't I cope with the situation? It was done for my own good. There was no information she could give me.

At the end of that little speech I said, "Can you at least tell me something about my mother? Is she Italian?" No. "Well, what was she?" We don't know.

Talking to her was a very frustrating thing. She didn't give me anything useful. She wouldn't even tell me how old my mother was.

I was very depressed. She told me I was sick, and that wasn't the last time I heard that. I dropped it for a while.

One day I wrote to the Bureau of Vital Statistics again. They sent back the same stupid thing, the amended birth certificate. I wrote back and said that I didn't ask for that. It was a worthless piece of paper. As far as I was concerned the information wasn't true. The people listed on it were not my real parents. That time I got no response.

Martin called them. He got a man on the phone who asked, "How old is your wife? Is she older than twenty-one?" I guess he didn't have the file in front of him.

"Of course she is," my husband said, laughing. He explained what I wanted, but he never used the word adoption, he just said that I was a foster child.

"Come on now," the man said, "your wife is no foster child."

"I don't know what you're talking about."

"Go ask your wife. If she were a foster child she wouldn't have an amended birth certificate." Then he told Martin, "Tell your wife to write me a personal letter and to request 'a full and complete copy of my birth certificate before it was amended.'"

So I wrote again and four weeks later I got it in the mail. Now I had something to go on. I had my mother's full name, Angela Pankovic. I had the time of my birth. The certificate listed as her address a town called Smithville. No state was listed, but since her place of birth was Buffalo, New York, I figured that she had been sent to Burton by her family in Smithville, New York, to have the child. I found out that there was a Smithville near Buffalo. I called the postmaster in Smithville and asked if there was anyone named Pankovic living there. No one.

"Well, this dates back to 1942. Could you check it?"

Nothing. I tried calling all over the Buffalo area. No Pankovic listed anywhere.

I felt I was at a dead-end again, so my husband said we would go right back to the hospital. They got to know me very well. They'd see me walk in the door and they would throw up their hands. Here comes the nut again.

It was a Saturday. This time the Mother Superior had me see their staff psychologist. She told me I was a neurotic, that I was maladjusted. She twisted things so much that she had my husband agreeing with her. There was no way that I would get any information because I was neurotic. I was neurotic for wanting information, and I couldn't have it because I was neurotic.

I told them I had some facts. I had her name—Angela. I had her place of birth—Buffalo. "Good," she said, "there isn't any more to know."

I could have killed her. I asked if my mother had any brothers or sisters. She said, "No, she was an only child."

My husband had business dealings in the Allentown area, so we combined these trips to the hospital with his business. We always stayed in the same motel. There were mountains in the background and I used to stare at them. I had the eerie feeling that my mother was somewhere in those mountains.

Martin said that we would drive to Smithville, New York, and find out what we could.

Sunday morning we were drinking coffee in the room. The television was on and a sermonette was droning on and on. We weren't listening. Then they broke for a commercial for a record shop. In Smithville.

I said, "Did you hear that? Is there a Smithville, Pennsylvania?"

"I don't know." He called a friend who did business with him.

"Where's Smithville?"

"Where are you staying?"

"At the Host."

"That's easy. Just take the highway in front of the motel across the bridge, turn right and it will take you straight into Smithville."

Smithville is right at the base of those mountains. We got dressed and off we went to Smithville. It took us ten minutes. We drove right to the address on the birth certificate. A man was trimming the lawn in front of the house.

I thought he was my mother's husband. "I can't get out of the car," I told Martin, "I can't."

"Excuse me," he said to the man. "I'm looking for a family that lived here a long time ago named Pankovic."

He thought. "Never heard of them. Wait. Let me ask my wife."

She came out and Martin asked her. "No we don't know anyone by that name. We bought the house from a family named Kowalski. But if you want any information like that, go to that house on the corner." She pointed. "There's an old lady living there. She's close to eighty. She's spent most of her life right here and she's known everybody."

With that we went across the street. I was wearing sunglasses. I didn't want anyone to see my eyes in case I started crying. Inside, a little old lady sat saying her rosary. I knocked. She kept right on until she finished. Then she came to the door.

"I'm looking for someone named Pankovic who used to live across the street," I told her.

"Who are you?"

"A distant relative." I took off my sunglasses. "This was the last known address."

She looked at my eyes. "You're Marie's daughter aren't you?"

"No."

"You're not the one from Berwick?"

"No."

"Come on inside." I went in. She looked at me again and then said, "You're Angie's daughter."

"That's my mother's name."

"I knew you'd come here some day looking for her." She pointed to a chair and I sat. She made us coffee. Then she started to cry.

"Why do you want to find her?"

"Because I'm her daughter," I said, "and I think she should know me."

"Your mother is dead."

With that the bottom fell out. It had taken me ten years and in just one instant it was over. It seemed to be over. I had concentrated on that one goal and it didn't occur to me right away that there might be other relatives. The mother seems to be the key when you are searching, the most important one. Dead.

"Who is Marie?" I asked.

"That was your grandmother. She and I were very close friends."

"Where does the name Kowalski come from?"

"When your grandfather died, Marie married a man with that name. Would you like to see where your mother is buried?" I nodded. She called an old undertaker and set up an appointment for me.

According to the old woman my mother had gone to live in a town called Warren, married, had a son, and died right after she had the baby. So I had a half-brother for a start. She didn't know the man's name. She never met him. My mother was thirty-two when she died.

We met the undertaker. He spent an hour in his basement looking for the records we wanted. He had death records for my grandmother, my mother, and my mother's twin sister Serena. So the nun had been less than accurate. Not only a sister but a twin sister. I was constantly finding out about new relatives. The undertaker and his son showed us the graves. From there we went to the church. The priest said he didn't have time to get any records for us, but I was elated to have as much information as I did.

I had so much information that I couldn't make up my mind where to start. Finding my brother seemed like the logical first step. My mother died in 1956. My grandmother died two days before I was married in 1960. My aunt died in an automobile accident in 1943. There were no other males in the family. The aunt in Berwick didn't seem like a good bet. A son of my grandmother's had also died in an accident. My mother had been married twice. I had both husbands' names.

I took the second one and wrote for a birth certificate for my brother. I knew that my mother had died in an Allentown hospital and I had the name of the attending physician. We drove to Allentown and stopped at the hospital. I asked the secretary in charge of records if the doctor had come in yet.

She checked and told me that he was off for the week.

I thought fast. "Gee, that's funny," I said. "He told me I could come in and look through the records and he would meet me here."

She said, "We never show this information to anyone."

"Well," I said, "I have the doctor's permission. If you'd like to call him, you're welcome to." I had my fingers crossed, sure I would be caught.

"If he told you, then I guess it's all right." She pulled the file. I found that my mother had died of a pulmonary edema with an additional notation about an embolism, a heart attack with blood clotting. Her son's name was Carl.

His birth certificate arrived. I took an Allentown directory and found his father's name.

My husband called and spoke to my brother's stepmother. Her husband wasn't home. Martin gave her no reasons. We wanted to be very careful not to create any problems for him since the boy was at a delicate age.

The next evening Martin called, explained who he was and that I would like to meet my brother. "If you have any objections, we understand. If you are opposed to a meeting, could you send a picture and perhaps one of their mother?"

Two weeks later an envelope arrived with a picture of my mother and pictures of my little brother from infancy on. An accompanying letter invited us to visit.

My brother is a quiet, shy teenager. His parents are quiet. They live in the mountains. I did most of the talking, but I know he was happy to see me because he sat right by my side the entire evening. He never knew our mother. She died when he was just a few months old. His father didn't have much to say about her either. They had only been married a short time before she became pregnant.

"Did you know anything about my father?"

"No. I knew Angie had a child. When she was giving birth to Carl she had a very difficult time. The doctor said it was a common difficulty. He told me, 'The same thing must have happened the first time.'" He said that Angie wasn't very talkative and kept everything to herself, but she did say that she had given up a child. Her husband never asked who the father of her first child was. He figured it was none of his business since it had happened a long time before. He said that the last time he saw my mother she was vomiting. Within an hour she was dead.

On that trip I started looking for my father in earnest. I had no information about him, no names or anything else. I called the hospital and a young nun answered. Her name was Sister Angela. I kidded her about being my real mother.

"Do you have any information about my father?"

She had the file right in front of her. "Yes, we have a page-and-a-half interview about him. But I can't tell you what's in it."

"Come on," I said, "Give me something to identify with. At least tell me what religion he was."

"Baptist."

"Was he married?"

"No, he was single."

"Was he older than my mother?"

"Yes, but not by much."

"What nationality?"

"His father was French-Canadian and his mother was Welsh."

That's all I got, but it was something. I went back to the old lady. Before we got into a discussion about my father that, based on the information I now had, would lead me to him, the old lady told me that my mother's twin had a child too, right around the same time I was born, and that she had also given her child up for adoption. The old lady didn't know if that one was male or female.

I went back to the hospital. I went straight to the Mother Superior and I made up the best story of my entire search. I told her that she lied to me when she said that my mother was an only child. I now knew that my aunt had had a child of her own. The rumor I heard from my mother's friends in her hometown was that my aunt's child had died from hemophilia. I knew that this was a hereditary disease handed down through the mother and contracted only by males.

I had never mentioned that I already had two children. So I said, "I am pregnant. If this child is a male and there's a chance that I am a carrier of hemophilia, I am going to have an abortion, and my husband is going to divorce me. If I kill this child it will be on your consciences as well as mine. I know that child died and I must know how. If you tell me nothing else ever again, tell me this."

After this long outburst I took a deep breath. The Mother Superior looked right at me and said softly to her assistant, "Go get the records."

She came back and handed me a card, just one index card.

"Read it," said the Mother Superior.

I looked at it. It had my name on it—Lisa Pankovic.

I looked at them. "You gave me my own card. This is my name."

"No, my child, check the date of birth."

The date was November 17, 1942. My birthdate is October 8, 1942. My aunt had a girl and gave her the same name my mother gave me. My mother and her sister were twins. Twins I'd known had dressed alike and acted alike. My mother and her twin had given birth a month apart and named us the same. Were they trying to tell me something? I had to find my cousin.

I thanked the nuns and left.

I had my cousin's birth name, her mother's address at the time of birth, and her date of birth. Everything but the date was the same as mine. Pretending to be my cousin, I wrote to the Bureau of Vital Statistics and said that I had my original birth certificate but that I had lost my amended one. Could they send me a copy?

They did it. That's how I got her name and her parents' names. Again I looked in the directory. Her adoptive father was the only one listed under that name.

Before I called my cousin's parents, my husband and I decided to devise a strategy for gauging how receptive they might be to our approaching her. At the time, a mother was making headlines by trying to regain custody of her child from the child's foster parents.

Martin called and said that he was from the Adoptive Parents League of Pennsylvania. He asked Lisa's mother if she was familiar with the case. Yes, she was.

He said, "We're taking a survey to find out how many adoptive parents have told their children that they were adopted and what their reactions were."

She was very pleasant and answered all his questions. They had told Lisa she was adopted when she was eight years old. She was a very good girl and beautifully adjusted, never gave her parents a problem.

I thought that, since Lisa was so well adjusted and her mother was so open, there was no reason I shouldn't call and speak to her. I wouldn't be presenting her with anything she couldn't handle. Since she knows that she is adopted, I reasoned, she must suspect that there are relatives.

I called her mother a few days later and identified myself. She hung up on me. I called her right back. I said, "This is a long-distance call and it's costing me a fortune, but I don't care. Each time you hang up on me I'm going to call again, so you might as well resign yourself to the fact that you're going to talk to me sooner or later, and tell me what I want to know."

She said, "Why don't you leave this girl alone? Leave Lisa alone. She's happily married. She doesn't need you to bring problems into her life."

"That isn't good enough."

I tried to explain what it meant to me to have a cousin so close in so many ways and how I thought Lisa might feel the same way.

At last she said, "I'll tell you what. I'm very sick and my husband is very sick. I don't think I have much longer to live. Why don't you send me a letter with all the information you've gotten so far on your family with a picture of yourself? I'll give it to my attorney. When I die, he'll give it to my daughter."

I agreed. This was in November.

She added, "Please don't contact my daughter." I never let on that I didn't know where Lisa was living. She described Lisa as blond and blue-eyed.

"Please don't contact her. Let us have our holidays in peace."

"I'll promise you that much."

After the New Year I wrote to this woman. Two weeks later I got a very nasty reply from my cousin. She said that she had just buried her mother, that I had a lot of nerve contacting her mother and upsetting her, and that she didn't know what my angle was but I had better be "open and above board" with her; otherwise she would sue me. She had already contacted her attorney to find out if there were any grounds.

I was flabbergasted. I could not believe it. For so many years I had hoped to meet someone. Here I had given my cousin a chance to meet me. I had done all her work for her and she reacted like this.

I wrote her a letter. I stifled all that anger and suggested as politely as I could that we might meet.

While I waited for a reply I had it out with my mother. She said to me, "Why did you want to find her? She didn't want you. If she loved you she wouldn't have given you away."

I said, "You don't know why she gave me up. You're not in a position to judge anyone. You don't know her circumstances. It was 1942 and she was eighteen years old. If you had a baby in those days without being married, you were immediately labeled. She had nowhere to go. She did her best to leave me in good hands. She didn't leave me in a garbage pail. I don't ever want you to say anything about her again, unless it's something good. If I don't hate her, there's no reason for you to hate her. She's not your competition. And furthermore, she's dead so you don't have to worry that I'll go off and take care of her in her old age instead of you."

And I meant every word of it. The anger I had felt earlier had disappeared as I began to understand more about my mother's circumstances.

Finally my cousin consented to a meeting. I drove down to Allentown with a girlfriend. We checked into a motel and went to eat dinner before our eight o'clock appointment. Service was very slow and it seemed that we could never finish our dinner and arrive on time, so I got up from the table and called my cousin to tell her we were going to be late.

She said, "If you're not here by eight sharp, forget it."

I went back to the table and said to my friend, "We have to move." We didn't finish dinner. In the car I said, "I'm not going to give her any information. I'm going to meet her and if she wants to know anything she's going to have to ask for it."

When we walked in her husband greeted us. She was warming her baby's bottle and wouldn't turn around to look at us. Among the other things her mother neglected to tell us was the fact that Lisa was extremely pregnant at the time I spoke to her. I might have felt a little better about waiting before contacting her if I had known. We sat for two and one-half hours. Her husband gave us drinks, but Lisa was cold and even hostile.

At ten-thirty, I stood up and said, "I guess we've taken enough of your time. Thank you for having me here."

She said, "Wait a minute. You haven't told me anything about my mother."

I said, "I didn't think you were interested. You've been sitting there for two hours and you haven't asked me anything. I didn't want to tell you anything you didn't want to know."

"I want to know about my mother."

I went through the whole process, but I didn't tell too much.

Then her adoptive father walked in. He was a sharp old man. He had listened to the story from the next room and I think he liked what he heard.

He said to Lisa, "Aren't you going to offer them a cup of coffee? Why are you sitting out here? The kitchen is a lot more friendly. You've been giving them liquor, but no coffee and cake. What's wrong with you?"

If looks could kill, he would have died right there. She didn't like him.

"Come on," he said to us. "I'll make you coffee." Then he went and got a family album. "This is some way to treat a relative. At least show her some pictures of yourself, when you were a kid and when you were in the convent."

"What made you leave the convent?"

She remained cold and vague. "I was there for five years. I don't want to go into it. I decided it wasn't for me. Let's leave it at that."

I was ready to let her have it but, instead, the old man and I got drunk and had a wonderful time. We stayed until 2:00 AM. When my girlfriend and I arrived back at the motel, I was fed up with my cousin.

"There's no way I'll ever see her again. I looked for all those years and look what I found. What a kick in the teeth."

At 7:00 AM the phone rang. "Hi, this is Lisa. I thought that if you weren't doing anything you might come for dinner tonight."

"I'm very sorry, Lisa." It was my turn to be cold. "We came to meet you and we did that. Now I'm going."

"But I want to meet you again."

"I didn't think you were interested. Don't feel you have any obligation to see me again. I wanted to meet you once. Let's leave it at that."

Then she sort of broke down. She had tried so hard to keep things to herself that to admit anything at all was a sign of desperation.

"Please see me again. I apologize for the way I acted last night."

"All right, but only for an hour." After the way she and her mother had treated me, I wasn't going to warm up to her right away.

When we met, we sat alone and talked. "It's clear to me," I said, "that you are a very bitter person. Why did you take it out on me? I don't deserve it. I thought that you and I could establish a relationship and become very close. I've never had any sisters and you haven't either. We're not only close in age, but I think we probably have a lot of other things in common."

"The reason I was so nasty is that you opened up old wounds. I didn't know how to handle it. I had put it out of my mind years ago. I searched the way you did and no one gave me anything. All my life I've been very lonely. My adoptive mother was so insecure. Every day I had to tell her that I loved her. She didn't want me to go away. She didn't want to share me with anyone."

"Your mother said that you were very good, that you never gave her any problems."

"As a matter of fact," she said, "I was a very rebellious child. I wanted to be an airline stewardess, and, although they said they couldn't afford it, they came up with the money to train for it. I decided I didn't like it and came back. My mother thought that I would stay with her. But when I told her I would get my own apartment, she was crushed.

"Then I went into the convent. All my life I had been searching for someone or something."

"Why did you leave the convent?"

"I thought they would give me the information that you have. I went back to St. Bartholomew's as a nun, thinking that they wouldn't refuse one of their own kind. They wouldn't help me.

"Even then I didn't want to leave. But I wanted to hold office within the convent and they told me that because of my illegitimate birth I could never hold office."

She hadn't wanted to say this in front of her father. We are close today. We had similar childhoods. Her mother's description of a happy, well-adjusted girl was an insecure woman's fantasy. We were both very lonely and rebellious as children.

I met more people who knew both my mother and my aunt, and that mystery of my early days got broader and deeper. One thing I found out was that I had been kept in the hospital for two months after my birth. I have always had a scar on my hip. The most they ever told me was that I had a growth removed by surgery, but they never told me what it was.

The undertaker told me that there is a male child buried with my aunt—an infant—but no one is sure whose son he was— Angie's or Serena's. Was he my brother? I asked around about it, and was told that my grandmother insisted that the child be disinterred when my aunt died and placed with her.

So in July 1973 I wrote to the Bureau of Vital Statistics, using my own file number, requesting a copy of a birth certificate and a death certificate for male infant Pankovic. In late August I received a reply which read: "We are unable to locate a death record for this subject. With regard to the birth, we have located a record which we believe to be the one in question. We are prohibited by law, however, from issuing a copy of this record to you."

In October, responding to a further request, the same man informed me that they were unable to locate a copy of either the birth or the death certificate.

In June 1974 I wrote again. The reply arrived: "A search of our records has been made and we have located the original record of the subject's birth preserved under the above file number. Before issuing a certified copy of the birth record, we must be furnished with a written request from the subject or a court order."

So the same man confirmed, then denied, then again confirmed the birth of my brother. I no longer know what to believe.

Emma Vilardi, ALMA genealogist, did some research for me in an attempt to petition the court for release of my medical records. Her research shows that there is much more twinning among twins than among non-twins, and that the prenatal casualty rate is much higher for twins than for non-twins.

As for that scar on my hip, one possibility is that I may have been a Siamese twin. If so, I also have—or had—a sister. According to Emma's research, "One may develop fully, one may not. Sometimes the undeveloped or partially developed twin is enclosed in a tumor, 'a teratoma,' like an embryonic graft attached to the fully developed twin." Research has also led me to believe that I was considered the weaker of the identical twins. Because of the position of my scar, I think I was on the left side and the left-hand twin is usually thought to be in greater danger. We were baptized at birth by the attending physician, a measure taken only when survival is in doubt. I wonder how many of us were born together. If I have a brother and/or a sister, I think I should be allowed to know.

I met a woman who owned a bar. She had been close to Serena, Lisa's mother. She said that both girls wanted to keep their children, but Mr. Kowalski was out of work with no prospects of finding a job. He said no to both.

Angela, my mother, had a nervous breakdown. She used to go downtown every day looking in every baby carriage for her baby girl. Her sister did the same. How could I be angry anymore? It was obvious that they had no control over anything. They really cared.

My natural mother hardly ever talked about herself, but she often talked about Serena. She went over to the old lady on the corner one day and told her, "Guess what? Serena's pregnant." She never mentioned that she was further along than Serena was.

The old lady said that both of them were mischievous and always in some kind of trouble. They used to pull tricks using their similarities. The twins continually fooled people into thinking they were talking to one, when in fact they were talking to the other. Both cut school quite a bit.

My cousin and I have been over and over the possibilities as to how closely we are related. Sometimes I think she might be my own twin.

The old lady gave me my cousin's father's name and told me

that he was killed in a bar brawl several years after Serena died, but she wouldn't tell me about my father because he still lives in the area.

I tried to talk her into telling me, but she said, "Please don't."

"Why not?"

"What if he tells you things you don't want to hear?"

"What can he tell me? That my mother was a tramp? A hooker? I don't care. I want to know about him."

The more she tried to convince me that I shouldn't see him, the more determined I became. The same as with everything people ever told me I couldn't do, whether it was smoking, finding out about my mother, or this.

I met her daughter and her daughter said, "Mom, you know who her father is. He was in the car accident with Serena."

There were five people in the car that my aunt died in. My aunt and another girl died and the three fellows survived, but it turned out that my father almost lost his leg.

I knew from my talk with Sister Angela that my father was French-Canadian and Baptist. A friend of mine worked in the credit department of a nationwide department store chain that had headquarters in Pennsylvania, so I asked her to call this man and do a credit card check and to somehow find out if he was French-Canadian.

She called. His wife answered. They went through all the standard questions. Then my friend said, "You have the same last name as a friend I had in high school. Are you French?"

His wife answered, "My husband's father was French-Canadian." I was saying in the background, "Ask if he's a Baptist." I was giggling and excited. My friend couldn't think of a way to work such a question in, but that was enough. She didn't take a charge account. Her husband made decisions like that.

We drove down to see him. There were major floods that year in Allentown. A note attached to his door said that he could be reached at a relative's house, so we went there to wait. We told them that my mother had gone to school with him. I didn't want to give myself away.

No one else noticed, but on top of the TV was a photograph of a young man and his wife. He looked just like me.

My father never did arrive that day, so we found out where he worked and the next time we came to town we went right to the factory. I didn't want to go to his home and raise any questions in front of his wife.

"I didn't know your mother very well," he said.

"Do you know anyone she might have dated?"

"No."

"That doesn't make any sense," I said. "High school kids have cliques, and you must have been in that clique." He never once looked straight at me. He kept his face toward the opposite side of the street. He still walked with a limp from the accident in which my aunt had died.

"I'm going to be honest with you," I said, "I'm looking for my father. I don't want to cause any problems. I want to know who he is and talk to him for an hour, that's all."

He kept staring across the street.

"Are you my father?"

"No."

Some time after I spoke to him, my husband called him. "We got your name from the hospital, sir."

The man who I am sure is my father said, "Any time your wife wants to go to the hospital for a blood test, I'm ready."

"You know that isn't conclusive," Martin told him. "You're a very shrewd man, but you're not shrewd enough. You know who you are."

He knows where I am if he wants to contact me. But I won't make any problems for him. I know he's had trouble with his wife. But this doesn't end just because someone says no or because I put it aside. It's so emotionally draining that you just need to stop for a while. I've learned enough that I've stopped for several years, but that doesn't mean it's the end.

Three years ago, I made another effort to find out what it was that kept me in the hospital for those months. I didn't ask for anything about anyone but myself, just for my own hospital records.

The Mother Superior said, "I can't give you any records because of the oath I took. I will turn it over to our attorney. You retain an attorney and have your attorney write to ours. He will give you what you want. After all he didn't take the same oath I did."

Our lawyer wrote, and we got no reply. My husband called and tried a ploy similar to the one I used at the hospital where my mother died. He said he was in the courthouse and needed some information from the file. The secretary was about to give it to him when someone walked in. She had time to think and said she couldn't give him the information.

He did succeed in establishing that those thirty-year-old records were in the attorney's office. Martin then called the Mother Superior. She claimed that she had never said that the records would be released, that I must have made it all up.

"I was there," he said to her. "I heard you say that you would give the information up through your attorney, and he hasn't even had the courtesy to reply to our attorney, let alone do what you said he would do."

She was silent. "Underneath that habit," my husband said, "you're nothing but a lying bitch." Nerves were wearing thin.

I called the attorney. He gave me a line befitting an officer of the court. He said, "I have adopted children of my own. They don't know their backgrounds. Why should you want to know yours."

I was so upset. "Why are you ruining my holiday? Why won't you give me the information?"

"Come in and we'll discuss it."

"You know there's nothing to discuss. Either I'm getting it or not."

"You're not."

"Thank you. I wish you nothing but misery."

My husband called him. The lawyer mentioned in passing that he had tried to contact my father. I don't know if it's true or not. If he did contact my father and he said no, then that might explain why the lawyer never released my records after the Mother Superior said he would. But I didn't ask for anything about my father. I wanted *my own* medical records which might have given me some clue to the truth about my own birth and whether I did have a twin. That has nothing to do with a man who says that he is not related to me.

I tried to get the Orphan's Court of the county to release my records. The legal requirement in these cases is demonstration of "good cause." Determination of good cause seems to be entirely at the discretion of the individual judge.

I spoke to the judge and asked him to define good cause.

"I can't say."

"If I came to you and said that I would die in three months unless I had full access to my medical history, would that constitute good cause?"

"I can't say for sure."

We decided to petition anyway. Emma Vilardi had limited power of attorney. She based her argument on the grounds that lack of full and exact proof of identity had caused me to miss out on certain rights of citizenship, such as employment and adequate medical care. She included research on the incidence of twinning and the probabilities that knowledge of brothers and sisters was being kept from me. My parents submitted an affidavit waiving their interest in confidentiality.

The judge released my adoption decree and I got very excited thinking that was the first step towards release of my full record. But it stopped there. Maybe the hospital got to him. I do know that neither my cousin nor I have been able to get any information about our own histories. Lisa last requested her records in mid-1976 and was rebuffed.

This fight hasn't stopped, I've just taken time off. I'm determined to find out whatever they are hiding from me. If I was born attached to an identical twin, I want to know. Did I have a brother in the womb with me or not? I'm entitled to know.

# A Racial Puzzle
## —— Ted ——

*Many adoptees view the present legal system that stands between themselves and their own histories as a foe to be outwitted. While working at ALMA, I saw people, diffident when making their first tentative inquiries about their search, change into effective, deliberate searchers in a matter of weeks. Suddenly they were able to direct their pent-up anger. The maze of bureaucracy and the system that seals off the past were obstacles to be overcome; condescending clerks and social workers were enemies to be beaten.*

*Ted Avery was never diffident. He grew up as a hard-hitting athlete. No affront would go unchallenged; no opponent would be allowed to strike first. But from his adoptive family Ted learned to care about other people—a habit which perhaps saved him before his hair-trigger temper could get him into trouble. Ted's search was conducted in order to discover his racial origins and he is proud of the personal history he uncovered. Today, as a policeman, Ted is deeply concerned about a law that stands so directly between adoptees and what they consider to be their natural rights. He has always resented the existence of a legal device that kept him unaware of his own heritage for so long.*

When I was a kid I didn't really know the meaning of bigotry. I grew up in a town that had both black and white people and most of my friends were white. I have very light skin and wavy dark-brown hair. My father was dark, but my mother could have passed for white. The confusion caused by my appearance went further than that. When I was about nine, my father took my sister and me to the beach in Atlantic City. I was running along the beach when a gentleman started taking pictures of me. My father got annoyed and asked the man what he was up to.

"I've never seen a real Indian before."

My father told the man off and took us away.

A year later I was playing with a girl from the neighborhood who started to tease me for being adopted. I didn't know what she meant. I went home to my mother and asked about it. To this day she insists that she had told me long before that, but I swear she hadn't.

After that I began to wonder what I could have done as an infant to have forced my mother to give me away, to say, "Here's a human life. You take it, I don't want it." Who wouldn't want a baby? What could a baby do that would cause a parent to give it away like a piece of property?

From there I created reasons. Well, she was raped. She died. She was broke or sick.

I became a tough guy. I began to get into trouble, not so much because I was naturally mischievous, but because my friends did things and I went along. I played sports all the time and so did most of my black friends. They also smoked pot and drank wine. I wanted to be accepted and admired, so I did these things too.

In sports the most important thing was to be physically heroic. It wasn't enough to tackle the guy in high school football. I had to hurt him too; he had to know I was the one who did it. People used to say what an aggressive player I was, but I don't think it had anything to do with being a good player. It was more a matter of "Here I am. I don't know who I am, but you're going to know."

My big lesson came when I was sixteen. I found out how deep friendships run when they are based on being one of the guys. I was with some of my friends at a party. A big black guy, a football hero from another high school, came in with his gang. Drunk, he grabbed me by the front of my shirt and ripped a button off for no reason at all. I was so small by comparison that I had to jump up on a couch to hit him. I knocked him out. I was so amazed that ...st stood there; then four of his friends proceeded to beat me up.

All my friends just stood around and watched.

I learned from that experience that hanging around with the guys would get me nowhere. I became a loner. I had never really developed a taste for alcohol and had never liked the feeling of being high. I became very straight.

Other things kept me straight. I hated to see what it did to my father when the police would come around to question me about something I had done. I became very close to him. He was diabetic and needed lots of attention. He had a leg amputated, then some fingers. He became more helpless and I looked after him. Every time I did something that hurt him, I felt I was taking time off his life.

I did poorly in school. My skin color and my hair and being adopted made me feel like I was alone in the world. There was nobody else in the world like me. I never kept individual friendships going for long periods of time, but went from one crowd to another, from person to person. My parents gave my sister money for bringing home good grades and they would have done the same for me except that, being a tough guy, I couldn't care less about school.

At seventeen I quit school to join the service. The army sent me to Virginia. It was 1962, well before the Civil Rights Act of 1964, and there I got my first exposure to prejudice. Blacks weren't allowed on the beaches or in public facilities. Still, since I was in the service, this didn't affect me right away. Then one weekend I got a ride up North with five white friends who were headed for New York. They were going to drop me on the New Jersey Turnpike so that I could visit my parents. We stopped at a restaurant in Maryland for lunch and the owner called an army sergeant over to tell us we would all have to leave unless I left myself. We left. That really shocked me. Hurt me. I had never faced it before. I had now been singled out for special attention for being "Indian" and for being black, or, as we said in those days, Negro. It made me wonder about being adopted. That was an identity crisis if there ever was one.

Being in the army also taught me that I wasn't as smart as I thought I was. Being tough didn't matter as much as being smart did, so I began to spend more time thinking and studying, finishing my high school education and learning a skill for when I left the service. I chose computer science.

After my father died, I looked around and saw that all my relatives, except for my sister, were in their sixties and seventies. My father's death left a big void in my life because I had cared for him so closely as he became more sickly. I developed a habit of caring for people, I guess, so I began to think more about my natural family and what they must be like.

I went into police work. Computer programming for the telephone company just didn't provide me with what I needed. I had a funny experience while working for the phone company which added to my feelings of curiosity. I started rooming with a white fellow. We shared our apartment for months before I told him I was adopted and he told me he was Jewish. We both had the same awkward feelings about our identities. Later he got busted for drugs and ended up in prison. I became a policeman.

As a policeman, my curiosity continued to grow. Once I had to handle a situation where a Jewish family complained of harassment of their children by those of their Gentile neighbors. I instinctively sided with the Jewish family. I could hear that little ignorant girl taunting me at ten. "You're adopted. You're adopted." I knew what it meant to be different.

Another time a father, an educated white man, stormed into the station house dragging his son by the arm, demanding that we lock the boy up to teach him a lesson. The son, eight years old, had tried for the third time to burn the house down with his parents in it, and the father wanted to scare him into behaving by seeing what it would be like in jail.

I lost my temper. "Can't you see that he's been scared already? He doesn't need more scaring. He needs help and so do you. If he's been trying to burn down the house with you in it, it's because of you."

I was reprimanded for handling the case that way. I should have told him the same thing, but subtly, quietly. I don't know if that kid was adopted or not, but I know that his father didn't know anything about being a parent and, being adopted myself, I sympathized even more readily with the child.

The more deeply I became involved with my police work, the more I appreciated my survival. Many of my childhood friends were in jail, or dead, or hooked on drugs. I once had to carry the body of a boy who died before he even got the needle out of his arm after an overdose of heroin. I gave credit to my parents for raising me to care enough about myself to survive, but I also wondered more and more about my heritage.

I've gone to college part-time for years. In a sociology class the teacher wanted to do a genealogical study of someone in the class in order to demonstrate just how varied our backgrounds were as Americans. Her explanation of the project made me uncomfortable. I could see what was coming. I looked like the most ethnically mixed student in the class. I was also the oldest. I stood out for a number of reasons.

When she picked me for this project I made an excuse about not wanting to be made into a subject for research of any kind. I didn't want anyone to know more about me than I knew about them.

In fact I would have loved to know where I came from, but it was easier to shut off the investigation before the truth became known. Telling thirty students of nineteen and twenty that I was adopted would have been embarrassing. Not knowing where I came from, or who I came from, made me, the oldest in the class, younger than any of them.

Finally, I began to ask my mother questions. She told me a few things: the name of the hospital in New York where I was born and that the adoption was arranged privately. But she didn't tell me other things that she knew.

My sister and my mother have always been closer to one another than I had been to either of them. I thought my sister might know something important. At first she said she didn't know anything, but a week later she called up and told me she knew my birth name. She had known for five years. At first I felt terrific animosity toward her for holding back this information for all those years, information that belonged to me and not to her, but at last I let it go.

My name at birth, according to my sister, was Neil Lipton. I did the usual amount of library research, but the thing that helped the most was that my doctor, through a simple request, secured my mother's hospital records. The whole search took only ninety days.

In my mother's 120 pages of hospital records the name of my aunt Nancy Lipton was listed. The rest of the names and addresses were all badly out of date, but Nancy Lipton was still in the phone book at the same address. I called her on December 23, 1975.

"I'm looking for Beth Lipton," I said.

"That's my sister."

"I believe she may be a relative. I'd like to try and locate her." We talked for a while. I could tell that she was a friendly, open woman, so I finally volunteered that I thought Beth Lipton was my mother. "I was born in July of 1945."

She laughed. "Oh no. Impossible. Beth has a lot of kids, but she wasn't pregnant back then. She had plenty of kids before the War and another after the War, but none during the War."

"Will you do me a favor?" I asked. "Will you give her my name and phone number? Ask her to call me if she wants to."

I was ready. I figured if she wanted to talk to me, I would accept it, but if she didn't, I wouldn't grieve. I didn't know what her status was and I didn't want to cause any problems.

The phone rang. It was my aunt. "I can't believe it," she said. "I talked to your mother and she said she did have a baby in 1945 and did give it up for adoption. Nobody in the family knew it."

She gave me my mother's phone number. I called. I said about twelve words. Then she told me everything.

She was married at the time I was born but separated from her husband. My father was in the army and stationed nearby. There were nine children and the relatives with whom they were staying said that she couldn't bring the new baby into their home. She never even saw me after I was born.

I don't know how she could do it. I know I couldn't give up a child of mine. Later on, my natural parents started living with one another. They had one more child, a daughter who married young, had three sons, lost her husband, and was later stabbed to death.

Beth Lipton, my natural mother, asked me to spend Christmas with her, but I didn't want to suddenly become part of a family scene that I had never known, so I waited until the day after Christmas before visiting them.

When I pulled up in front of my natural mother's building, I almost decided to leave without seeing her. After all those years the answers were waiting for me, but I didn't know if I wanted them.

I did go in and found that I am almost the mirror-image of my mother. I am the lightest of all of them, but we have many of the same features.

We have had many problems of adjustment to one another. My mother is so proud of me that I have to stand back from her to keep my perspective. Our tastes are different and our interests are different. They enjoy bingo and playing poker, while I prefer a quiet competitive game of chess with some good music.

Getting to know my brothers and sisters has been difficult too, because my mother insists that I check in with her every time I go near any of them. I don't want to offend her by disregarding her wishes, so it becomes easier to avoid driving to New York. She holds me up as an example, and that strains my relationships with all of them. I am the baby and yet, because I have achieved as much as I have and because it meant enough for me to come back and find her after all the years, my mother places me on a pedestal. Her children don't have jobs with the status of mine. Some of them are on public assistance. They all live in housing projects. Most ironic of all, I have relatives who run numbers. I'm a policeman and they make their livings from gambling.

The thing I am most grateful for is the knowledge of my heritage. It turns out that I am part white, part black, and part Indian. My mother's family comes from a group called the Jackson Whites. Scholars disagree about the exact origins of the Jackson Whites. They live in the Ramapo Mountains of New Jersey and New York. The Negro blood is thought to have come down from a settlement of runaway slaves. The Tuscarora Indians passed through the Ramapo Mountains in fleeing the extermination campaign waged by white people in North Carolina. Slaves were used by the whites as soldiers in that campaign. Most of the Tuscaroras settled in northern New York and Ontario, Canada, but some probably remained in the Ramapos.

The white genes come from European immigrants, primarily Dutch, who settled there over centuries. Many are thought to have been fugitives. Although the term Jackson White is derogatory in the same sense that Okie used to be, implying inbreeding and degeneracy, I couldn't be happier to know that it applies to me because it gives me a history that I have traced to Holland in the seventeenth century.

My mother's mother's father was a Dutchman named Alfred Dupont. Her mother's mother was full-blooded Tuscarora. My mother's grandfather on her father's side was Alfred Boucher, part Dutch, part English, and part Indian. I've read about all these families in books and articles.

So I know about my skin color and my hair texture. I feel a part of all these ethnic groups and free from any labels at the same time. My mother doesn't. Somewhere she developed a tremendous hatred of white people. I asked her what she would do if I married a white woman. She told me never to bring her around. If I had any children by a white wife, I should keep them away.

My mother cried so much when I asked about my sister that I had to get the whole story from others. This was my only full sister and I wanted to know as much about her as I could. Her husband came home from work one day and went to take a nap. He died of heart failure. He was twenty-four. My sister then began going out with a guy. She realized that he wasn't good for her and was trying to break up with him. Her three little boys were away staying with an aunt overnight when the irate boyfriend stabbed her to death. No one heard from her, so someone went to check up and saw her lying on the floor.

I feel a tremendous sense of loss. If I had been around three years ago when it happened, perhaps I could have been a stabilizing influence on her and helped her avoid men with criminal tendencies. Her boys mean so much to me now. They live with another sister. If I were more settled I would want to have them around me, but my work doesn't permit it. They were shy at first, especially the oldest who remembers his mother more than the others. But they like me and get a kick out of seeing how much I resemble their mother.

I also missed my father by a couple of years and, again, I feel I could have helped him. My mother gave me his name and told me where his people came from. I called an aunt and she said that my father had written to her when I was put up for adoption, telling her that I was born with my heart on the wrong side of my body and had been put in an institution. He couldn't live with the truth and had to invent an excuse for this thing that was done to me, this severance. I found his invention most interesting too. But, excuse or not, he wanted his family to know that he had had a son.

My mother said that, after they lived together, my father settled in New Jersey and married another woman. She told me that both of them drank and that my father had been arrested a few times for stealing batteries and things like that. He had supported all ten children for some time on his salvaging of scrap. That's what led him to steal batteries.

Using my police contacts I was able to see a "rap sheet," an arrest record. My father spent a considerable amount of time in jail. The most serious charge he ever faced was for threatening to kill someone. This charge, like most of the others, was related to his drinking problem.

He was killed in a traffic accident in 1974. I sent a letter to the chief of police in the town where the accident occurred and requested a copy of the accident report. He wrote back that he never sent copies of accident reports to anyone, not even other policemen but, when I told him what my interest was, he responded with a beautiful letter. He knew my father well and was acquainted with his problems. He invited me to meet with him any time. He is also in possession of the only photographs of my father that exist anywhere—his mug shots.

For all his difficulties with the law, my father was known to love children. Not only had he supported all my mother's children for some time, but his own son by his New Jersey marriage was his pride and joy. He took him for long rides in his truck. That's just the kind of thing I would like to do with my kids if I had hours to spend with them, showing them new things and talking. But by a couple of years, I missed this man.

I have confused, mixed feelings about my life. When I look at my half-brothers and sisters, I think that I had the better break. But I don't know how anyone could give up a child, one child out of eleven.

My adoptive mother and I get along the same as ever. I see her about as often as I did before. I've never told her about finding my natural mother, because I don't want to upset her. She obviously feels very sensitive about it. She used to cry when I'd ask her questions and tell me that she and my father loved me. She even told me that adoption was her first choice, although I've known for a long time that that was not the case.

It would please me to discuss it with her, but I feel that she has earned an old age free of disturbance. I hate the idea that she felt forced by society to lie to me. I know about her lies now. Now that I have discovered the truth by my own means I can accept them.

As a policeman, I don't think that adoption as it exists today encourages respect for the law. We all have to lie to get what we are entitled to.

I've been lucky to see both sides. I listen to my fellow police officers speak very politely to black people and then turn around and call them niggers. I've gone back to the same beaches that were segregated when I was in the service and seen all kinds of people swimming. And now I've seen where my face comes from.

# A Foundling

## —— Anna ——

*Foundlings do not concentrate on trying to get information from sealed adoption records. The facts of their births lie elsewhere—in the minds of their natural mothers. While there may well be a record of the birth in a hospital, there is no way to match the discovery of an abandoned infant with that specific birth record. Foundlings have petitioned for police records of investigations into their abandonment. In some cases, these records indicate that the investigations ended prematurely, perhaps to avoid interfering with adoption proceedings that were under way. What may have been the only possible opportunity to find the name of one's natural mother disappeared when the investigation was halted.*

*Newspaper files may be of help to foundlings, since they often include photographs in stories about discovery of abandoned infants. Responding to requests by searchers, newspapers have often shown a willingness to update these old stories by recounting a foundling's life story and addressing appeals to the natural mother to come forward. There is always the chance that such an appeal will work, but I have never heard of a single success.*

*Anna Johnson's story is unusual even for a foundling. Discovered in a hallway on Christmas Eve in 1934, she went on to become a child actress and nearly lived the Hollywood dream of the cute little bundle who grew up to be a star. While the Hollywood dream never came true, Anna thinks there is hope that her search for her mother will succeed. That would be the happiest ending for her story.*

"Did you find your mommy today?" my kids ask me when they come home from school. They don't really understand what I am doing. I don't fully understand it either. You really start to go crazy in this search. On subways and buses you see people and you stop and stare. In the supermarket you find yourself scooting around the aisles to look at women your height. My kids look like me. I must look like my real parents.

The first thing I remember is auditioning for a radio program, the Horn and Hardart's "Children's Hour." It must have been 1937. The "Children's Hour" was a program of live entertainment that went out over radio every Sunday for years and continued on television. Even that part of my life has a little mystery attached to it because of my adoption. The announcer said I was two and one-half years old, but I was really closer to four. My adoptive parents considered that I was born in 1935 because that's when they got me, so I have always thought of myself as younger than I really am.

I sang my song at the audition and became a regular on the program, first as a singer and then as a tap dancer as well. I stayed with the program until 1955.

Mom was never the typical stage mother. She was retiring and shy. She would never go anywhere while I was working, but would sit in the corner of the studio and watch. It helped that I had talent, and she nurtured it. My parents kept a balance, sending me to Catholic schools and public schools, never to professional schools. I lived the life an ordinary child leads. I was not a little celebrity.

My sister Edna was fourteen years old when I was adopted. My mother couldn't have any more children of her own. She had taken in two foster children, Eddie and Ruth, before I was adopted. My parents took care of Eddie from the time he was a baby until he was five or six. Then his mother wanted him back. My parents kept contact with her and she always made it clear that she loved Eddie. He went back to visit them from time to time after he returned to his mother, and they remained close even after I was adopted, but my sister liked Eddie so much she felt her little brother had been taken away from her.

Ruth, a little girl from someplace in Vermont, had come to stay with them for a few years until her mother wanted her back.

I guess my parents had decided that if they ever did get another chance they would go through a legal adoption so as not to worry about losing the child again.

When I was a few months old, my parents received a letter from the New York Foundling Hospital offering me for adoption. My parents always kept that letter hidden from me, but I found it when I was thirteen and it confirmed my belief that I was an adopted child.

I first began to believe I was adopted when my mother took me to a doctor's office for my physical examination before entering school. She asked me to leave the doctor's office after he had examined me and through the closed door I heard her tell him I was adopted. She never told me.

As a child I had bright prospects for an acting career. When I look back upon it now, I like to think that my mother kept putting me before the public in hope that the woman who had abandoned me would see me and come forward.

Mom had a way with children and ran a dancing school. She gave Edna lessons, but my sister didn't like dancing and soon gave it up. I took to dancing easily, and Mom encouraged me. Maybe Mom was realizing her own ambitions through me. I don't know. She was also a talented seamstress, and every Sunday while I was performing I had a new coat or a new dress to wear. I think she may have kept too busy in those days. I remember wishing that my Auntie Bess had been my mother, because when we visited she always had plenty of time to play with me.

When I was four or five, I appeared in three movies. We filmed at the old Warner Brothers Studios on Long Island. Shirley Temple set the style for little girls in those days. The studio warned my mother not to curl my hair. They didn't want me to resemble Shirley.

In one scene I remember, the male lead was locked out in the rain while I was indoors. My mother was near me off camera. The technician turned on the shower they rigged for rain and I got so frightened for him that I started crying. He had to come over in his wet bathrobe and explain that it was all a game.

In another film I made, the star played a soda jerk who loved to juggle while he worked. He would collect crowds of kids by juggling plates and glasses and spoons in the store window. I was his favorite, of course, and he looked at me while he juggled. It was supposed to be snowing in one scene. They dropped white corn flakes as snow, but it was so hot under the lights that my ice cream cone kept melting. Finally they put a rubber ball in the cone and poured chocolate syrup on it. Another time he was making me a soda. Since he wasn't too good at it, he kept forgetting his lines. I kept whispering them to him, which made him laugh. He couldn't get over it. This little girl was cueing him, and that made him laugh all the harder. Finally the director called a break and gave me a stern lecture about not feeding lines to actors.

Those three films were all I ever did, but I had a close call with real fame. My dancing teacher had set up a screen test for me and my mother took me to it. The casting director told me what to say because I couldn't read well yet. When I had finished and the rushes were done, the casting director called my mother and said, "Well, Mrs. Smith, what do you think of your daughter going to Hollywood to be in a picture with Clark Gable?" She was thrilled. Unfortunately the dancing teacher thought he was being left out. He called the casting director and claimed to be my manager. That put the casting director off, I guess, because some other little girl got the part. The picture was *Gone with the Wind*, and I would have been the daughter of Rhett Butler and Scarlett O'Hara.

I finally gave up my dreams of an acting career. Sooner or later you have to decide whether you really have what it takes. As a young actress in New York, I saw too many talented people around and not enough work for all of us. I just didn't have it.

My dad was an engraver who worked for the same company throughout his career. But even though he stayed in one job all that time, Mom was a restless soul. We seemed to move every year, all around New York and sometimes New Jersey. My father always ended up having to commute to work an hour each way except for one year when we lived one block from where he worked.

I never thought about why we moved so much. It seemed normal and I thought everyone did it. I know one adoptee whose mother kept moving her family around to keep anyone from telling her daughter about the adoption, but I don't think that was the case with us. Wherever we lived, I always worked with the same kids on the radio and, as I found out later, they all knew I was adopted.

Every Saturday night we went to New Jersey to Auntie Bess's and Uncle Jim's to sing and have parties. Uncle Jim played the guitar and a friend of his played the banjo. I got a chance to perform for the people I loved.

Edna was separate from most of this and very distant from me. I hardly remember her being around much after the first few years of my childhood. When I was adopted she was old enough to be my mother. Whenever she traveled on the bus, she would tell me to call her "mommy." She always worked and dated as far back as I can remember. She was married in 1941 and moved to a town in New Jersey.

I was eleven when my mother died. My father and I went to live with my sister and her husband who had two children. Bad feelings sprang up between my sister and me. She had always been much closer to my mother than I had been, and I think she resented all the attention Mom gave me because of my acting career. Now that I was living with her, she thought she could be my new mother and, at the same time, get free baby-sitting and help with the housework.

My father came to my rescue. He insisted I should have time of my own. After my mother died, he had told me I could quit show business. I guess he felt mother had put too much pressure on me. But I chose to go on with it for some time. He had always been a fantastic father. He had been my buddy, taking me to the zoo and places like that, while mother had always taken me to lessons and the studio.

I don't believe I thought too much about the question of who I really was until my mother died, but the problem began to occupy me from then on.

Finally it really bothered me. My mother had often told my father to hide the box that contained the family papers. He did until we moved in with my sister, but then he became careless. One night Dad went off to a meeting and my sister and her husband went to the movies. I was left alone to look after my niece and nephew.

I decided it was time to find those papers. I went to his room. The box was easy to find, and I went through the papers carefully so as not to disturb anything.

A white envelope from New York Foundling Hospital was addressed to my parents and dated March 1935. I opened it. "Dear Mr. and Mrs. Smith: We have a little girl here presumed to have been born December fourth, if you would like to see her. . . ."

There was my proof. I had known, but now I had proof. I cried. I think that's the first time I ever cried about it. And I prayed for strength not to tell anyone. I also vowed to go to the hospital one day and ask about it.

I was in high school when I began to talk about my adoption. Up in Vermont, where my father had a summer home, I shared my secret with a friend named Sally Mills. It felt good to tell her. Sally called me Scottie. "Yeah, Scottie, I know you're adopted." I was shocked. My father had told her parents, and they had told her. But no one had ever told me. I asked her not to tell my father that I knew and she never did.

In New Jersey, later that same year, I told another friend, Annette Hastings. I made a production out of it, swearing that she was my best friend and if she weren't my best friend I wouldn't tell her my great secret. But she already knew. Everyone I told was my closest friend, but they all knew. Only I hadn't been told. Yet I liked talking about my secret with them.

Later on I moved to Manhattan. I was on my own and I shared an apartment with two other girls. There was more freedom to talk about the secret, but I still told them not to mention it to my father when he came to visit.

My father was sixty-eight when he died in 1964, and I never discussed my adoption with him.

In those days, I suppose, adoption was kept more secret than it is now. I'm sure Dad wanted to protect my feelings. Other people who adopt may fear that the child will not be theirs any longer if the secret gets out, but I think my father wanted to protect me against confusion. I protected him too. "Don't tell him," I thought. "It might hurt him. He might think you don't want him any more."

People have said that I'm different from some other adoptees because I'm cheerful and outgoing. When I was a child, I was told all the time that I had a great personality. I didn't even know what "personality" meant when they said that, but I was glad I had it.

Since childhood, being cheerful and outgoing or even being able to discuss my feelings has taken a great deal of hard work and psychoanalysis. My father and mother always fought, and my sister and brother-in-law always fought. I was determined not to be like that. I had the burden of a great secret before I started school. I felt that strong emotions could bring it out. Being an entertainer meant that I could only speak words written by others. I was comfortable with that.

I had an even disposition. I never displayed anger. It bothered some people. When they made me mad they never knew it. My father would bawl me out, but I never answered back. He asked me what I was really thinking, but I never told him.

When I began my psychoanalysis after my first marriage broke up, Dr. Gordon recognized my shyness and told me to write down at home the things I really wanted to say so that we could discuss them. I wrote for him every night. After years of therapy, when we finished, he handed me hundreds of sheets of paper on which I had written.

"Here's your book," he said. When I read of his death recently, I felt sad. He would have been thrilled to hear of my progress in searching. His partner told me I should at least make an effort to find my parents, that I would be true to myself if I tried.

My first step in my search was to apply for a copy of my birth certificate. My name was Anna Wright and I was born at 260 East 85th Street in Manhattan.

I got very excited. "That's the house. I must go to look at it."

I went to New York Foundling Hospital to ask about myself. I didn't realize how hard it would be to learn anything about the past. The social worker told me, "If there are any names, we're not allowed to tell you. We're not allowed to give you any direct leads."

The social worker got the records and began to tell the story. "You were not born at that address. You were found there on Christmas Eve in 1934 by a woman named Mary Santillo. Mrs. Santillo called the police, and the police took you to Bellevue Hospital."

I thought it over for a month before I returned to Foundling Hospital. I remembered that the letter to my parents had been dated March 1935. Could I have been in Bellevue from Christmas until March? When did I get to Foundling Hospital? There had been two precinct numbers in the police report. Why? I was a beginner at searching and didn't know what to expect or how to interpret the information. And, of course, I wanted to believe that the information was there, that somehow I could get it from them.

Back to Foundling Hospital. "How come it took from December to March before I was adopted?" I didn't know then how long it takes for an adoption to be completed. I really was not legally adopted until 1937, when we lived in New Jersey.

I had been at Bellevue for two months. The Child Welfare Bureau had given me the name Anna Wright for no apparent reason. The social workers at Foundling Hospital told me everything they could. They were more cooperative than I thought they would be. I have since found out that New York Foundling Hospital has assumed a relatively lenient attitude in cases such as mine and has even arranged family reunions in certain cases. The only detail the social workers could add was that a religious medal had been pinned to my shirt when I was found. Because it was a Catholic medal, I was given to a Catholic family.

In the past year certain events have given me new hope of completing my search. In November 1975, my husband Richard and I went to the New York Public Library at 42nd Street and Fifth Avenue to look for some mention of my birth. Richard is a great leveler for me. He kids me and warns me not to get my hopes up too high. But every time he says that, something new happens to buoy me up.

After going through all the newspapers on microfilm without any luck, we were told that copies of several newspapers were kept at the Public Library Annex several blocks away. I went there myself the next day and began to leaf through them. When I got to the centerfold of the *Daily News* Christmas edition of 1934, I saw a picture of a baby with the headline "Santa Sent Her."

I stopped and told myself, "Don't get excited. It may not be you." But the caption said that Mary Santillo had found the child at 260 East 85th Street!

I didn't go any further. I went to the desk and tried to have a copy made. The people who do that work were out to lunch. I left to get a sandwich. As I ate, I remember thinking, "I'm going to go back and they're not going to let me have that paper again. I'll never see that picture again."

I had never seen myself as an infant. The earliest picture I had was taken at two years old. I went back to the library and sketched the picture myself while I waited. Then the excitement began to wear off. "Great," I said to myself, "you found the picture but you don't have any real news."

As Christmas approached in 1975, a friend contacted a newspaper reporter who had done a story about the adoptees' movement the previous summer. My friend told her about the Christmas Eve picture of forty-one years before and suggested it might make a good story for Christmas Eve.

The paper ran the story, telling about Mary Santillo and reprinting the old picture.

The response was both gratifying and disturbing. One call came from a man who had worked with me on the "Children's Hour" from the time I was seven. He was a few years older than I. I asked him whether any of the kids knew about my adoption. He said they all did. There it was again. Everyone knew but me.

A number of religious books and pamphlets came in the mail. One woman wrote telling me she was my mother. She said I had been born in Harlem. "I know you're thinking," she wrote, "what was a white woman doing in Harlem? You see, I'm not white. I am Puerto Rican with a little Negro blood mixed in me. Your father was a Cuban so there's no way in the world that you are white. I just had to tell you to get it off my chest."

If it were only the truth. She didn't give an address, of course, but insisted that I get the newspaper to run another article saying my mother had stepped forward and supplying my home address so she could visit me. She said my name was Anna Martinez.

One letter carried a Flushing, New York, postmark. It was from someone who called herself Aunt Susie. "You say you have children but you don't mention a husband, could you be taking after the whoer [sic] that hatched you?" She advised me to get a decent husband. Doesn't such a person realize that an adoptee's fantasies take into account all kinds of possible mothers?

I also received a letter from Mary Santillo.

On the Sunday after Christmas, I went to meet the woman who had found me.

I was nervous when I started out. I was supposed to call her as soon as I reached Staten Island, where she lived. I made the call, but I was told she had already left for the ferry station. I asked myself, "How will I know her?" I went up the ramp from the ferry station and saw that a car was waiting. A man and a woman were in it. The man got out and looked around. He had a copy of the newspaper that carried the story. I knew I had found Mary.

Mary started talking as soon as I got in the car. She introduced the man as her brother. They were glad to see me. They had been together forty-one years ago when Mary found me. At 11:30 PM, Christmas Eve, they had been on their way from their mother's house to fetch Christmas presents from Mary's place a few doors away. Mary lived at 260 East 85th Street with her husband and three children.

"There were only three people on the street, the two of us and a well-dressed young woman ahead of us who kept looking back. I said to my brother, 'I'd like to know who she's looking for.' We walked into the hallway, and my brother said he heard something that sounded like a cat. I said no, it sounded like a baby. We found you in back of the cellar door all wrapped up. I picked you up. You were a darling baby."

People came out into the hallway. There was a commotion and Mary remembered the woman on the street. She said to her brother, "Go find her." He couldn't.

Her brother said, "If we had been a minute and a half earlier, we would have run smack into her."

People were crying and calling the young woman all kinds of names. Mary told them not to say such things because they had no way of knowing why she had done it. Then people got mad at Mary for calling the police. "Any number of them wanted you right on the spot. They just wanted to keep you."

For depression times the girl was well dressed. She had a nice black coat and a hat.

The police came and Mary went to the police station with them. They all thought I was a boy because I had a blue blanket around me. The police asked her to undress me. There was a striped blanket under the blue one and a white coat and a pink dress. My booties were flannel and homemade. My hair was all over the place. I had a St. Theresa medal pinned to my shirt.

Mary eventually gave birth to seven children of her own, and she has twenty-eight grandchildren. The Santillo family moved to Staten Island in 1935, but they showed me a photograph of the old building where I was left. Mary's daughter told me that Mary remembers me every Christmas. She always referred to me as Theresa because of the medal, and she named one of her own daughters Theresa.

When I returned to the ferry, the full impact of what I had just experienced hadn't yet hit me. I had just met the woman who had found me forty-one years ago. She had seen a girl who could have been my mother. After all the years of imagining, this was no fantasy. It was real.

I overhear two women talking in a supermarket. One of them says, "What do you mean they won't tell you about your family? That's your legal right. You just tell them you've got to know." The other one says something to the effect that her father had disappeared when she was a youngster. She is trying to find him. "For all I know, he could be walking past me on the street right now, and I wouldn't even know him."

I have no earlobes. When I see a stranger I always check his earlobes. As I board a subway train, I see a tall, thin man with gray hair. His earlobes are smaller than mine. His build reminds me of my son. His nose is long, like mine. I want to stop him and speak to him. I almost go after him. But he looks kind of disheveled. That stops me.

Later I keep thinking I should have tried. That conversation between those two women might have been some kind of prediction.

You get hung up finding people who look like you.

Another person has read my story—a young telephone company employee from Queens, New York. Her name is Pat Merrill. When she saw my picture in the newspaper, she thought I looked like her grandfather. She called me and said, "I think we're cousins."

Pat's grandparents, the Herberts, came to the United States from England in 1930. They had four children—Rose, Jennie, Lynn, and Pat's mother. Jennie was fifteen when the Herberts arrived in this country. She went to work as a governess for a family named Black who lived on West 91st Street.

Jennie fell in love with an Italian boy and her father objected strongly. The family was English Protestant. Jennie became pregnant and gave birth about the time I was born. The parents disowned her. The last time anyone saw her was in 1935, when she visited Rose in Jackson Heights, New York. Rose wanted Jennie to make up with the family, but Jennie disappeared. When Rose was dying, she wanted to see Jennie, so Pat began to search for her aunt. Rose died a year ago, but Pat has continued the search.

There is confusion about just when Jennie's baby was born. Some say autumn, others winter. December 4 is right on the borderline.

The last concrete trace of Jennie is a 1933 telephone listing for a Jennie Black at the address where she worked for the Black family. The children she looked after are grown now and have no strong memories of their governess.

The chance that I am the daughter of Jennie Herbert is as promising as any other. It means a great deal to me that I have found the woman who picked me up. Pat's search is now my search too. We are working together on it.

Some of Pat's relatives resemble me. Her grandfather died in 1963. His photographs are not unlike me, especially the shape of the nose and the lines around the mouth. But when you look for resemblance in photographs, you find it. Besides, his earlobes are enormous.

I see Mary Santillo from time to time. She now seems to look at me more closely than she did at first. Does she think she remembers someone from the past? My imagination takes hold.

You have to become a detective for this. Fantasies and longing don't count. Still, you have to use your imagination to make sense out of clues. It's not like a television program. The clues don't just come together all by themselves.

A friend suggested recently that Jennie Herbert might have left me at 260 East 85th Street because so many Italians lived there. Jennie's boyfriend was Italian. Maybe he lived nearby. Someone had pinned a St. Theresa medal to me, and St. Theresa is popular with Italians.

The newspaper story has given me two other leads. A woman has written to tell me of a girl named Jackie who had come to board with her family in Queens, New York, in 1935. Jackie kept a picture of a young movie actor she claimed was her boyfriend. The woman had even gone to the trouble of looking up the actor in film directories to pinpoint the year. She remembers that Jackie made sandwiches for her that were even daintier than her own mother's sandwiches. Jackie spoke with a Canadian accent, she thought, and visited her sister every week.

After Pat's family contacted me, the newspaper published a follow-up with photographs of Jennie, her father, Pat, and me. Another woman has written, recalling a Queens, New York barmaid she had met in 1949 who resembled the photograph of Jennie.

Pat's Aunt Lynn, Jennie's sister, says she thought she saw Jennie on a subway train in Jackson Heights, New York, fifteen years after Jennie disappeared. Lynn called to the woman by name and the woman fled.

All these stories center around Queens, where I now live.

Pat says that Jennie's baby was born two months early, but Mary says I looked full-term when she picked me up. The people at Bellevue have promised help in trying to discover why I was kept at Bellevue for those missing months. There was no name for the baby, so we will have to go through the microfilm record inch by inch.

Somehow the newspaper articles have come to the attention of my sister Edna, who has been living far from New York for several years. Her memories are bitter. I would like her to be able to accept what I am doing and, if she wants, to know me again and let go of the past. She doesn't seem to be capable of it yet.

We both were hurt by the secrecy surrounding my adoption. She claims she wanted Mom to tell me about it, but that my father wouldn't permit it. When I was a teenager, my sister found out I knew the secret and fought with my father about discussing it. He said I wouldn't be able to put on such a good act if I knew. I had been an actress since the day they brought me home, so I should have been capable of putting on a good act.

How was my sister hurt?

She says that after the foster children, Eddie and Ruth, were given up, my parents promised to bring home a blond, blue-eyed baby brother. Her version of my adoption claims that when they went to Foundling Hospital and walked through the ward, my mother was drawn to me. I was small and sickly looking. When she went near me I held up my arms to her. She felt my motion was a sign from God. The nuns were reluctant to let me go because I was ill. My mother pleaded and they gave in.

My sister was sitting at the kitchen table when they brought me home. Mom placed me in front of her and said, "She's yours."

"You were so small," my sister has told me. "I thought you were a doll. And then you moved."

I feel sorry for my sister, but we don't feel any closer. She has said such things as, "I loved you and you kept hurting me. When they write books about adoption, they don't talk about how people like me feel." She speaks only of her own problems when we talk on the phone.

When things are open, they are easy to dismiss. When things are subtle and unspoken, the way they were with us, they don't stop hurting. My husband took the phone away from me during a recent conversation with Edna. He felt I was too upset. He told my sister to leave us alone if she can't do anything but make me feel guilty.

Richard is a good man. He is always logical and practical about my search for my real identity. That helps me. When I tell him stories about people I see in the supermarket who look like me, he says I'm going crazy. And, when I'm going to meet new people, he warns me to find out as much as I can about them and not to put too much stock in what they say so that I won't be hurt.

I don't think it has been so good for my kids to know that I was abandoned. They have known some pretty unstable times. It's hard to ask them how they feel. I don't want to put ideas in their heads that will make them feel worse. But I let them tell me what they want to say.

I have spent many evenings with friends who have hauled out the family picture albums and shown photographs of their grandparents, brothers, sisters, and parents. They always take delight in their family memories. Sometimes they know my background and sometimes they don't. Such evenings always get me started again thinking about who I really am.

So I go on looking at all the evidence, trying to find something significant. Maybe Pat's family album is also mine.

If I could send my true mother a message, it would be:

Dear Mom,

My search is ever constant that some day I will find you and write the book of my life into yours for any time that is left to us.

Love,
Anna.

# Black-Market Baby
## —— Danielle ——

*Black-market adoptees may not be helped by open adoption records. The men and women who operate black-market baby businesses are usually careful to hide the true identity of any child they place. These people take advantage of laws that permit private adoptions. Because of their ability to supply children on request, black marketeers can demand great sums of money for the service they provide. There is no need to go through long, formal adoption proceedings.*

*Recent stories about black marketeering indicate that enough money is involved to corrupt whatever legal mechanisms are set up to fight profiteering. A shortage of healthy white infants has caused prices to skyrocket. The going price for such infants is in tens of thousands of dollars in some cases.*

*Danielle Rosenthal was adopted through a black market. The woman who arranged her adoption worked on the staff of a licensed child care agency, which gave her access to a ready supply of children whose mothers could not care for them but had not placed them for adoption. The same woman went on to participate in a scheme that brought children from the South to other parts of the United States. Danielle's birth and adoption records have been altered repeatedly, so there is little chance her search will succeed without the cooperation of the woman who arranged her adoption. Danielle's story is an example of the often insurmountable difficulty of trying to find one's origins after they have been obscured by illegal transactions.*

When I was three, my mother sat me down and told me I was

adopted, and I think my gut reaction was that there was something wrong with me. I've never stopped wondering. My life since then has been comfortable but rootless, successful in ways that can be measured, as in school and college, but uncommitted.

I did a great deal of traveling. Antiquities always fascinated me. My first choice of careers was to be an archaeologist, but to be safe I chose social work, thinking that by solving other people's problems my own would somehow solve themselves. Four years ago I returned from a trip to the Orient and someone asked me where I was going next. At that point I didn't feel like going anywhere. Instead I read *The Search for Anna Fisher* and became preoccupied with finding my natural mother. The traveling and the social work had been substitutes for a more basic need. Since I began there has been no relief. The more I learn, the less I know.

My amended birth certificate gave the name of the Zilker Park Hospital, a twenty-bed maternity hospital, as my place of birth. I hired a private detective who did one useful thing. He found the doctor who delivered me. The doctor and his wife lived in their retirement home in Florida. He had suffered a stroke and his wife did most of the talking.

The doctor's wife, the hospital's business manager, remembered my case. I was one of the last children to be born at Zilker Park. She said they kept no records except for due dates. Something happened, she didn't say what, and the couple went to Atlantic City for a holiday and decided to close down. She remembered my mother's face but not her name. I've written to her several times, but she insists she knows nothing more. Today the hospital is an apartment building.

I have always respected my parents' wishes not to be involved in my search, but I asked family friends and relatives what they knew about my adoption. There are a number of other adoptees in my family. An aunt gave me the name of a woman, Nanette Bernstein, who, I discovered, was widely known among Jewish families of means who wanted to adopt. The rumors included the names of a number of Jewish celebrities.

I didn't find Nanette Bernstein right away. I began to follow standard search procedures, but this was frustrating. Obviously the filing of vital statistics was subject to corruption.

My birth certificate had the number Special 22426 with delayed registration and delayed filing date. Some delay is normal in adoption, but the dates were four and ten years after my birth. It has since been explained to me that the term "Special" is attached after such delays have occurred. Obviously someone was tampering with the records many years after I was born. In the New York Public Library I searched through six thousand numbers until I found 22426. But, according to the birth index, that number belonged to an Italian boy in the Bronx who was born on another day in October. I was stumped.

I wrote to Emma Vilardi, ALMA genealogist. She informed me that New York State only uses a number more than once in the event of a multiple birth. On her suggestion I sent for a full transcript of my original birth certificate. I received nothing.

The lawyer in my own case was dead. The lawyer who handled my sister's adoption had become a judge. I had gone to school with his daughter and knew him personally. I went to see him to ask if he could give me any help in locating information about myself. He was very nice about it, but gave me the name of another judge who would know more about it.

The second judge promised to help. He asked some questions about why I was searching, but there was no trace of judgment. He had never handled such a request and wanted to know for his own future reference.

Six weeks passed and I heard nothing. He called one evening just to reassure me that I had not been forgotten. He hadn't been able to find any files about me, just a docket slip saying that on a certain date Kathleen Graham would be adopted by Anthony and Meredith Rosenthal.

In the meantime I located Nanette Bernstein who still lived in New York. I called her and she was very nice to me. I identified myself and she recognized me instantly. She had visited our home when I was sixteen, she said. Her memory was so good she named the town where my parents lived. All she told me was that my mother was an unmarried college student. No names and no places, but nothing fuzzy about her recollections. I thought it would be just a matter of time.

I wrote to a librarian at the New York Public Library, giving him the name Kathleen Graham, born October 3, 1939. He sent back a certificate number and I wrote away for that birth certificate.

Then I called Nanette Bernstein again and told her that I had found my birth certificate number. This time she became hysterical. She was scared. She told me I was crazy. She said I was lower than the leather on the sole of her daughter's shoe. Then at the end of her tirade, her tone abruptly changed. She called me "dearie" and suggested that we have dinner the next time she came to Philadelphia. Maybe someone came into the room where she was talking and she didn't want to sound like a lunatic.

When the certificate was sent, it became apparent that Nanette Bernstein had something to hide. It was a birth certificate, by adoption, for someone named Martha Ryder, born the same year, the same day, in the same city, but in a different hospital. At least three different typewriters were used. Names and dates were crossed out and changed.

The names of the adoptive parents, Anthony and Meredith, are the same as my own parents. Their last initial is also the same. Nanette Bernstein had been party to a fraud, but I couldn't tell how many others were involved. Maybe Martha Ryder did exist and our identities were switched. Maybe Kathleen Graham was me disguised to look like someone else. There were so many confusing possibilities. The public records, which should have been concrete evidence, made the mystery more baffling than ever.

By contacting realtors and using voter registration records, I was able to establish that an Anthony Ryder had lived at the address on the birth certificate, but he was married to a woman named Sandra and had a two-year-old daughter.

Another adoptee, doing research for herself, brought to my attention a series of articles from 1949 in *The New York Times*. The first article was headed: "Baby Ring Suspect Held on 3 Charges—Woman Accused of Assaulting Detective—Father Escaped With Address Book."

The article said:

[Mrs. Nanette Bernstein, 48 years old, of 733 Second Ave.], who is being investigated for her alleged connections with a Black Market in babies, will be arraigned today in Felony Court on charges of felonious assault, resisting arrest, and preventing an officer from performing his duty.

At 1 PM yesterday, Detectives William [Burns] and James [Crews] of the Manhattan District Attorney's office were admitted into Mrs. [Bernstein's] apartment. Present at the time were Mrs. [Bernstein's] daughter, [Diane], 17, and her father, identified only as a Mr. [Kresge].

As the detectives began searching the apartment Detective [Burns] picked up Mrs. [Bernstein's] pocketbook. Suddenly, according to police, Mrs. [Bernstein] attacked [Burns], kicking and scratching. She is said to have grabbed the purse from his hands and removed from it a memorandum pad containing names, addresses, and telephone numbers.

As Detective [Burns] struggled to retrieve it, she threw it to her father, who escaped down a back stairway. Police of the West 100th Street Station were notified, and an alarm was sent out for [Kresge].

According to the District Attorney's office, Mrs. [Bernstein] is being investigated in connection with a "baby ring" that allegedly operated in Florida, and in connection with which [Eugene Simpson], 38, an attorney, was arrested on Thursday.

[*Brackets indicate names which have been changed from those appearing in the original article.*]

Nanette Bernstein and two attorneys, Simpson and his partner, went on trial eight months later. Mrs. Bernstein was represented by a lawyer who argued that her only contacts were with foster parents, "hungry to adopt children." Fees ranged as high as $2000.

Prosecution witnesses included two young unwed mothers who claimed that they had answered ads in Miami papers that read, "Childless couple anxious to adopt child." On answering the ads, both mothers were met by Eugene Simpson.

One mother, seventeen years old, said that she was given $100 cash and her mother was given another $20. A twenty-four-year-old received $15 per week for several months before entering the hospital. She received her final payment after signing the adoption papers. Medical bills were paid. An adoptive mother claimed that she and her husband paid $2000, while an adoptive father said he paid $1650.

Conspiracy to bring children into New York was never proven, but Eugene Simpson and Nanette Bernstein were convicted for illegal placement of babies and accepting compensation for such placement. Simpson was sentenced to a year in prison, while Mrs. Bernstein was fined $2500.

In the Polk Directory for New York in 1934, I found Nanette Bernstein listed as the secretary of a kindergarten and nursery in Manhattan. Later the name and the address of this institution were changed. I went to the home just before the start of a holiday weekend. Everyone but a secretary had left. When I mentioned the name of Nanette Bernstein she turned pale. She told me to write to the president of the organization and then said, "We never had this conversation." I wrote and received the reply, "We have no records." So the kindergarten was very sensitive about being used as a front for a baby-selling racket.

Finally the judge's secretary called up and informed me that they had found my file. I didn't ask how. I didn't feel I was in a position to ask questions. They let me copy the petition and decree of adoption in the office.

The space provided for the signature of the mother, identified as Charlotte Graham of Hartford, Connecticut, is blank. Two character witnesses for the adoptive parents signed the petition— Nanette Bernstein and an uncle of mine. Mrs. Bernstein told me that my natural mother had been present when my uncle signed, but he claims this isn't true. He claims he would do anything for me and I believe him. At any rate, Charlotte Graham never did sign.

I packed my bags and went up to Hartford. It seemed that Kathleen Graham must be me and that Martha Ryder must either have the same identity or be an invention.

In Connecticut you are not listed in town directories until you turn twenty-one. If my mother was a college student when she left for New York to have me, she probably wouldn't be listed in any directories until she returned and settled. I checked marriage certificates for the five years after my birth. I made charts of ages. I acquired stacks of information, but none of it has helped.

One Charlotte Graham I tracked down was very nice. She invited me to see her doll collection, but she wasn't the right one. One moved to Massachusetts. Another had disappeared. After five days I returned to Philadelphia.

I have tried so hard to spare the feelings of my adoptive parents. After my third phone call to Nanette Bernstein, this convicted baby-seller did something that makes me wish I could spread her name over the front pages of every newspaper in the country. She tracked down my parents to their retirement home and asked them to tell me to quit bothering her. Then she had her daughter call me and tell me that if anything happened to her mother I would be responsible.

If Nanette Bernstein wants to live quietly for the rest of her life, she must give us the identities she has obliterated for her own profit. She has gone beyond the boundaries of civilized behavior, and still she asks to be spared the consequences.

Forgiveness, for Nanette Bernstein, is something I am incapable of, until I find my mother and learn to forgive her. I don't think people can learn to forgive until they've had the opportunity to forgive someone who means something to them. I think of my mother with real anger sometimes, I call her names, and yet I know that she may have had some plausible reason for giving me up. She may have been cheated out of raising me. Nanette Bernstein knows the truth and she is a proven scoundrel.

I once heard a fifty-five-year-old woman tell about finding her seventy-three-year-old mother and cultivating a friendship for a year and a half before revealing who she was. They did things together; the daughter visited her mother in the hospital, cautiously increasing the old woman's dependence on her and finally revealing who she was.

It upset me to hear about this because that is one of my fantasies. Somewhere there is a woman of about sixty who has never, with all the publicity about adoptees' rights, been able to come forward and acknowledge me. My frustration has led me to some harsh thoughts about her.

I've been rootless because I've never been able to take seriously the idea that anyone could love me or want me because for some reason the most important one of all didn't love me or want me.

I've been depressed all my life. I have no way of knowing how much of it is reactive and how much is genetic. Every doctor I've ever gone to for treatment asks me the same questions about my family medical history and they all express the same dismay when I tell them that I was adopted. I've cataloged my physical problems according to whether they are hereditary or psychogenic. Recently I came down with tendonitis. I went to the doctor and was surprised to find out that it was a hereditary condition. I was used to being told that my aches and pains were all in my mind.

So I'm looking for a depressed woman with short hamstrings. Not much to go on. There are times when I've wished that I had never heard of adoptees' rights. Years have come and gone and I've watched dozens of scared, insecure people begin to search and find release, but for me this hasn't happened. I've become locked into a search that doesn't end. If I had been less bold, I might be plagued with a wistful longing instead of the anger that I feel. There are a lot of us who will not be helped by open records. For people who start looking for their natural parents, the thing to fear is not what they might find, but the chance that they will never find anything at all.

# Memory's Effects

## —— Donald ——

*By issuing a birth certificate that names only the adoptive parents, the law severs the early life of an adoptee from the rest of his life. Many adoptees have long waits between birth and adoption, and these early months affect them forever. Adoptees taken straight to their adoptive homes from the hospitals where they were born are thought to be least troubled by adoption. They form bonds immediately with their new families. The longer the wait before adoption, the more severe adoptees' problems are likely to be. Since early experiences leave a child with memories of strange faces and strange events that may later cause difficulty, it would make good sense to give people access to whatever information they request so that they can work out their problems. Certain children become aware of their surroundings earlier than others, and individual adoptees are the best judges of their own needs.*

*Donald Wilson is one of many adoptees whose psychological problems are thought to be directly attributable to events in the fourteen months between birth and adoption. A social worker provided Donald with information about his early background that helped to confirm a psychiatrist's explanation of Donald's bisexuality.*

My bisexuality started me on my search. I wanted to find out what, if anything, my adoption had to do with my being gay.

I don't really remember what happened in the fourteen months between my birth and my adoption. Under hypnosis during psychotherapy, however, I have mentioned beatings by one of my foster mothers. My adoptive parents told me once that I wouldn't allow my mother near me for a long time after they brought me home. My therapist thought this might partially explain my sexual problems.

The earliest memory I have is of the day my parents took me home from the agency. I was fourteen months old. It's just a flash. Two images stick in my mind. I am in an office. A man in a gray suit comes into the room with my parents. My new father walks toward me and hands me a toy car. Then I am outside the building and getting into the family car.

My adoptive mother is from a closely knit Italian family with twelve children, six boys and six girls. My father's family is German-Polish. They have never gotten along with my mother's family. At the time I was adopted, Dad had two sisters and one brother. Other children had died earlier. Dad's father was a foreman in a Westinghouse plant. One day a cable suspended from a crane snapped, and the load landed on my grandfather. Dad was only fifteen when he took over support of his family. Things were rough.

On December 6, 1952, the day the adoption agency called my mother about me, she was pregnant and didn't know it. Dad wasn't home so she went down to see me by herself. After she left she got violently sick and miscarried. She didn't tell the agency. She was afraid that if they knew she could conceive they wouldn't let her have me. Twenty days later I was in my new home.

At that time my family was well-to-do. Dad was in the construction business and Mom owned a beauty parlor. She sold it to her brother so she could take care of me. Mom and Dad found a big house in a residential neighborhood when they were told they would be adopting me, and we moved into it very soon afterward. We never lacked for anything and seemed to be influential, Dad through business and Mom through social and charitable activities. Mom had a new Cadillac every couple of years, and Dad drove big cars. We went on long vacations and socialized with rich, important people.

I think I have always known I was adopted. I guess I came along too late for my parents to pretend, even if they had been inclined to do so. But I don't think they were. The agency told them nothing about my natural parents, so when I asked they made things up. The first story I ever heard was that my natural parents had been married when they were quite young, and my natural mother had died in childbirth. My natural father, the story ran, couldn't afford to keep me. I believed that story until I found out people could have children without being married.

It never bothered me that I had been adopted, except when the kids in the neighborhood wanted to needle me and would make remarks. Yet I didn't care too much. My parents treated me so well, and I couldn't see any real benefit in living with one's natural parents.

When I was eight, there was talk of adopting another child. I said, "Great. I want a brother." Two girls, four- and five-year-old sisters, came and stayed with us for three weeks. They were nice, but my mother was forty and didn't feel up to taking on such a load. We didn't take them.

In January 1959, we took a trip to California. After we returned, I was at home one day while my mother was taking a nap. I heard a knock on the door and answered it. A woman stood there with a little girl.

"This is Cynthia," she said.

"Oh yeah," I answered. "So what?" I was some kid. The woman didn't say anything for a while. I couldn't figure out what was going on. Then my mother came down and asked the woman and the child to come in. They spent the day with us.

When they left, Mom asked, "How would you like to have a sister?"

I thought it over and said, "No. No sisters. Besides, she's five years younger than me." That should have settled that.

A month later, there was another knock at the door. Same woman, same girl. And baggage.

This was it. I was in a state of shock. I hadn't been properly consulted. A little girl had come to disrupt my domain. I did my best to get rid of her and we didn't get along for years. At every opportunity we'd beat each other up.

I had trouble adjusting to the fact that I would never have a brother. I tried to talk my parents into adopting another boy. Then my mother had a menopausal pregnancy and fell down the steps and lost the child. Her menopause lasted for years, although it took me a long time to figure out just what was going on. When I was in high school she got pregnant again and needed a surgical abortion to save her life. That was that. No brother.

We had regular visits with doting aunts and many girl cousins, but there were only four boy cousins and I hardly ever saw them. I could be very mean to the girls. One day one of them who had hair down to her waist insulted me. I sneaked up behind her while she sat on a swing and started swinging her by her hair.

My mother tried to get me to wear good clothes all the time, but I didn't want to be a goody-two-shoes. I'd go out and play and come back a mess. They wanted me to take tennis lessons, but I didn't want to.

Dad and I fought. We're closer now than we've ever been but he tried to be a pal when I was little and it didn't work. I can see now that the hardships he went through after his father died had a lot to do with his remoteness. He could never display much emotion. I could tell from the way he disciplined me. I did bratty things but my punishment usually consisted only of being kept indoors, and that never lasted long. I knew how to get around him. He would end up buying me off. "Here's a new airplane model," he would tell me, or "Here's a couple of bucks."

I also did some pretty bad things, and there were never any real consequences. A few times, before Mom and Dad went out for an evening, I let air out of the automobile tires. My father, who had worked his way up through all kinds of manual labor, would call a garage and have them come out to change the tires. He wasn't too old to change them, but too advanced socially.

Another time I stole all my mother's dresses and hid them in the crawl space above the attic. When I finally gave in and retrieved them, they were sooty and black.

When I was a child, my father held me in his lap when he drove. Later he would take me out to the country and let me drive. Starting when I was fourteen, I would gather up my gang when my parents were out of the house and we would pile in my father's car and drive around. I got caught once. My mother's new Cadillac needed some adjustment so they left it home one night. I called my friends and off we went. One of the girls didn't know how to drive so I decided to teach her.

A few days later my father took the car to the dealer for repairs, and a cop he knew came up and told him he had seen the car wobbling all over the road on the night in question. My father claimed it must have been another Cadillac just like it. "No," the cop said, "I took down the license number. A girl was driving. I would have stopped them, but I was off duty." My father muttered something about his niece who stayed with me that night. From then on all the car keys were accounted for when my parents went out. I didn't drive again until my parents bought me my own car when I turned sixteen.

I did some thinking about adoption when I was fifteen. One of my unmarried cousins had a baby and gave it up for adoption. That's how I found out people did not have to be married to have children. I asked my mother to tell me the truth about myself. Knowing the facts of life, I felt the story of my natural mother dying in childbirth didn't ring true. Since my parents really didn't know anything about my beginnings, they sent me to the agency that handled my adoption. I spoke to a social worker named Margaret Miller. She wouldn't tell me much. She gave me a description of a woman she said was my mother, but it could have fitted anyone. I asked if my parents had been married and she said no. That settled that.

The things I loved to do as a child that I still like are to draw, read, ride horses, and ski. Solitary things. I used to write Gothic mystery stories with characters like me, only more glamorous. Of all the things my parents tried to get me to do, I am grateful they forced me to take piano lessons.

I have very good memories of childhood, generally speaking, and I'm glad I was raised the way I was. My parents had rich, often eccentric friends. I got to see the insides of yachts and mansions with peacocks strutting around the grounds. When I wrote my Gothic mysteries, with their haunted houses and shorefront settings, I knew what I was talking about. Still, I didn't grow up to be a snob, the way I could have. I've always gotten along with all kinds of people.

Things started to change near the end of high school in 1969. My father lost a lot of money in a business deal. It didn't ruin us, but we couldn't raise the cash we needed without some sacrifices. He had always been so proud of material things and the fact that we never wanted for anything. Suddenly the luxuries weren't there. He began to drink.

Most of my personal problems started in college. My freshman year was one of the happiest years of my life. Sophomore year things started to slide. I took up dramatics. Theater people tend to be bitchy and gossipy and I got caught up in it. Friends were hurt because I became less trustworthy than I had been. I did something dumb, said the wrong thing, and lost my best friend.

I couldn't be happy. My school work fell off until I did nothing at all and finally got suspended for the first time in 1971. I thought, "Good. I'm going to take the next six months to find out what I'm all about." I planned to rent a cottage in New England, write, and catch up on myself.

But I couldn't go. Something was keeping me there. I figured it might have something to do with my adoption. I was also having trouble with my homosexual feelings.

I have known from about age twelve that I had these feelings, but I buried them. I remained a virgin in both ways until I was twenty-one. Being gay in a small city involves all kinds of difficulties. I didn't want my family to find out about me, but I kept running into straight people I knew in gay bars. They would see me and tell the world about it.

I was suspended from college again and developed a drinking problem. I had picked up my father's temper. But the only times he ever hit me were after I had hit him first. I began flying off the handle and crying over stupid things.

One day a psychiatrist lectured in one of my classes. He said at the end of his talk, "If you've got a problem, do something about it." This was in March 1973. A month later I read an article in *Newsweek* about a couple of adoptees' rights groups, but I didn't join any of them right away. I still didn't feel any definite commitment to find my natural parents.

In late May I got an appointment with the same psychiatrist. He hypnotized me. When I was under hypnosis, I was instructed to have a dream that dealt with my problem. He said I would wake up after the dream and not be able to sleep again until I had written it down.

In the dream I was working in a shop in a train station. A man, somehow familiar to me, entered and asked for a suitcase that was supposed to have arrived by train. I told him to wait and went out. I found a black bag and thought it must be for him. But the name didn't match the one he had given me. I returned and he asked, "Where are your vacuum cleaners?"

I turned and pointed, but he disappeared. I went outside but he was gone. Then the dream switched to a house.

I was with two guys I had grown up with. We weren't supposed to be in the house, and we were going up and down the stairway. I found a photograph of myself and the others and someone else. We were stuffed into a single costume I had worn in a play. The costume tore because there were too many of us in it, and I was left alone in one part of it.

We left the house and we were in our own neighborhood. I said, "We'd better get out of here so we won't be caught. Let's go in my car."

My convertible was parked in front of my house. I got in it and got wet because the top had been down during a rainstorm. My friends said, "Come with us. Your car won't start." The car started. They got in and wiped the back seat with a blanket.

The psychiatrist told me that whenever you dream about a house, you dream about yourself. The stairs in my dream represented a search for something, and the familiar stranger represented a father, my natural father. The psychiatrist went on to say that a car represents a man's sex drive, and those two friends who claimed my car wouldn't start were saying, "Come with us—you can't be straight." I did start the car, so it meant I could go either way. But I still haven't been able to consummate a relationship with a woman.

I had suspected that my problems were related to adoption, so I started to search. I went to the adoption agency. I refer to the social worker who spoke to me as the Squirrel. She turned white and shrank back when I told her I wanted to find my natural parents. She said, "You can't do that."

"Why not?"

She was flabbergasted. She told me to wait and went to get her superior. The next woman said, "This is highly irregular."

I asked to see the head of the agency. Mr. Tyler was busy. I waited. When he finally saw me, I told him what I wanted. He said I should get a lawyer and speak to the judge at Children's Court. Until then he could do nothing.

I asked where I could get hold of Margaret Miller, the woman who had spoken to me when I was fifteen. Margaret had retired. He gave me her phone number.

A few days later I called Margaret Miller and she invited me to her home to talk. It was mid-July. She said she was on my side, that even though she had been a social worker for thirty years, she could change with the times and understand my need to find my natural parents.

Margaret Miller had never met my natural mother. Another social worker had dealt with her, and Mrs. Miller had counseled my foster and my adoptive parents. But she had a lot of information. My natural mother had approached the agency while she was still pregnant and said she wanted to give me up. She came from a town outside the county. She worked as a waitress and started seeing a man who ran out on her when he found out she was pregnant. She was in her mid-thirties and couldn't afford to support me.

Mrs. Miller told me my natural mother had neglected to sign the final papers, so I was put in a series of foster homes. The last foster parents I had expressed interest in adopting me. The social worker had called up my natural mother several times to make appointments. She wanted to discuss whether my natural mother might want to take me back, but the appointments were never kept. At last the agency sent a letter. It came back stamped "Moved. No Forwarding Address."

I remarked on the clarity of Mrs. Miller's memory. She said the case stood out in her mind because in my third foster home, the last one, the man worked nights and played with me during the day, and we got along very well. His wife, however, would come home from her day job and ignore me. When I cried, she would beat me to shut me up. The husband finally came in and told the agency what was going on. It was then that they tried to get my natural mother to take me back.

At last I thought I had an answer to some of my sexual conflicts, but the search had raised too many larger questions about my identity for me to stop there.

I said, "I realize there's a code of ethics involved, but can you tell me anything specific? Like where she worked."

Mrs. Miller answered, "I can get access to the files if I want them and find out a lot more information. But you have to give me time to think about it." Then she said that my natural mother had been a waitress in a diner on Orange Street and that the place had been demolished fifteen years before.

We talked for a while about other things. When I got up to leave, she wished me luck and told me to call if I needed anything else. She also said she would contact the social worker who had worked with my natural mother.

Two days later Mrs. Miller called to say, "She can't remember. She's half-blind and senile. Your case goes back twenty-two years."

I had trouble getting an appointment with the judge. I was a factory security officer at that time. I worked nights and got up too late to reach him, since he only had morning office hours. One day I got up early and went to the court, but he had left town for a week.

I couldn't afford to pay an attorney to try to get my records, and I didn't want to tell my parents what I was up to. I went to Legal Aid, where I spoke to a lawyer. She said she would get some of her assistants to check on the law and then she would file suit if I wanted. The problem intrigued her.

I knew such a suit would take a long time, so I continued to work on my own. I went to the library and got a 1951 city directory. I looked up the restaurants and found the New York Diner, 59 Orange Street. Then I got the October 1951 newspapers to study the birth notices. I was sure this wouldn't help because I was illegitimate. And I only checked the notices for one of the city's hospitals. I found out later that I had been born in the other one.

The city directory listed the name of the owner of the diner. I checked the current telephone book and found he was still living in town. I called and asked whether he remembered a woman who had worked for him in 1951, who had been pregnant and given up the child for adoption. He didn't. He had thrown out his records after he had sold the diner. Although he couldn't help me, he appeared cooperative.

I found out that the judge had returned, and I lined up an appointment. I told him everything. The judge was a friend of my adoptive parents so I figured he would be sympathetic, but he was not. He said he would look at the records and see what was there. He told me to come back that afternoon.

When I came back, he said, "The records don't really have anything except names, and I can't tell you names. Your mother's name is so common, it is probably phony. Many women give false names and then disappear because they don't want to be traced."

I was furious. I went back to the agency and screamed at them, "I demand that you tell me everything you can. I've got a law suit in progress. I don't care what the hell I have to do, I'll get you for something."

Mr. Tyler was embarrassed and asked me to go quietly into his office. "I'll go through the records and pull out everything I find that is in my power to give you."

A couple of days later, I picked him up in my car outside the courthouse and drove him to his office.

He told me my natural mother had worked in a diner. I already knew that. He described her. The description would fit anyone; it was probably the same one Margaret Miller had given me seven years before. Mr. Tyler told me she had come from elsewhere within the state, but not the county she lived in when I was born.

He wouldn't say where she had lived at that time.

I inquired about my father. They didn't have much information. He was a salesman who came to town occasionally.

As I left I announced grandly that he would be hearing from my lawyers. From there I went to the Bureau of Vital Statistics, where I applied for a copy of my birth certificate. To hide what I was doing from my parents, I used a friend's address. They mailed me a copy of the amended certificate, so it contained nothing useful. Only my adoptive parents were named.

I went to see the restaurant owner and described my mother as she had been described to me. He didn't remember anyone like that. I asked if he remembered any waitress at all from that period.

"Edith Dawson worked for me," he said, "but she's been married and divorced so many times I couldn't tell you what her name is now."

"When was the last time you saw her?"

"I don't remember, but I did see her working out at Hanson's Diner."

I called Hanson's. They had a waitress named Edith and they gave me her hours for the next day. I went out there for lunch with one of my cousins. Edith waited on us.

I asked her if she had ever worked at the New York Diner. She said she had. Did she know another waitress who had a baby sometime about 1951?

"Oh my, yes," she answered. "That was Alice Kelly. We were very good friends. I used to baby-sit for her older boy."

I was floored. Nothing I had learned until then pointed to any other children. Maybe she hadn't been able to keep me because she had had too many to support. Why hadn't the adoption agency told me that at least? I began to feel some compassion for the woman who had given me up.

"What was she like? Where was she from? What does she do now?" I started asking everything I could think of. I was so excited I didn't give her a chance to answer.

Edith said, "She was from Mansfield. I remember that because in 1950 there was terrible weather at Thanksgiving and she was supposed to go home, but the weather kept her here. She ate with me instead."

I had my mother's hometown. It was something to go on.

Edith continued, "I haven't seen her for about five years, but I know she stayed on here because her son was in school. I don't remember where she lived. Say, why do you want to know all this?"

I said, "I think I'm the kid she gave up."

That did it. She sat down and talked. Her other customers got impatient. Then I looked up the Alice Kellys in the phone book. The only one lived a few miles outside of town.

Before I had a chance to go to see her, I had to go to court with my mother to testify for some friends who were involved in a law suit.

My mother said, "I know what you're doing."

"How did you find out?"

"I won't tell you. Why didn't you mention it to your father and me?"

"I didn't want you to be hurt."

She smiled. "The only thing that hurts is that you didn't tell us. We could have helped you."

"How? I thought you didn't know anything."

"We don't, but our lawyer has everything. I remember the day we signed the papers. When we told him we didn't want to know the name, he covered it up, but he said, 'If Donald ever wants to know, have him come and ask.'"

At first I was relieved she wasn't upset. I kissed her and felt really close to her. I would do anything for my parents. Dad told me he would do the same thing in my position.

It turned out that a cousin in whom I had confided had told her mother, my aunt. This aunt has always had a grudge against me. Her husband died when their son was young, so my cousin never had the advantages I have had. She's tried to put me in a bad light many times to make her son look good. She told my mother I was searching. She just wanted to stab me again.

That same afternoon I went to see Alice Kelly. She came to the door of her house. She was about eighty-five. I told her I was looking for an Alice Kelly who was about fifty-five or a little older.

"There's another Alice Kelly living downtown," she said. "I used to get my mail mixed up with hers all the time. Why don't you try over there?" She gave me the address and I tore downtown.

The address was a big Victorian house that had been broken up into apartments. I used to hang around there with a friend who lived a few doors away. A man came out and I asked if Alice Kelly lived there. "No, she moved eight months ago."

"She has a son, doesn't she?"

"Yes," she said. "Joe, that's his name."

"Do you know where I can get in touch with him?"

The man looked at the ground for a minute. "Sorry," he said. "It's somewhere in New Jersey. I'm not at all sure."

Terrific, I thought. She probably went off to live near him.

"Last I heard she moved down around Harrison Square on the other side of town. She was on welfare. Disability. Has real bad asthma."

That helped. I had a friend who worked in the welfare office. I called her up and asked if she could trace Alice Kelly for me. Then I went off to the post office and asked if they had a forwarding address for Alice Kelly.

"Why do you want to know?" they asked.

"She's my aunt. We lost track of her. We were all wondering what happened to her."

"That'll be a dollar."

The address they gave and the address the welfare office had were the same. I went right away. The building was in a run-down neighborhood. I parked the car and went in, nervous as hell. In the hallway I looked at the mailboxes to see which was hers. Her apartment was at the end of the hall. A man stood outside banging on the door I wanted. He was drunk, although I wouldn't call him a derelict. I hoped he wasn't one of my mother's friends.

"Oh, you looking for Alice?" he said. "I am too, but I don't think she's home."

Through the peephole in the door you could see into the apartment. There was a back door.

"Excuse me," I said to the guy, and I went around back. He followed me. I knocked on the door. She answered.

"Mrs. Kelly," I said. "My name is Donald Welles." I gave her a false last name, because I wasn't sure what was going to happen. She invited me in. The man outside started calling to her.

"Oh my God," she said, "How am I going to get rid of him?"

I turned and told him, "I'm seeing Mrs. Kelly privately." I slammed the door in his face. It happened so fast he didn't know what was going on. He didn't knock again.

"I have some personal questions to ask you." She looked at me for a second, then went to the window to see whether the man was still hanging around.

"Did you ever work at the New York Diner?" I asked. She nodded.

"In 1951?" Again she nodded. "I have come to find out through various means that you may have had a baby that you put up for adoption." She didn't say anything. Then she looked through the door.

"Yes, I did," she said. "How did you know?"

"I'm here to confirm it."

People have told me I'm not really very emotional when I repeat this story. There was a time when I could do anything to avoid attention and stifle my feelings. But at that point I was trying desperately to hide them, and I didn't have anything to say. Finally the questions came out one after another, like a prosecutor's.

"Can you tell me the sex of your child?"

"It was a boy."

"Could you tell me the name you gave him?"

"I called him Jay."

"When was he born?"

"It was so long ago. I've blocked it out. I know it was in the fall of 1951. Why do you want to know this?"

"I think I'm that baby."

"What do you know?"

I told her the story, vague as it was.

She said, "I think I'm your mother." She was in a fog. I didn't want to tell her too much about myself. I wanted to hear her talk. I wanted her to tell me things that I knew would fit. I showed her a picture of myself taken the day I was adopted.

"I knew who you were when you walked in," she said. "You have a cousin who looks just like you." She took out some photograph albums and showed me a picture of Chuck. Chuck is older than I am, but we look like twins except that he has blue eyes.

She showed me a picture of herself taken in 1948. She had been quite attractive. On the mantle I saw a high school graduation picture next to a photograph of two little boys.

"This is my other son Joey and those are his two boys." She showed me a snapshot of Joey at three. He had the same round face I used to have, although he's heavier than I am.

"Well," I said, "What can you tell me about my father?"

She gave me a funny look. "I don't think I should tell you anything about him."

"Why not? I've come this far. I ought to know the rest."

She shrugged. "Before I tell you who he is, let me tell you about him and about us. We were seeing each other. One night something happened and that's where you came from."

She had met him in the summer of 1950. He had owned two restaurants, one in town and another in a suburb. She worked in the diner at the time. He would pick her up and they would go nightclubbing. One place they went to had a bad reputation. It was supposed to be a Mafia place. He used to sing out on the terrace with his band. People used to come over to him to talk about going out to the airport and picking things up. It went over her head at the time, but she had since figured out that they were talking about drugs. Once she went out to the airport with him to pick up a package in a landing field.

She had known he was married. Toward the end of the year he sold the restaurants and moved to New York. He left his wife, who was pregnant at the time. When Alice told him she had the same problem, he offered to arrange an abortion, but she refused. Alice never saw him again.

Joey was about five at the time she was pregnant. She put him in a private school and went to stay with friends out of town. She returned to have me, then moved to the suburbs. When Joey went into the service, she returned to the city.

"What's my father's name?" I asked.

"You've probably seen him in the papers. He's a businessman around here again."

She looked in that day's paper but he wasn't mentioned. She told me the name. I hated it—Vic Mars, shortened from Vito Marzullo.

I got up to leave and said I would be back the next day. I went to visit a friend, and had a few drinks. I called home and told Mom what had happened. She was amazed. This was one day after she and I had discussed it for the first time. Then I called Vic Mars and made an appointment for eleven the next morning.

He opened the door of his office, and I decided I couldn't stand him. He looked like me.

"What can I do for you?"

"I'm not really here on business, Mr. Mars. Is there someplace we can talk privately?" He took me into a back room.

I asked if he had ever known Alice Kelly. I showed him the photograph she had given me. He shook his head. I told him she was my natural mother and had named him as my natural father. He said he hadn't even been living in the city at the time. He had lived in New York.

"What were you doing there?" I asked.

"I was in show business for fifteen years."

Then I said I was an actor and a nightclub performer. I didn't tell him I was an amateur. He didn't say anything for a time.

Finally he said, "It is impossible for me to be your father. Sure I might have fooled around a little, but my own wife was pregnant at the time. I have a daughter around your age."

I said, "That might stop a woman, Mr. Mars." He seemed to be getting upset, so I changed the subject. He told me about his kids and why he had returned from New York. I let him believe I was convinced he wasn't my father, but before I left I said, "I hope that when I meet the right man he has the integrity to admit it."

I went back to see Alice. She said, "I could have told you that was going to happen."

"I had to find out for myself." Then I said, "If it's going to be a hassle for you to see me, I'll stay away."

"Oh, no. The worst thing was not knowing where you were or that you had a good home." She had called her sister the night before and told her what had happened. No one in her family except one brother had ever known about me. Her sister's daughter was getting married on Sunday and wanted to know if I wished to go to the wedding. I accepted.

I arrived at the church before Alice did. The usher came up to ask which side I wanted to sit on. I said that I was waiting for someone else and that I would remain in back until they arrived. Then my cousin Chuck entered and saw me. He just stared. He didn't know yet. Only the bride's mother knew. She was too busy to do anything but wave. I heard people talking about the guy who looked just like Chuck. After the ceremony, Alice called everyone over to introduce me.

I had to leave the reception before I got too drunk. I was appearing in a play that evening in the community theater. I was a little embarrassed over creating such a stir. I said so to the bride, but she said, "Don't be ridiculous." Joey hadn't been able to make it to the wedding, and we agreed that Alice should tell him.

The next time I spoke to her, she said Joey wanted me to call right away. He was very excited and I told him I would take some time off on my way to New York in three weeks. His kids were excited to have an Uncle Donald all of a sudden.

When I got to Joey's house in New Jersey, we played with the kids, and then Joey and I sat down to talk for a long time. Among other things, he told me that he and Alice were both musicians.

Finally he said, "Get ready for this. There's another one of us. His name is Larry."

When Alice's husband walked out on them, Joey was two and a half and Larry was one. Alice couldn't afford to keep both of them, so she put Larry in foster care. The social worker knew of a family who wanted a child. Alice once told Joey it might have been someone in the social worker's own family. The social worker put a lot of pressure on Alice, who finally signed a paper, thinking it was just something preliminary. When she went to pick Larry up one day, the social worker told her that she had surrendered Larry for good.

Now Joey and I are looking for Larry.

# A Chance of Incest
## —— Sarah and Jerry ——

*Adoptees and their natural parents sometimes are reunited by acci-
dent. In this case an adoptee has a date with a young woman who
turns out to be his half-sister. This is the first situation I encountered
that had the potential for incest. By one estimate there may be as
many as fifty thousand incestuous marriages in the United States
involving adoptees who are unaware of a blood relationship with
their partners. In fact, one adoptees' rights organization is basing a
class-action suit against sealed adoption records in part on the
grounds that adoptees have no way of protecting themselves against
incest.*

*Sarah Mayer is a mother whose daughter is attracted to the son
Sarah had given up years before. Sarah's response to this situation
is but one example of the courage with which she has faced the many
misfortunes of her life.*

*Her son Jerry's version of these same events shows that finding
one's natural mother is more complex than a simple reunion. Jerry
had not begun to search and had no clear idea of what he wanted from
the newly discovered facts of his identity. The accidental meeting
that led to his reunion with his natural mother raised many questions
he had long ignored. He has not yet found answers to all of them.*

When I was nineteen years old I had a son I gave up for adoption
for a very good reason: I could not support him, and there was no
way I was going to leave him with my family while I went out and
worked for a living. My parents raised me to be, at nineteen, so

unsure of myself that I didn't have the sense or self-respect to avoid getting pregnant.

My mother was raised by a neurotic aunt and a neurotic mother. She used to make a great show out of being afraid of my father, because, I suppose, there were no men around when she was growing up. When my parents met, my mother had already begun looking for something to replace her mother's influence.

My father was very bright. He went through architecture school on a scholarship when quotas limited the number of Jews in universities in New York. He became a civil engineer, started his own firm, and built the lift span on the Triborough Bridge.

My mother began to attend Christian Science meetings with a friend soon after she got married. Dad told her he didn't care what she did, as long as she didn't try to rope him into it. But my father had a great capacity for self-delusion, and they both soon became fanatical about the religion.

I learned a lot about my father when my husband went to work for him. Although he was an engineer, Dad's mind was not very logical in many respects. He made excuses when things went wrong in business. If he couldn't deliver some material on time, he would tell a client that the steel had arrived but it hadn't been unloaded. Then he would go around blaming whoever was in charge, as if the story he had told his client were true.

They were very strict with me, but they were never consistent. They wouldn't let me date. I couldn't go to the movies because people smoked in the balcony, but they left me home alone when they went out and I had visitors. They hired a man to clean our house and he started making passes at me when I was eleven years old. If they knew, they never said anything.

We didn't communicate. They were cold and self-absorbed people. Every phase of life had to fit into their scheme of things. If I got sick, according to them, my thinking had to be faulty. They never changed. When my husband died, my mother came over. It was three o'clock in the morning. She sat down on the couch next to me and the first thing she said was, "I wonder what he was thinking about."

In 1945 when I graduated from high school, I went to a junior college in Connecticut. I really had fun. Most four-year colleges were full of veterans studying on the G.I. Bill, so there were no college boys, but older, more experienced men. I edited the newspaper and became close with the adviser. I found that I could make friends after all.

The government was spending a lot of money on psychological testing at the time. So many men were receiving training with government sponsorship that it was felt there should be efforts made to find the right niche for everyone. I took the test and scored high in "written persuasion." A new department of public relations opened at Boston University. My adviser went up to take a look and talk to the faculty. He approved it, so I applied and was accepted for January 1948.

Since it was a new department with no upper classes to compare ourselves with, I felt right at home. I still didn't have enough confidence to match myself against others. We had our own classrooms above some stores, and we became very clannish.

It was in this setting that I met Mick in September 1948. We had classes and played bridge together. He had a wife and a daughter in Vermont. He shared an apartment with two other guys, and pretty soon I was living there along with the three of them and some other girls.

I never learned too much about Mick. The whole situation discouraged serious talk, and I had no experience with that anyway. His roommates didn't even like him very much. In addition to being a married man and a father, he had already been named in another paternity case. He was a reckless Irishman, but I didn't care at the time. It was enough that I belonged.

While I had always resisted the rituals of the family religion, I had grown close to an older woman who was called a Christian Science practitioner. She was my safety valve, and I confided in her when I became pregnant. She suggested an abortion, but they were hard to get in those days. Besides, I had no experience with doctors. To have an abortion as my first medical treatment would have been too much.

So she laid the groundwork for telling my parents. I don't know what she said to them or how much of it they listened to. My own direct approach to the problem was to write a note to them while they were out and promptly go to sleep.

They read the note and woke me up. They surprised me: they were very good about it. I returned to school to finish the semester and they wrote to me. They visited, brought me a present and took me out to dinner. My mother couldn't resist asking, "If you wanted to have some fun why weren't you more careful?" "Having fun" was something alien to me, but she couldn't see that.

My father insisted that I shouldn't live with Mick "as man and wife." I continued to live with him. Not only did it seem practical, but I guess I harbored some illusions of my own about staying with him. He was a Catholic. I wasn't going to be the cause of a divorce, however, and I never pushed him. At the end of the semester I went to New York to stay with my parents, and Mick wrote to me—for a while.

From the beginning it was understood that my father would pay the bills, so I went about the task of finding the right home to board in during my pregnancy. I saw a Salvation Army home that looked like a prison. I didn't feel as if I had committed a crime, and I wasn't about to put myself behind bars. There was a home called St. Catherine's in a small New York town that seemed like the right sort of place, more like a boarding school than a maternity home.

I got a job for a few months to save money for maternity clothes and spending money. The employment agency sent me to a publisher of girlie magazines. My job was to invent a system for filing models' photographs according to their looks. I wore loose-fitting tops, and it took about two months before the pregnancy began to show. The boss always ran up and down the aisles shouting things like, "You'd better touch up that crotch or it will never get through the mails!"

With a tolerant atmosphere like that, the story I told when I could no longer pretend, that I was secretly married and would have to return to my family in Boston, found ready acceptance. I'm just not the kind of person who can disappear when it suits me. They gave me a shower before I left.

When I first entered the home, I had the same fear of not being accepted that I had when I went to college. But, as at college, we were thrown together for a common purpose in a dormitory, and we enjoyed ourselves. We discussed impersonal things like politics. There were counselors from an adoption agency around for very private thoughts. I think that ninety-nine out of a hundred had made up their minds not to keep their children. One girl kept hers, but she had a supportive family. It never crossed my mind while I was pregnant that I could keep the baby. I knew that I could never leave the baby with my family.

We all helped with the housework. We made our beds. My job was to cut and square the butter every morning. We went to the movies and the post office together. We had church services at the home. Rules were established to protect us from abuse by towns-people, and our movements were restricted, but we did take a certain delight in marching off to the post office knowing that people were thinking, "There go all the bad girls."

One girl's stomach extended in an odd shape. It came to a point and reminded someone of Dennis the Menace's pointed head. From then on her child became Dennis. If it were a girl she swore to name her Denise. She had a Dennis.

Looking back on it, I think this is the most sensible way for an unwed mother to live, assuming that she is not in a position to keep her child. I felt a bond with the other girls. I recently spoke to a young girl who had been placed in a family home by a "right-to-life group." To me, her feelings of isolation were not mitigated by that situation. She felt freakish. The emphasis was all wrong. To them she was preserving a life and they didn't pressure her to give the child up, but to her the child was just a beating heart. She felt like a brood mare. They fed her and sheltered her and took her to the doctor, but they were more interested in the baby than in her.

Not that we were so tolerant in the home. We had our own outcast, a girl who described in lurid detail all the different positions she and her man had made love in. There we were, all in the same boat, and the one who confessed to having a good time became a pariah.

My baby was born on July 10, 1949. I changed my last name for the birth certificate. They urged all of us to do the same. So my name became Sarah Kay.

I looked after "Baby Jonathan" for two weeks, then went to stay with my family while he went into foster care. Then, for some reason, I hesitated about signing the surrender papers. My father would say "When are you going to sign the papers?"

I would answer, "Maybe next week." Perhaps I thought that by some miracle I would get to keep him. Then, near the end of August, he convinced me that further delay would hurt my son. So I signed. We went off to Cape Cod for a vacation. From there I returned to finish at Boston. I roomed with a doctor's family off campus, so I was unaware of any rumors that might have accompanied my departure. The friends who counted had kept in touch, and several visited me while I was away.

After I graduated I got a job as a typist for a public relations firm, although I could hardly type. The typewriter I used had no letters on the keys, so I came in early my first day and with the help of a kid from the mailroom I painted the letters on. My memory was good and I could memorize whole paragraphs and type them while looking at the keys.

One day my boss grabbed me and said, "We're going for a ride." In the car he told me that my name sounded too Jewish and ordered me to change it in a hurry, so for the second time I had a new name. This time it was Stern. We went to a hotel in midtown Manhattan where a closet had been equipped with a typewriter. He told me to sit down, handed me some information, and told me to write a news release. He took the finished copy with him. A call came from the office later. The boss came in and said, "Damn. That girl can write a news story."

So I was set for a long time doing publicity for hotels. I went to openings of all kinds and met interesting people from all over the world. As a favor to the management I went out with one of the richest men in Spain. I sat through the entire meal with one hand on my fork and the other on a Spanish-English dictionary. By my parents' standards I led a very decadent life.

One day I noticed that a man from the accounting department was making an unusual number of trips past my office, and all I could think was that they were not very busy. Then at a Christmas party I met the fellow who played Santa Claus. We began to date.

When he proposed to me, I told him about Baby Jonathan to test him. I wasn't about to marry anyone who objected to my "scarlet past." Accept it or not, he had to know. He listened and we never mentioned it again in all the years we were married.

In 1952 I began to feel twinges on my left side. One doctor after another checked me and no one made any definitive diagnosis. Multiple sclerosis is a very subjective disease. They test you for everything else, and when they've exhausted all other possibilities they decide that's what it is.

Because of my upbringing, I punished myself with the question "What am I thinking and what's wrong with it?" When my mother visited me I would hide my cane, sit as much as I could, and struggle around trying to appear as if there were nothing wrong.

She recently bought a new place to live, a split-level ranch house with stairs all over the place. She apologized to me, but I know she thinks that if her eighty-five-year-old aunt can get up the steps, her forty-five-year-old daughter should be able to.

Despite my deteriorating health and restricted mobility, I tried to lead a normal life. I pushed myself to do housework, drove, and looked after my daughters. The only doctor who could give me any relief at all was the infamous Dr. Feelgood—Dr. Jacobsen—whose license was lifted because his vitamin shots were supposedly laced with amphetamines. I don't know if that was true or not, but he treated me at all hours of the night, arranged for me to park at his building, and never charged me anything. And if there were amphetamines in his medication, they weren't as potent as the diet pills that another doctor gave me. I testified on his behalf.

Dan was a great husband and a great father. He worked in two jobs most of the time, one in New York and another closer to home, and then settled into the second job full time when he began to have trouble with high blood pressure. With my handicap, he took over more and more of my chores. He was sure of his masculinity and nothing was beneath him, not even setting his daughters' hair.

Spending more and more time at home in the mid-sixties, I began to write a humor column for our local paper and did other bits of freelance writing. The humor column meant so much to me. I have a logical mind, and my life had become so illogical that being funny kept me sane. The column was very popular, and my editor tried to get me syndicated, but Erma Bombeck's editor convinced me that the market couldn't make room for competition.

In 1972 my husband died, and suddenly I couldn't even be funny anymore.


I never told my daughters about my first pregnancy. I didn't feel there was any need to, especially since I had so effectively blocked it out for myself. I raised them to be open and honest, to care enough about themselves so that they wouldn't ever end up in the position I was in.

I was asked by a reporter once how I would react if one of them came home and announced she was pregnant, and I answered that, in all candor, I couldn't imagine it happening. They value themselves too highly.

My husband's younger brother Charlie is an easy-going guy who drives a truck and lives in a town nearby. His best friend is a bartender. My mother-in-law doesn't like any of her son's friends. To her they are all a bunch of lazy bums and this bartender, Jerry, was no exception.

My eldest daughter, Jane, likes her uncle, looks up to him, confides in him. On Valentine's Day in 1974 she promised him that she would treat him to an evening out, but never got around to it until the following July. She and another friend met him in the bar and they made up their minds that they would go to the ball game. Then they tried to decide whom to take as a fourth.

The bar management was throwing a birthday celebration on that day—July 10—for Jerry. They had a cake and decorations, and so Jane invited Jerry along to the game.

They had a wonderful time, drank a lot of beer, and when Jane returned that night she had a real crush on Jerry. She told us about his sense of humor and his good looks. She began spending more and more time at his bar. One day she took her sisters down to bowl at the alley where the bar is. My youngest, Leslie, remarked to me that Jerry looked like someone she knew. I became concerned that Jane spent too much time with Jerry and that he didn't seem to be interested in her. She insisted that Jerry was shy and that some fellows need to be prodded.

"He never calls you," I said.

She answered, "It's because he keeps such late hours."

"He never takes you home," I said.

"He doesn't have a car of his own. He borrows his father's car."

Every time I raised a point she had an excuse. Her uncle tried to convince her, but she wouldn't listen to any of it. Jerry wasn't exactly sweeping her off her feet.

One night in the middle of a serious discussion, she left and took the bus to the bar. Jerry was sitting at the bar reading a newspaper article about an adoption search and he told her that he was adopted and was thinking about looking for his natural parents.

Jane got very excited and announced that she would help him. She had something she could do for him at last. She came home that night full of enthusiasm and told me what she was going to do. She knew his birthdate already and he had told her where he was born. When she repeated them to me, alarm bells began to ring. I stopped her and said, "I think there's something you should know."

When she heard my story and the possibility that Jerry was her brother presented itself, she was more gung-ho than ever about helping him. She stayed home from work the next day and we called my cousin who's a lawyer. He told me to write to the adoption agency right away. While I was talking, a friend of my daughter Leslie overheard the word "adopted" and she told her. Leslie began to think that she might have been adopted because Jane and I obviously had some secret we were keeping from her.

I wrote to the agency and made the circumstances seem more melodramatic than they were, hoping that the thought of an incestuous relationship might spur them into action earlier. But I didn't expect a prompt response.

Nora, my other daughter, was sleeping in my bedroom a couple of nights later because there was a thunderstorm and she couldn't stand the lightning. She overheard me talking about Jerry with a friend. She came out and asked if there was something wrong with him. I didn't tell either of the younger girls what was going on. If it wasn't so, I didn't want anyone to be hurt.

Jane took a job at a camp. Before she left she said, "If you hear anything call me right away." Off she went. The next day was a Thursday. I received a letter from the Sunday *News* saying that they had bought an article I wrote about having multiple sclerosis. And then my cousin the lawyer called.

"The agency told me it's one chance in six million," he said, "But he's the one."

Nora was sitting in the room at the time, and I spoke in the vaguest way, confining myself to "Uh huh, yes" without saying anything of substance. He asked if I was prepared for the consequences of telling people. The agency didn't want it spread about. All I kept saying was, "Yes, I understand."

Then the agency called and offered any counseling I might need. The social worker said, "I know how you must be feeling," but she couldn't know what I was feeling. For her to know what I was feeling she would have had to go through the same thing before, and, if it has happened before, I should think they would want all the records open and I know that they don't. I didn't need her help, but I hadn't made any decisions myself.

I called Jane's camp and left word that I wanted her to call. Nora was still there when Jane returned the call. I said, "How nice of you to call to see how I am." She thought I was being sarcastic because she hadn't called of her own volition.

"I'm not mad at you, just ask questions," I said.

"Is it good or bad?" she asked.

I had to laugh. "How do you qualify good or bad?" I paused and then said, "It's true."

We hung up. She finished her work that day, and it must have been difficult. We didn't know how to tell Jerry. We had no idea how he would react. He had only expressed his desire to meet his natural parents in the most wistful terms. His closest friend was practically his uncle. The girl who had chased him for a month was his sister. We lived so close for so long. And his own family problems were enormous.

Jane arrived home that night. There are some advantages to being in a wheelchair, and one of them is that I have to be wheeled into the bathroom. This gave Jane and me a chance to talk privately. We decided that she would go to see Jerry at the bar and tell him. We also decided to tell the girls that they had a brother. If Jerry chose to come right back here with her, it would be too much for them to hear the news as he walked in the door.

I was still in the bathroom when Jane told them so I don't know exactly how they took it, but Leslie was relieved to find out she wasn't adopted. I put together a package of things to send to him—mostly baby pictures, but I still had a ring that Mick had given me. It occurred to me that Jerry should have it. He might not want to meet me after all, and I didn't want him to feel that anything that belonged to his father should be a condition for coming to see me.

Jane asked a friend to drive her, and she invited a third along to keep the driver company while she went to speak with her brother.

She spoke to Charlie when she got to the bar. How would he react when she told him? Jerry's sisters were also there. They looked at the baby pictures, and they both said there was no doubt that the boy in the pictures was their brother. They knew the name of the adoption agency and it was the right one of course. They hesitated, and then finally decided that he should know right away.

Jane walked up to where he was sitting and said to him, "Your mother is my mother."

He climbed right up the wall. He was almost delirious for a minute and then said, "I always wondered why I had a Jewish nose and Irish eyes." He was right on the mark.

Jane called me and told me that Jerry was going home that night to tell his family and that he would call the next day. I thanked her for calling and hung up. I couldn't sleep that night. I didn't know if he would want to meet me or if he would like me. The only thing I was sure of was that I wouldn't try to force a meeting if he didn't want one.

The next day he had to work again. At two-thirty in the morning, Jane came into my room and said, "Jerry is going to sleep on the couch tonight. I'm telling you now so that you won't be surprised in the morning."

I wasn't going to wait. I put on my robe and went out there with my walker. He came through the dining room door and hugged me. We both babbled for a while, and we cried. Then we sat at the table to talk. By then all the girls were up and sitting with us, and Jerry and I both felt inhibited. They were involved, but at that moment their involvement was only peripheral. After all, both Jerry and I had been around longer than the rest of them. W happened twenty-five years before belonged to him. He told me that in one picture of the two of us I looked like Joe Namath. People were always saying that he looked like Joe Namath, and when he saw me he cried and laughed at the same time.

I told him to ask me anything at all, nothing was taboo. He asked me about his father, only he referred to him as "that guy up there." I chided him for this.

"For better or worse, he was your father. You have to try to understand him if you want to get to know him."

Nora got very nervous at this point, and when she gets nervous or tries to impress someone, she begins to chatter. She wanted to convey an impression of me to him, and told him that I once threw a frying pan at her. It wasn't even true. The frying pan just hit her. But she went on and on in copious detail until Jerry turned to her and said, "Look, this is my life, and you're talking about frying pans."

We retired at five o'clock, and Jerry got up at ten to take his father's car home. We agreed to meet that night, just the two of us. We were also concerned about telling friends and family. My mother-in-law was coming to pick up the two younger girls. I was especially worried about her reaction. Not only would it be a matter of dredging up something of my life before I knew my husband, but Jerry was also one of those "bums" who had robbed her youngest son of his ambition.

When I told her, she said, "I always thought he looked familiar." Then she apologized for bad-mouthing him for being one of Charlie's friends.

Jerry got lost on the way over. When he arrived I felt like a girl on a first date. I had to go to the bathroom every five minutes. We talked for a long time, looked at pictures, and made arrangements to meet the next day. The next day he brought me flowers.

We had lived in adjacent towns for many years. The chance that our paths crossed at some point is very good. I told him that there were times early in my marriage when I thought about trying to find him, and if he hadn't been adopted I would have tried to get him back. There were also times when I thought about trying to marry a guy I was engaged to before I met Mick, and raise him as this fellow's child.

We continued to meet almost every day, and we got along beautifully. The other family problems on both sides resolved themselves, at least for a while. My mother-in-law invited us over for a picnic on Labor Day. She asked him to set up some chairs, and, as he busied himself with that task, she tapped him on the shoulder and said, "You'd better listen to me. I'm your grandmother." That pleased me, since there was no blood relationship and she might have felt threatened. He visits her son more than before.

While I wouldn't say that I was terribly troubled about Jerry all those years, I had my bad moments, particularly on his birthday or if I allowed myself the luxury of daydreaming. I'm noted for my self-control, however, and I never permitted too much of that. Still there was a lot of scar tissue, and all of this stirred up a great deal of pain. Having him around made everything worse for me for a while.

People with good intentions would say, "It will be good to have a man around the house again." But things started to come to the surface with a vengeance—all the pain of growing up in a home where emotions were stifled, all the insecurity that led to my getting pregnant in the first place, my multiple sclerosis, the death of my husband.

With Jerry around, my relationship to the world grew more complicated because I could have leaned on him and that wouldn't have done any good. I didn't want him to assume my problems, and I didn't want to be dependent upon him. I didn't want him to be a husband, and I didn't want him to be a son. I didn't bring him up. We discussed it. We decided that if we could be close friends, all would be ideal. You don't have expectations of friends or make judgments of them.

And this is how it has worked out, although inevitably there have been lapses. I would get depressed and he would feel that I felt disappointment in him. It was hard to work it out for myself, let alone explain it to him. It had something to do with him, but not with him personally. It put a spotlight on a situation that wasn't too good to begin with.

Everything seems to have fallen into place now. The most important thing is that he make the most out of his life. I owed him some sort of a relationship, but we cannot make up for all the years we were apart.

I don't think that *any* children should grow up feeling that they are always your children, duty-bound to repay you for everything you've done for them. The most important thing is that they are whole human beings. If you're lucky, they like you.

I have no real sympathy for mothers who sign the adoption papers and then try to find their children while they are growing up. When I was twenty-three and newly married, the temptation to find him was very strong, but I knew that it would be wrong to turn up that covered ground. I just couldn't. I had made a decision based on my concern for him. And whatever benefits I expected him to derive from an adoption would be shattered by entering his life at that point.

And if the family situation wasn't ideal, he would have to develop the strength to survive on his own. No *deus ex machina* can rescue anyone from a bad family situation. I don't believe that a mother should make God-like decisions based on her own feelings. It's a very impersonal view of her child's needs. If you expect to control a child's life, you're going to get your comeuppance one way or another.

After our story attracted some local publicity, a reporter asked me, "Do you think you have a right to him after all these years?"

I answered, "It's not a matter of my rights. He has a right to a relationship. I'm not going to grab him and dress him in swaddling clothes."

A letter to the editor of our local paper from an adoptive parent claimed that Jerry's adoptive parents are his real parents. She said that adoptive parents are not caretakers. She referred to an account of an unhappy reunion, in which an adoptee found a parent in sordid straits, and commented, "I can't believe this child was not better off not knowing her all-important roots."

I feel sorry for this woman, but I feel sorrier for her child. I never made an issue of the term "real parents." And, in fact, this woman is a caretaker because she treats her child as an inanimate object with no feelings or critical faculties or needs of his own.

Everyone wants to belong, to have some continuity between past and future. I don't care how happy he is or how much he loves the people who bring him up, he lacks that connection. It is every natural parent's responsibility to supply these links, no matter what pretenses their subsequent families are founded on.

I have tried to give Jerry every clue to finding his natural father. Mick came from a small city in New England. Another of the fellows from the apartment in Boston comes from the same city. He tells us that the family has a business. I really don't know very much, and that is one more measure of the scared, insecure, friendless girl I was. They wondered, years ago, what I ever saw in Mick. Not much. And I didn't see much in myself either.

For Jerry and the girls and me, learning to accept one another has not been easy. When Jerry spent a lot of time with me, the girls felt jealous. They are teenagers, after all, and have many needs. He received a lot of attention and he was an adult. I felt at times like Solomon trying to decide fairly and keep peace among my own children. Sibling rivalries are inevitable, and when an adult enters a home to claim a parent's attention, there are bound to be more.

I know Jerry has had a difficult time with his mother. He must have unresolved feelings towards her and now she is past reaching, so he has to work them out for himself.

Now he has me too. He sees my house needs repairs and he wants to help. It must be as difficult for him with me as it is with his own family. He made a commitment to improve things for me and I feel I must restrain him. He makes a conscious effort, but I refuse to be a burden. It wouldn't be normal for a mother to be dependent on her son, but reaching an agreement has taken a lot of hashing out.

I've wondered how I got so lucky. I didn't clutch at my other kids and I won't clutch at him. I think that's the right decision for all of us.

*Jerry tells his version of the same story:*

My adoptive father comes from a long line of doctors and preachers. He has a book at home with the family genealogy that goes back to the seventeenth century. All doctors and preachers. If anybody did anything else they left him out of it. My adoptive mother is Irish Protestant. Her father died when she was fourteen. He worked for the First National Bank. My mother and both her sisters ended up working there too.

My father is a doctor too, although I really think he might have been happier as a preacher. He has very strict ideas about how people should live. My mother has been like a ghost to us for eight years, although she still walks around and eats and smokes cigarettes.

They adopted me when my mother couldn't conceive, and then, soon after they got me, she became pregnant. Now I have three sisters. My father has always liked to fish. The first thing I remember is going on a fishing trip with them to Canada. I was really quiet. I still am, in cars. Then we reached a bridge and I started screaming. I was about two. I didn't stop screaming until we reached land again.

When I was eight, they told me I was adopted. A lady who lived down the street, married with two kids, had the news sprung on her when she was forty. She went wacky. This affected my parents and they didn't know how to handle it. So they read up on it. They did it very intelligently, the way they did most things, according to the latest thinking. They told me I was chosen, the usual. I don't know if it really affected me right away. I used to sort of laugh to myself. As we were growing up, my sisters and I would fight and their main ammunition when they were losing or when we reached an impasse, was to say, "You're adopted." I would act like I was hurt, although I really wasn't, but my mother would be infuriated. It was only when I reached adolescence that it started to make any difference.

My father is a very fine man, although I think he's too sensitive for his own good and gets hurt too easily. You couldn't find a better doctor, though. His father used to tell me stories about going out on house calls in the middle of night in a horse-drawn buggy, and my father is the modern equivalent of the country doctor. If you are his patient, there's nothing he won't do for you at any hour.

When I was six something happened that made me lose respect for him, and for ten years I hardly ever spoke to him. The lines were clearly drawn in our house. He went to work and my mother kept house. He left all discipline to her. She was very strict and very protective at the same time. She did her best, but she would get sick of it. One night at the dinner table she was yelling at me and then yelling at him. He just sat there. So I said, "Are you a man or are you a mouse?" I didn't even know what I was saying. I think I picked it up from a cartoon. He was hurt. I could feel it, but I figured that a man should have smacked the hell out of me and her. He sort of sulked. That was when it started. That's when I started getting mad at him for not putting his foot down.

My mother tried to keep things simple. She was a complicated woman who tried to keep things running as smoothly and as simply as possible. If I did well in school, fine, as long as I didn't do too well. Don't be a wise guy or you'll get smacked. At first everything was great. They wanted the little bundle they adopted, but when I started turning into the wise-ass I am, neither one of them understood.

Our neighborhood had lots of kids, most of them older than me, but I was bigger than most of them so I enjoyed myself. I lived in a fantasy world. School and home were places I could function, but outside I had my own world, and the kids in the neighborhood liked to get in on it.

I was the greatest center fielder the Yankees ever had. I watched all the Yankee games and then hit all their home runs over again in the yard. We were all excited about Mantle and Maris and their home runs. If there were other kids around we hit our homers, ran around the bases, and shook hands at home plate. If I was alone, I shook hands with the trees.

I had a passion for antique cars and remodeled a baby carriage into a car. My mother worried about me. Sometimes she told me to get out of the yard and play with the other kids. She wanted more than anything for me to be a normal child, well-balanced, mediocre, and bland. My father wanted an educated son, maybe another doctor like him, his father, and his brother.

She never talked about what I was going to be when I grew up. They told her at school that I was above average in intelligence. When I wanted to, I did fine. So she just let it go. My father didn't know what to do about my real talents. The closest I came to anything biological was planting a garden once. I started writing stuff when I was twelve or thirteen and he would read it and praise it. I guess he thought maybe I would be a sports writer.

Outside the house I invented my family all over again. A new kid moved in when I was ten. I told him that I had five brothers and ten sisters, named them and gave them characters, and put them safely in different parts of the world where they did interesting things. I only invited him over when my family was out, but one day he came over and asked my father how Johnny was getting by in Alaska. My old man looked at him and said, "What are you talking about?" I explained, apologized, and was really embarrassed.

My mother began to have real problems. They sat in the kitchen in the evenings. I had a desk next to the kitchen and I would hear them fighting through the wall. My father's brother was a doctor and he married a doctor who hired a maid and kept up her practice. My mother got in violent arguments with my aunt. "How can you leave your children with a maid? You should be home with them."

"I'm a career woman," she would say. "I have a career of my own." I heard my mother tell about these arguments and I know she felt frustrated because of the implication that my aunt was smarter, more highly trained, and had a worthwhile vocation. My mother might have finished high school, but I'm not even sure of that. She was smart, though, and she had always worked before marriage. All she did while she was raising her kids was volunteer for hospital work sometimes.

She liked to talk and have a few laughs. My father wasn't very sociable. He worked hard and liked to have some peace and quiet. Once I saw him put his arm around her while they were watching television and I was shocked.

My mother's problems got worse and worse. My father, being a doctor, tried to deal with it medically. In the late fifties that meant starting with drugs and, when drugs didn't work, psychiatrists, institutions, shock treatments, and finally neurosurgery. He used up at least three years of income trying to make things better with medicine, the only thing he knew or trusted.

The drugs made things worse. She began having hallucinations.

Once I told them I saw a rat in the garage. Two weeks later, my mother got into a mysterious panic about my sister. "Cathy swallowed a rat in the garage! It bit her, then she swallowed it!" She was going berserk, and I think she knew it and that made her worse.

My father went back and forth to work and never really saw the worst of it. She began to take long naps, then finally there were three suicide attempts. I tried to talk to her, but I didn't really comprehend what was going on. She was so proper, tried so hard to be normal. That was probably one reason she had trouble having kids before adopting. She couldn't discuss her real feelings about my father. She couldn't tell him that she had her own life and interests, that she resented being handed a set of responsibilities. But I was fourteen and I didn't know. I didn't know what to do when she broke down crying. I could see that she got desperate. She took an overdose the first time.

One day my youngest sister came home from school and went up to her room and found that my mother had slit her wrists and drunk half a bottle of ammonia. She called an ambulance. I don't know how my father felt coming home from work and finding an ambulance and all the neighbors around the house. I blamed him for not rising to that, but I couldn't talk to him. He was still a mouse.

He never could hold his liquor, but he started to drink more and more. A couple of martinis and he's a different person. If he has a couple more, he can hardly stand up. And in the morning he's Mr. Perfect. You'd think he never touched a drop the night before.

In one year, 1966, he lost his whole life. His father died in January. His brother died in a plane crash in May, and in July my mother had a minor lobotomy. After that the drinking became more regular.

The first lobotomy improved nothing. It seemed to eliminate the wrong emotions. When she spoke she was aggressive and offensive. She would go on and on about the days when she worked for the bank. One of us might say, "That's a nice dress, Mom."

She would answer, "Don't tell me it's a nice dress. I worked at the First National."

She lashed out at everyone, including her best and oldest

friends. Her anger was totally irrational. It made no sense at all.

My father hadn't taken a vacation for a long time. All his money went into treatment for her. He had an old friend who had gotten divorced and married to his secretary, then retired to Bermuda. Every week my father got postcards telling about the weather and the fishing. So he decided to go to Bermuda for a week with my mother. He couldn't resist the fishing. He had two weeks' vacation and he would spend a week of it fishing. The night before they were supposed to leave, my father was drinking and my mother was going on and on about life at the First National. He yelled at her. Dishes started to break. Then, finally, one big crash. I went to see what had happened. I heard my father moaning. There was blood all over the place. She was sitting in a chair.

He got so mad at her that he picked up a milk bottle and started to swing it at her head, but at the last instant he blocked it with his arm and slashed himself. I had just got my license and now I had to drive him to the hospital, his own hospital. He was still drunk and playing back-seat driver.

They brought him in all covered with blood. He was quite humiliated. They didn't go to Bermuda. He spent two weeks sitting in the back yard. He's such a good man when he's sober. It hurts to remember the bad times.

He was very aware that I was adopted. I think in the beginning my mother made believe that I wasn't, but it was something that had to be dealt with because he said so. When it became apparent that I wouldn't become a dentist or an eye, ear, nose, and throat man, I think he filled in the puzzle and figured my natural father for a good-for-nothing. He knew I had potential, but consciously he resigned himself to whatever happened, or didn't happen. And I think he loves me, more than I can handle sometimes.

He doesn't say this, not directly. He talks in press releases. His press release when I got out of high school was, "You do what you want. You have your own talents. I'll support you as much as I can."

I'm twenty-seven years old now and I'm still getting the same press release. But when he's loaded and the real truth comes out, he's disappointed. He doesn't like me tending bar. He comes in once in a while, but he doesn't like it.

I have good, decent, honest friends in the bar, but he doesn't understand them. To him you're not decent unless you have a routine job. In the last year or two, I'd say he's come to respect me. Now he understands, whereas before I couldn't bring up the fact that we have real differences.

I wanted to say to him, "I just go home to you, but we're not related. We're not the same people at all. We don't think the same way." I wouldn't say it because it would wound him. But after what's happened I think he has begun to understand.

When I went to college, I invented my family again. I didn't tell the truth about them at all. The stories I made up were based on the truth, but I put a different emphasis on what really happened.

I turned my father into a wild man. I took that story about the milk bottle and told it as if it were typical. My father became a brawler and a drunkard. If you tell that story right, it becomes hilarious. You leave out the neurosurgery and the pain of course.

My imaginary father came out very close to what I always figure my real father for—a drunkard, a wild man.

After a time at school I began to drift. I took a job at a race track as a hot walker for a dollar an hour. I walked the horses after their work-outs until they cooled off. My professors let me miss class and just go in for exams. I began asking myself for the first time questions like, "What are you living for?" "What are you doing?" "What are you all about?"

I had girlfriend problems. Everything started to fall apart at the same time. I worked at the race track and wrote term papers for other people in order to make money. Then I left and got a job on a horse farm, thinking that I might become a trainer. My girlfriend asked me one night when I had been drinking if I had any idea what my real parents were like. I had never told her I was adopted, but it's something that gets around. I was mean about it. What difference does it make? We started to fight and that came to an end.

I started traveling. I felt there was no one I could turn to. I had no focal point to my life. I went all over the eastern part of the country and ended up down in Florida. I had a job tending bar, a little cottage that I fixed up, and a new girlfriend. Things calmed down for a while.

Then I came up North to help my father move. I was supposed to stay a week and ended up staying a month and a half. That's when he started to raise all his objections. He couldn't understand that I felt content in my life in Florida. I had sunshine and love. Our fights made me think more and more about where I came from. He brought up things from years before and harped on them. And after going through his disappointment, he would come back to his own failings. The mouse.

When I returned to Florida, I had lost my job and lost my girl-friend. I've felt really burned by girls three times in my life and it really sets me back each time. It makes me think, get morbid, depressed. I had spent more time by myself than anyone I knew and knew myself better than anyone else knew himself. I had found a contented situation and then lost it. I drifted, living out of my Volkswagen for a while, and then came North again.

Somewhere along the line I began to look at pictures and faces on the street, trying to figure out who looked like me, or whom I looked like. I read Jack Kerouac's books and began to place myself in that situation. Kerouac's scene was going on around the time I was born. I thought I was a lot like him in some ways. Both of us always hung out with wild men, but both of us were always hanging back just a bit and watching and listening. He went to college near where I was born. But mostly it was looking at pictures and looking at faces. I thought about it a lot, but never did anything about it.

I've worked in the same bar for two and a half years. I've met thousands of people, seen thousands of faces. People come in and literally tell me their life stories.

For six months I had known this guy, Charlie, casually. He was loud-mouthed. I didn't like him much, but I didn't know him. One night he fell asleep at the bar and I tried to wake him up. He woke up fighting, so I grabbed him by the hair and threw him out.

The next night he came back, considerably quieter. We talked for a long time and we became good friends. He came from a strange family. His mother was widowed. His older brother had died at forty-three, and he and his girlfriend lived with his mother.

I had seen his niece Jane once when they came in together. On my birthday she came up and said, "Hey, how would you like to go to the ball game?" Sure. After all, I used to be the greatest center fielder the Yankees ever had.

We went to the ball game. Everyone had a lot to drink and we had a good time.

I saw her a couple of times after that. She would stop by the bar. She told me that her mother was in a wheelchair, and I had seen her father around town before he died. One time she came in and I was reading an article in the paper about adoption. We talked about being adopted. Then I didn't see her for a few weeks. I had no romantic interest in her whatsoever and I didn't miss her. I knew she was only nineteen, and that seemed a little young.

I hadn't done anything to follow up the article in the *News*. It was something I wanted to get off my chest, but I had other things on my mind. I had been going out with this other girl, a teacher named Jean, and the night before, Wednesday night, we had had a fight. I came in on Thursday night to talk to her. She was going on vacation the next day for two weeks, so I didn't have much time.

I came over with my sister Cathy. Charlie's niece was the least of my worries. I hadn't thought about her at all. I wanted to talk to Jean. She was talking to Charlie. They are good friends. I left them alone, since I didn't want to get into it right away, so Cathy and I sat at the bar.

A half hour went by and in walked Jane. She started coming towards me. I thought, "Oh Christ." But she ignored me and went to Cathy and said, "I have to talk to you."

I thought she was chasing after me and I had no need for that right then. They went to a corner of the bar to a table and started talking. I wasn't paying any attention, just watching TV. Then Cathy came up and grabbed Charlie and said, "Come with me. It's important." So just Jean and I were left at the bar and we started talking, which was all I wanted in the first place.

After fifteen minutes, Charlie came up and said, "Jane has something really important to tell you." I was annoyed. Then I saw that Cathy had tears coming down her face. We're pretty close. I'm close to all my sisters. They're nice, gentle people. They like life to be simple. They are like my mother at her best, but they don't realize that, the two younger ones anyway. They just remember her going crazy.

I went over and said, "What's going on?" Jane told me I should sit down.

"I know who your mother is."

This was three weeks after I had told her. "Bullshit."

I looked at Cathy. She was still crying but she nodded. Jane handed me an envelope with a ring and a birth certificate and some pictures.

She said, "Your mother is my mother."

I went home and stared at those pictures. There I was with my mother at the maternity home. It was the first time I ever broke down and cried over it. Cathy was stunned too. She stopped in my room and said, "How are you doing?"

"She looks like Joe Namath," I said. People were always saying I looked like Joe Namath.

I stayed up all night and told my father about it. He didn't say anything for a whole week. He saw it as a reality now, not as an abstraction. I was an adopted son with parents out there. He's a reasonable guy and he went about dealing with it.

The next night I went back to the bar. I sat with Jean and Charlie and the other bartender, who kept pouring me shots of Irish whiskey. We were good friends but I never mentioned I was adopted or anything. Now I knew I had some Irish in me, so the Irish whiskey was appropriate.

Jane came in, and at two in the morning we headed up to her house. I was still numb from the shock. She went in and told her mother I was there and out she came with her walker. I went over and held her. It was quite a moment.

We went into the kitchen and started talking. The other girls were there. I had met them once before. Nora could only talk about everyday things. To me everything seemed so small compared to finding my mother.

If my adoptive mother weren't in the state she's in, I doubt if I would have gotten very close to Sarah and her family. It would have been quiet and discreet, more a matter of curiosity than anything else. I could never have foreseen the problems that arose.

My half-sisters are just growing up. They were used to being where they are with very little interference from the outside, and I know they feel jealous of some of the attention I've received.

For both my natural mother and me there have been problems. This has pointed out some things in both of us that we would rather not have to deal with.

She's handicapped, and she wants so much not to burden me with that. I feel compelled to help, but I have tried to limit myself to things like repairing the house. At first I did more. I spent a lot of money on a color television for them. But I can't become the man of the house.

My adoptive mother was always so simple, even before her serious problems. She never went too far into things. My natural mother is so analytical, so open that it hurts at times. I wish there could be some happy medium and that I still had real access to both of them. An interesting thing is that when my natural mother comes to my father's house, my adoptive mother is very good to her. She is neat and quiet, as if there is some sort of bond between them.

Things are better between my father and me, although some of the same distance will always remain. He's begun to copy me in some ways. It's as if he is convinced since this happened that I am my own person. I bought a funny hat and he went out and bought one like it.

This reunion came at a good point for me. Two years earlier and I wouldn't have been prepared for it at all. It's lightened up in a year. I need it that way for now; I've had enough of this heavy stuff. But my natural mother is so probing. I feel I need something a little lighter, like Mick.

From everything I've heard from my mother and their college friends, he's a wild man. He's supposed to be able to see a picture of someone or read a headline and make up a whole story to fit that person, a whole character. He's supposed to be a good storyteller.

I'm still mad at myself. I make a decent buck and I have time on my hands, but, instead of putting that time to use, I drink and talk and play golf.

I would like to find Mick and see if the father I made up for myself is really true. My father knows who his father was. He knows who his brother was. Who is my father? Who is my brother?

*Some time after this interview was completed, I talked with Jerry again. He had been to see Mick's family in New England. His adoptive father and he drove up to the Canadian border to fish. Jerry borrowed the car for two days and drove to Mick's town. Mick's family owns a fairly large business, and locating people who knew the family was easy.*

*The first relative he spoke to was a great-uncle who seemed to recognize him when he came in the door. In discussions with various relatives and one ex-wife of Mick's, Jerry formed a complex picture of his natural father. Mick had not been heard from in almost twenty years. People seemed to either love him or hate him. There was liitle indifference.*

*When Mick was sixteen, the day he got his driver's license, he asked a man if he could take his expensive car for a spin around the block. The man consented, and Mick disappeared for two days. A wild man. And yet he did not drink.*

*Jerry was one of three children born between May and September of 1949 with the same father. Jerry's half-sister knew their father and his disappearance has hurt her. She wants to know him too.*

*Mick was a very smart man. People say that if he had gone into business with his brother, they would now own the whole state, but his brother couldn't stand him.*

*After Boston University, Mick attended MIT. He returned to his home state and taught at the state university. At some point Jerry will head out West to look for Mick. He says, "It would have been easier if I had just found out he was a drunk."*

# A Brief Reunion
## —— Hannah ——

*Most adoptees who find their natural parents feel the reunion has been a success if they are able to fill the gaps which have existed in their own self-images. They want to know where they came from, where they received certain traits and characteristics. Even if they do not establish a friendly relationship with their natural parents, fulfilling this need enables them to call their reunion successful. Any subsequent friendship with their parents is strictly a bonus.*

*Hannah Ward traveled around the world before she met her natural mother. Born in England, she was taken as an infant to Australia by her adoptive parents. She later emigrated to the United States, then returned to England to find her natural mother. While she still has a longing for some additional contact with her natural mother and particularly her half-brother and half-sister, her primary desire has been satisfied.*

My adoptive father was a sickly child. He was very well-read, but his childhood illnesses prevented his getting any formal education. He was a bricklayer by trade and, because work in England was scarce, he beat around the world, stopping where he could find work. When he came to New Zealand he decided that was where he wanted to settle. He returned to England, married Mum, and adopted me.

He had a chest ailment and the army rejected him. We set out for New Zealand. War broke out as we reached Ceylon so we had a destroyer escort to Sydney. My mother said to Dad, "There's a war on. I'm not going any further. I'm not going to get off this ship and onto another one."

They agreed to remain in Sydney until the end of the war. Dad took work anywhere, contracting to go off to New South Wales or into the bush for a week or two at a time. We traveled with him too, but after a few years of traveling all around, living like pioneers, we bought some land and built a house in the country a few miles outside of Sydney. There weren't any roads to speak of.

After the war, Dad made plans to go into the contracting business himself. He sold almost everything he had and put the money into his business. Then he started feeling pains in his chest. At the hospital they opened him up and found that he had cancer. Three days later he died.

Mum was left with a nine-year-old child, a house, and nothing else. She went out to work because a widow's pension wasn't enough to live on. We stayed in the house for a year and we were very lonely. The closest houses were some distance away. We were both depressed. Mum would cook a meal, we would sit down and stare at it for a while, then throw it out. Then our little dog was poisoned by a neighbor and that was the last straw. We sold the house and lived like gypsies, moving into a house where Mum would do domestic work, then into a room somewhere, and back into another house.

I wasn't told I had been adopted until I was fifteen, although I did wonder why I grew tall and thin, while my mother stood four-feet-eleven and had an hourglass figure. She was outgoing while I was introverted. We just weren't alike.

When I was a little girl, something annoyed me and I cursed, "Blast it."

My mother heard me and nearly had a fit. "What did you say?" I was stunned by her anger. I just stood there. She shook me. "What did you say?" She nearly shook the insides out of me.

"All I said was 'blast it' Mummy." She let go.

"Oh, I thought you said something else." I wondered for years what she thought I had said. Then I learned the word "bastard." And when I was fifteen I figured out why she had been so sensitive about that word.

I led a very lonely childhood after my father died. With my

mother working, I had to come home from school to an empty house and it was as if I had lost them both. When my mother gave up domestic work and started at a factory, I missed her in the morning too.

School made me feel out of place. I did very well in certain subjects, particularly in geography, but being English-born in Australia made me strange. It's like a family squabble, like cousins who don't get on. If you put an Englishman in Australia there's friction. The same with the Australians in England. If you put them together in a foreign country they stick together.

In school they would ask where everyone was born and the answers would come back Sydney or Brisbane, but then little me would pipe up, "London." Silence. I wasn't one of them.

At fifteen I applied for a government job in which I could use my shorthand and typing. I needed a birth certificate. I came home from school and told my mother about it, all excited because at last I would be able to work using skills that I had studied. When I asked for my birth certificate she said, "There's something I have to tell you."

My life up to that point became a lie. She hadn't wanted to tell me about it. No one knew except the doctor who arranged it and my father's family. We went through a great crying scene. I said I never wanted any mother but her.

She said, "You'll always be my daughter. I've loved you like my own child. It never made any difference to me."

Taking my adoption certificate to the head of personnel was embarrassing. I was the only person I knew who didn't have a birth certificate. We skirted the subject at home. We fought—teenagers always fight—but even in the heat of our battles we avoided adoption. I never stopped thinking about it.

At nineteen, just before Christmas, I left for New Zealand to work. I promised my mother I would return for the following Christmas. I went because there really wasn't much for a nineteen-year-old girl to do in Sydney. New Zealand was wonderful. While there was no more entertainment—theaters, movies, or nightclubs —the New Zealanders entertained themselves. But when I returned to Australia the following year I became restless again, and I knew I had had enough of New Zealand.

My mother and I took a trip to England. There I felt out of place. I was British to my Australian classmates and Australian to my British relatives.

I also felt the burden of my adoption in England. At least no one knew the terrible secret in Sydney. My mother's relatives didn't know either, but the whole time we spent with them, I wondered if they didn't suspect that the tall thin girl with their sister was not related. I felt like an impostor, a child of unknown background impersonating a respectable girl.

With my father's family things were worse. They knew I was adopted. Arranging to see them after twenty years was about as warm as a dental appointment. They were all polite, but they didn't consider my father's wife to be family and they didn't consider his illegitimate daughter to be family either.

For years I had thought of these people as aunts and uncles, but upon meeting them for the first time, those labels didn't mean a thing.

Not being at home in Australia, tired of New Zealand, and uncomfortable with England, I decided to move to New York in 1963. I discovered that most New Yorkers are either the children of immigrants or immigrants themselves. They don't care about your accent or who your family is. It's now my home.

Still I was looking for myself, for an identity. All my moving around had been a part of it, attempting to forget my curiosity about my natural mother. It didn't work, and New York, with all its cosmopolitan atmosphere, couldn't erase my curiosity.

I began to go into psychotherapy. Invariably I was asked, "Why do you want to find her?" I would tell the therapists I had no strong sense of who I was and they would respond with unctuous psychological jargon. "It comes from inside yourself. You are you. You have a right to be here. You are what you make of yourself and you don't need to know more. All this comes from inside yourself. Your adoption shouldn't mean that you feel any less yourself."

The standard phrases. But society tells us to keep adoption secret and so it becomes a shameful thing to be adopted. My adoptive mother, whom I love, who took care of me through the measles, the mumps, and the chicken pox, who as a young widow worked so hard to keep us going, even this strong, wonderful woman felt the need to hide it from me. Then, after being conditioned that there is a stigma, you are told that it means nothing, to forget and get on about your business. You learn one thing and then are told the opposite is true. It doesn't resolve anything to be reassured in this manner.

Then I started with a therapist who gave me an ultimatum.

She told me, "You've spent your years sitting on the fence and it's immobilized you. Either do it or forget about it."

That put the decision on my shoulders. None of this pandering and saying, "You're all right . . . being adopted doesn't mean anything . . . you're a human being." None of it.

"Make up your mind. Do it or stop talking about it." I knew that I'd been thinking about it and fantasizing about it since I was fifteen. I sometimes berated my natural mother for giving me away. Other times I would imagine that I'd found her and would go to look at her without letting her see me, because she had given me away and I wasn't going to give her the satisfaction of knowing me.

So I resolved to look for her. I asked myself all the questions I wanted answers to. What does she look like? What kind of person is she? What is her background? To forget these concerns would have been like forgetting a part of myself. I had to fill the void with knowledge.

And yet it still terrified me. I feared being rejected.

I wrote a long letter to my mother in Australia telling her that while my love for her meant everything, this question of my identity wouldn't leave me alone. I feared what it might do to her. She was old and this could break her.

I posted the letter and waited until I thought the letter must have arrived, then called her. I did not want her to just pick up a piece of paper. I wanted to make contact with her.

"Have you received the letter?"

"Yes." Then she said, "I've often wondered why you waited so long. I feel it's been a barrier between us."

I didn't know she felt that way. I wondered why she had never broached the subject. We always hedged around it, not making contact, not really being mother and daughter. All had not been as it should have been and now we were closer than ever, her in Australia and me in New York.

The barrier was down. She didn't want to repeat what she had told me in her letter, which had already been sent by registered mail. She did speak very highly of my natural mother, whom she had met. She described her as an intelligent, thoughtful, respectable young woman. When I told her how frightened I was of rejection, she tried to reassure me.

"Your mother and I corresponded until the War reached its peak," she said. "Then we stopped. I'm sure she will be very pleased to meet you."

When her letter arrived, it contained all the information she had: my name at birth—Jill; my mother's maiden name—Julie Clarke; and an address near Nottingham. I wrote to some old friends who lived in London, telling them only that I would be visiting the United Kingdom in July. These people are like aunt and uncle to me. After my experience with my aunts and uncles twenty years ago, I wanted to stay with people who had proved that they liked me. They welcomed me like a long-lost daughter, and provided me with a base to come back to and be fussed over, something I wanted since I had no idea what I would be going through.

I took a train to Nottingham after a few days, then looked in all the area telephone directories for my mother's maiden name. I found one man who lived in the same town and called. I said I was the daughter of an old friend of a woman named Julie Clarke and I wanted to meet her. I gave her probable age.

"Do you perhaps have a sister of that name and age?"

He answered, "Yes, I do." His voice was thoughtful and suspicious. "She's married. I don't like to give her name to strangers."

"Where does she live?"

"She lives in the south of England, but I can't tell you where. I'll have to contact her and tell her that you want to see her."

I gave him the name of a hotel. This was a Friday. I told him I would remain at the hotel until he called. I stayed in my room, hardly going out except to eat. I had no idea what he thought. He might know about me and suspect.

On Monday night the phone rang. A woman's voice.

"Hannah?"

"Are you Julie?"

"Yes."

"This is Jill."

"I know who you are. I'm shocked. I'm still getting over it. My brother doesn't know about you. He called my sister and my sister called me."

"I'd love to see you," I said.

"Yes, I'd like to see you too." She was rather reserved. Then she asked, "Are you married?"

"No, I'm not. I believe you are married."

"I'd rather not tell you that."

"Where do you live?"

"I'd rather not tell you that either."

"Where can I see you?"

"I'd rather that you not come to see me at all. I'll come up and see you in Nottingham. I'll take the train tomorrow afternoon and come to your hotel on Wednesday at ten."

I could tell that she was frightened and hesitant, protective of her present status. I could hardly believe it. I would see my natural mother in two days.

Tuesday night the phone rang.

Julie again. "I'm sorry but I can't make it. You did say you would come to wherever we arranged to meet?"

"Yes."

"Do you know the British Museum?"

"Yes."

"How about meeting me there. In the Autograph Room, by the Magna Carta. Is tomorrow all right?"

"No. I don't know the transport system that well. I'll need time to collect myself. How about Friday?"

"At ten," she said. "What do you look like?"

"I'm about five-feet-eight. I have reddish-brown hair. I will be wearing a blue outfit. What will you be wearing?"

"I don't know yet."

"What color is your hair?"

"White now."

So after my fantasy of going to look at her and observe her without letting on who I was, she knew what to look for and I didn't. I went back to London and took a guest room rather than return to my friends right away. I didn't want to return to them immediately after seeing Julie if I became terribly emotional.

I was in the Autograph Room at a quarter to ten shaking all over. She would know me and I wouldn't know her. I looked at every woman's face, trying to see my features in any of them. I saw a woman with white hair walk into the next room, then quickly leave. I wasn't close enough to see her face. She wore a raincoat so I had no idea what her figure was like.

I told myself to calm down and be patient, forced myself to look at the exhibits. Ten o'clock came. No sign of her. Then at five past ten, the woman with white hair came toward me. She had taken off her raincoat and I could see she was built like me. At twenty feet away I could see my face. My legs were shaking and I couldn't walk very well, but I went toward her. I began to cry. She laid her hand on my shoulder and said, "Let's walk."

The Museum is vast, and the silence enforced by museum etiquette helped me to compose myself. When we got outside, I said, "I knew you were Julie." Then we talked about minor things —theater and television.

Finally she said, "I'm still getting over the shock of hearing your voice. I named my second daughter Hannah."

She didn't say why. My mother must have told her my name.

She still wouldn't tell me her last name. I asked if she lived nearby. "No. Not really. I drove here."

"What does your husband do?"

"I don't want to tell you." She didn't want to tell me anything about her life. I didn't know what to ask. I was frightened to ask anything because of her reserve.

She did say that she had two grown children and four grand-children, but she had never told them about me and it would kill them if they found out now. Her husband knew about me. She told him before they married.

"My son is in Rhodesia," she said. "So you see I have worries of my own."

"Where is your daughter?"

"She's overseas." I knew better than to ask where. She took me to lunch after walking for a bit. We walked some more and drank numerous cups of tea. She thanked me for not divulging my identity to her brother.

I learned a great deal about her from looking across the table at her. She doesn't wear jewelry and perhaps that's where I get my disdain for it. She smokes cigarettes. So do I.

She told me that she was tops in her class in geography. So was I. She was very good in sports. So was I. She is basically very quiet, as I am. And something else really weird: both of us had our two front teeth capped. That part has nothing to do with genetics.

"I had lovely straight teeth, but I chipped them and had to get caps. They were so nice before that people thought they were false."

The same thing happened to me.

"I knew who you were," she said, "because of the family resemblance."

Here was the link. We have the same build. Although her hair had turned white, I could see that it was like mine. I was looking at my face as it would look at sixty. Here was the genetic continuity I was looking for. I wasn't just sprung into the world. I had a history. I belonged to others through my genes. I wasn't made in a test tube. My adoptive mother gave me everything I have, but I always wondered if anyone anywhere looked like me.

When the conversation stopped for a bit, I said, "I was very lonely as a child. I had no brothers and sisters. My parents planned to adopt a brother for me, but the War came instead, and then Dad died."

"Having brothers and sisters doesn't mean that much. I hardly see mine." Then she went on to tell me that when she became pregnant she never told her parents, but came to London to stay with her sister. Somehow she didn't make the connection as she downgraded the importance of brothers and sisters. She had had someone to turn to.

I asked her about my father. They had been childhood sweethearts, but after she became pregnant she could see that he wouldn't make a good husband. "He was young and wild," she said.

"Well, he was young. I'm sure he would have grown past the wildness."

"I'm sure he would have," she said. "Had he lived. He joined the navy and was lost at sea in 1941 or '42."

Three or four times during the day she asked when I was returning to New York, and each time I told her. When I asked if I could see her again, she told me that she would be going away with her husband the next day. They traveled much of the time. I had been fortunate to see her.

I asked if I could take a photograph. She didn't want me to, since I might show it to people and find out who she was and where she lived, but at last she allowed me one.

When it was time for her to leave, she insisted on walking me to my guest house. She didn't want me to see her car. I began to cry again. At the door of the house I said, "Please don't go out of my life again. No matter how tenuous, please keep some sort of touch."

"Yes, I will. Some day I'll tell you everything." I gave her my address in London, my address at work, and my residence in New York.

I guess I left a lot of things unanswered because I didn't want to push her. It's hard for her to see a child she gave up nearly forty years ago. I wanted her to have time to absorb it. She didn't know if I was alive or dead and presumed that I had remained in Australia. I expected to hear from her, and I mentioned my birthday in September, but my birthday passed and I heard nothing.

I feel she has rejected me because she doesn't want anything to disturb the life that she lives in England. She doesn't want anyone coming into it, and I certainly don't intend to embarrass her. If she feels uncomfortable in trying to explain my existence, I'd rather avoid the situation. I have my pride too.

I have seen her face. That's the most important thing. I don't feel that I'm anything to be ashamed of. My mother in Australia has always been very proud of me. I've made my own way, just as my mother did after my father died, and it's her example that has given me strength. Her love for me was confirmed by her willingness to give me all the help she could in finding Julie.

As for my natural mother's claim that learning about me would kill my half-brother and half-sister, I can't believe that she could have raised two children, who are themselves parents, who would look on this news with such dismay that it would hurt them. They have traveled and made their own ways just as I have.

I would like some sort of contact. I would love to hear about their lives. I think they would be interested to know that they have a sister with a different life, who has lived in different parts of the world, and become a person in her own right. We have only one life and it seems a shame to keep people apart just because society dictates it.

I hold out no hope of something magical happening. I've reached halfway. I know better than to expect miracles. I waited for Julie to contact me again but, when she didn't, my disappointment didn't last. If I meet any of them, it will be a treat. I know what I will look like when I am old and it doesn't frighten me.

# Neighborhood Adoption
## —— Maria ——

*Because adoption agencies have traditionally ignored the problems of children outside their own religious and racial groupings, minorities have been left to form adoption systems based on their own customs. Chicanos, Mexicans living in the United States, usually keep their children, but when there are adoptions they are generally by private agreement. When everyone in a community except the child himself is aware of an adoptee's true history, the sense of powerlessness can be more frustrating than usual.*

*Maria Valez had a childhood punctuated with violence. For a long while she avoided asking about her natural parents. As a child she had met her natural mother and her brother, but she later refused to admit to a longing to know her own origins. After she was hospitalized with severe depression, Maria decided the time had come to assert herself. She still does not know her full story, but it seems that Maria was adopted at least three times within the same community.*

I may have set some kind of record. I believe I was adopted three times by two different couples. Juan and Rita were fifty and thirty-six years old the first time they adopted me. My second adoptive mother was Juan's mother, and her husband was just her husband.

Juan was the only one who treated me well, but he had to work and could never spend enough time with me. Rita worked some of the time and the rest of the time she didn't want to be bothered, so I spent a lot of time with other people, her relatives and friends. She also has a daughter eight years older than me named Ella, and

Ella always took most of Rita's time.

One day Juan took me to live with his mother and she adopted me. All this was done through a lawyer, not an agency, and the records don't show exactly what happened. I was just a little kid, always getting thrown back and forth. When I went to Juan's mother, she was very strict. They both used to whip me all the time. If I came out of school a minute late, her husband would be right there with his belt in his hand. Our house was just about fifty feet from the school. He used belts, hoses, sticks, anything. He gave me ice cold baths to "cool me off." He used to threaten to kill me all the time.

When I had lived with them for two years I had to go to court for a hearing. He told me that I would have to say who I wanted to stay with. Juan's parents, my adoptive grandparents, said they wouldn't give me back to my natural parents because of their problems, and Juan and Rita also had problems. I don't know why my grandmother's husband wanted me to stay with them, but he told me that if I didn't say that, he would kill me. I stood in court and didn't look at anyone; I just said that I wanted to stay with them. I thought, if I don't say it I'm dead.

Once my friends in the next house were looking out the window and saw him beating me. I was screaming and he told me in Spanish to shut my mouth or he would kill me. The kids and their mother heard and soon the story was all through the neighborhood.

He never gave any reason for wanting me there. I figure now it's because he wanted his citizenship. I also think he wanted to show that he was doing a good deed by taking care of an adopted child. The way I see it, that way he thought he could be assured of citizenship and welfare.

I couldn't think of anything to do. I was only eight years old so I couldn't run away. Everyone in the neighborhood knew me. They all belonged to the same Apostolic church, and there was no one to hide me.

Juan hated for me to suffer. One time he almost got in a fight with the old man, but before he could hit him, he saw me and ran off because he didn't want me exposed to violence. He figured, I guess, that if he reported the old man I would be taken away for good, and he had so much trouble with his wife that he didn't want me back with her. Rita had boyfriends. She would lock me in the car when she went off to visit them. I used to see them hugging and kissing.

I always had this fear of death. Once when I lived with my grandmother I had to walk to the bus past a field that had a store at one end and a camp where winos lived at the other end. They had to walk to the store to buy their wine and then go back. One morning at 7:30 I was walking to the bus and a man in a car honked his horn at me. A wino heard the horn and turned around. He spotted me. I don't know what got into him but he started chasing me with a machete. I was terrified and desperate. I ran to this house where I knew some people. I banged on the doors and the windows trying to get in. The man was still coming and I thought, "Christ almighty, he's going to kill me!" Then I saw an old couple walking up the road. No one answered the door so I took off and ran. I got in front of these two people. I didn't say anything, but just walked ahead of them. The wino stopped chasing me.

I never told anyone that story until I started going to a counselor just last year, and it happened when I was eight. I didn't tell my friends at school, I didn't tell anybody at the bus stop, I didn't tell my teachers. I certainly didn't tell my grandmother because the old man would have beaten me. He would have said it was my fault. I had dreams about people coming after me for years and years, and the whole time I would feel desperate and scared.

Everything in my life was split into at least two parts. My first adoptive parents spoke English in our house. The second spoke Spanish. The first didn't beat me, but they neglected me. The second didn't neglect me, but they beat me.

Also, when I was very young, my natural mother came to visit us three times with her two little boys. I never thought of them as my brothers. The old man used to tease me. "That's your mother," he'd say. "That's her right there." I didn't say anything.

He tried to get me to kiss him on the lips. If I hadn't gotten out of there when I did, he probably would have tried to rape me.

My grandmother never used to buy me anything. They didn't have much money, but that wasn't the only problem. One time

Rita's daughter Ella, her husband, and Rita's parents came over. It must have been my birthday because I remember this dress, a pretty pink dress they bought me. I never had any nice clothes when I lived with my grandmother, so when I got this dress I was very happy. My grandmother said she couldn't stand these people so they had to leave right away. They were always fighting.

There was a little window high up in the kitchen and I stood up on a chair to wave goodbye. My grandmother grabbed me off the chair and just started beating the hell out of me. She didn't want me even to look at them. I don't know what she did with the dress, but I never saw it again. They hated each other and I don't know why. I felt this hatred very strongly. When I got older and finally had it out with Rita, this was one thing I asked her about.

My grandmother died when I was eleven and I went back to live with Juan and Rita. The day she died was a Sunday. The church choir used to hang around a cafeteria near the church after they finished singing. All the kids would go and sing for them. My grandmother was really short. She was crossing the street and dropped her keys. She bent over to pick them up when a guy backed up his car and knocked her over. He didn't see her and kept on going. The bottom of the car crushed her chest.

A big crowd collected and I saw an orange coat covering the body. I knew the lady this coat belonged to and I thought it must be her. But it scared me and I stayed inside. My teacher knew who it was. She grabbed me and hugged me tight against her. Her daughter said, "Maria, it's your grandmother." I said, "No, it's not." Then two kids told me the same thing. I still denied it.

Then I looked and saw my grandmother's shoes on top of a table. It had to be her or her shoes wouldn't be there.

They took me to talk to her and she was lying there all bloody. She was trying to talk to me and she told me to get her purse. I was hysterical, crying, and couldn't talk. The pastor's wife handed me the purse. They asked me if I wanted to go in the ambulance. I was wondering who would take care of me. My grandmother's husband was away, but I didn't want to go back to him at all.

I ended up going home with the teacher. That night they told me the old lady had died. I couldn't go to sleep. They all assured me that I would get over it. And when I started to comb my hair that night, it started to fall out. That's how scared I was.

The next few years were rough, but luckily I learned to take care of myself so that I didn't suffer too much. Rita didn't pay much attention.

Once when I was thirteen a woman I believed to be my natural mother spotted me in a grocery store. I acted like I didn't know her because I was scared. I just walked away, but she kept staring.

A few weeks later I was at the same store and a woman came up to me with her husband and kids. She said, "Hi, do you remember me?" I said, "No."

She said, "I'm your aunt."

"No, you're not."

"Yes, I am. You just don't remember me." She walked away with her family mumbling about how I didn't recognize her. Things like that only made me more curious.

I could never figure out why Rita ever adopted me, because she took no care of me. I could never figure out why my grandmother ever took me, because they were always beating me. No one loved me. I felt lonely all the time.

When I was fourteen, Rita gave me one explanation for why she adopted me. She said that she adopted me because Juan had an affair with my natural mother. Since they were married, she figured that whatever was his was also hers. She was depressed when she told me. I never told anyone else that story. I didn't believe it anyway. She was the one who fooled around.

When I was fifteen I got pregnant, but I never told anyone until my eighth month. My husband's family was closer to me than my own.

I didn't really want to get married, but I felt I had to to give my baby his father's last name. Some girls gave their babies their father's names without being married, but I couldn't.

When Juan found out I was pregnant he felt hurt because I didn't tell him. I never even went to the doctor. A girl named Carol lived with us at the time. She didn't get along at home, so Rita took her in. I told Carol and Carol told Rita. Rita didn't come to me, but asked Carol if I were going to get married. We never talked about anything, never communicated, and so we couldn't start then.

Rita then asked Carol if I had thought about giving the baby up up for adoption. When I heard that I got angry. What's she going to do, I thought, give my baby to one of her friends? That's the way most Mexicans adopt. I figured her friends would be just like her. Then my baby would go through the same thing I did. And I would go through life staring into the faces of little Mexicans the way the lady in the grocery store did.

So Freddie and I got married. He is eight months older than me.

After my baby was born, people would tell me that he looked just like my brothers. I hated that. I would yell at them to shut up. I pretended that I didn't want to hear it, even though I did. I was just afraid to find out anything, because if I started thinking about it and asking questions, Rita would get all hysterical.

When I was seventeen I worked in an electronics factory. One day I just started to cry. I couldn't control myself. I went to see a doctor and he put me in the hospital. Juan came to visit me.

He was sensitive. He started to cry and he didn't want to cry in front of me.

"How come they put you up here?" he said. "You're not crazy." I couldn't explain things to him. I didn't want to hurt him. By telling him that I wondered why Rita adopted me, I would be telling him that I wondered why he adopted me, and I didn't want to hurt him.

I told him how I hated his mother. I knew that hurt him too, because he loved her even if she was no good to him. But he took it.

The reason I flipped out at work was that I hurt all the time. I had nightmares about people dying and people chasing me. They went on for years.

Juan died in 1971. He was seventy years old. He had leukemia and died a slow death. Rita called me up at three o'clock in the morning to tell me. She was crying and everything but I just went back to sleep. I thought about it for a little while and told my husband, but I just fell asleep. I didn't miss him right away. Maybe I was numb, or maybe I expected it, but I hardly cried at all until the funeral. They all went up to look at him in the coffin, but I didn't want to. I got hysterical. So then I had no one except Freddie.

Around Christmas in 1975 I started to have a lot of trouble. I had terrible nightmares. If I wasn't dying and going to hell, I would see Juan in his coffin. Sometimes Rita would be in a coffin. Sometimes Juan would be sitting up talking to me, wearing the suit he wore in his coffin. Either I died or some dead person would be talking to me.

My adoptive mother's daughter Ella was jealous of me. Any time Rita paid attention to my kids she got mad. If I called Rita at Ella's house, Ella would say sarcastically, "Your daughter's on the phone."

Rita bought things for Ella's kids all the time, but not my kids. If she did buy things for my kids, she bought things for Ella's that cost more.

Rita's sister is the one person I can still talk to. She had two adopted kids of her own, and she told me that none of their family ever really accepted me or her kids.

Freddie started drinking a lot. He had his own business and the pressures started building up. We fought all the time. Everything started flashing back. When we had these fights, the feelings of hurt and loneliness would take me back to my childhood days. I'd remember that was exactly the way I felt when I was a kid. I'd feel like I was a little girl and I was getting punished. No matter what went wrong, whether it was big or small, I always felt guilty. I tried to live for today and forget about the past, but I felt like I was trapped in my own little dream world, trying to make it better. I used to get so frustrated. Everything upset me.

I felt something stirring inside me that wouldn't go away. All the troubles were building up. I was crying more and more, losing my temper more and more, and finally I went to the hospital for a rest. All my friends came there to visit me. My in-laws came to visit me and I was glad to see them. I felt fine when they were there.

Then Rita and Ella came to visit and I realized they were part of the reason I was in the hospital. I wanted them to get out. I was on medication and all sleepy. I told them to get out. They started to cry. Then I tried to go to sleep, but I could tell they were still there staring at me. I turned over and told them to get out again.

They didn't leave. I screamed as loud as I could, "Get out of here!"

Rita asked how come I let my mother-in-law in but not her. I said it was because I resented her, but never had the nerve to say it. All the time I tried to pretend that I was happy and it wasn't so. I said I didn't want to have anything to do with her. They left.

It was the first time I ever let out any of that resentment. I finally told her what I really thought, but it wasn't over then.

I had to start putting things together because nothing made any sense. Why did they adopt me? I had to know.

Freddie's drinking became a problem but he started to go to Alcoholics Anonymous. I started going to AlAnon, which is for the families of drinkers. When I started going there and getting counseling, he stopped drinking. I kept on. When he was no longer drinking, I didn't have that to talk about anymore, and all my other problems started coming out.

I had plenty of problems at home. I would burst into tears for no reason. I would yell at Freddie and the kids for no reason. It was not knowing the truth that bothered me.

My counselor promised to help me.

I visited Sacramento. The woman at the place where my records were kept wouldn't give me any names, but she told me that most of the information on my amended birth certificate was correct. I'm still not clear about who told the truth in all this. I've heard so many different things through the years. I believe I was adopted three times because I had to change my name when I registered for school, but I can't be sure.

I knew my mother's name. I had always heard people talking about her, but had never wanted to know before. I also remembered that when she had visited our house she had called my brother Richie. So I asked around if anyone knew where I could find Richie Ortez, or Richard Ortez, because I thought his name must be Richard if his nickname was Richie. I told my husband to look out for him. I tried to picture the way he looked as a little boy and described him to my husband. I lived in the same area my whole life and I was pretty sure they weren't far away. I told Freddie that if he found him, he should invite him over and I would talk to him.

But Richard wasn't his real name. If it had been I would have found him right away. He knew a lot of the same people I knew. We went to the same school. He dated some of my friends.

I knew my natural mother belonged to the same church my grandmother had gone to. I figured that she must still be going to church because the Apostolic church is very strong, a lot like the Pentecostal. It was only five minutes from my house. I thought I might see her if I went to church, but I was scared so I called up a man who used to be pastor. I looked him up in the phone book. His wife answered. She's known me since I was a baby. I was lucky to reach them since they were moving away later that day. Her husband had gone to their new place in Modesto.

I told her that it was very important that I talk to her husband so she gave me the new address and phone number. It took me a month to get up the nerve to call again. He knew who I was.

I asked if he knew Vivien Ortez. I heard him ask his wife if she knew her. He said, "No, I don't think so." Then he stopped and said, "I know one—one Vivien Ortez."

"That's her. Do you know where I can find her?"

"Sure. Just go over to the church and ask anyone about her."

I went to my counselor and told her what had happened. I didn't want to go to the church.

She said, "You know what? I have a sister-in-law who goes to that church and she might know your mother." She called her sister-in-law and asked her if she knew Vivien Ortez.

"Oh sure. She goes to church every Wednesday, Friday and Sunday. She's there all the time. All you have to do is go there and you'll find her."

My counselor said, "Can you find out her address and phone number? I'm calling on a family matter. Somebody she hasn't seen for a long time wants to see her."

She gave my counselor the number of the new pastor. I called and his wife said he was out of town and would be back Saturday. I chickened out, so my counselor called on Monday. The pastor was out. His wife didn't have the keys to his files. Then my counselor asked her if she knew Vivien Ortez. She did.

"Could you ask her to call me if you see her? It's a family matter."

The pastor's wife agreed.

On Wednesday morning Vivien called my counselor. "I hear you've been trying to get hold of me."

"I was."

"You said it was a family matter?"

"Can you come into my office? I can't talk about this over the phone."

Vivien said she could. The next day, April 14, 1976, she went to my counselor's office. My counselor asked her if she knew anyone named Maria Valez. She said no. Then my counselor gave one of my previous names—Maria Vasquez. For a while she acted like she couldn't remember. Then she said she did.

"Is she in trouble?" Vivien asked.

"She says you're her mother."

"Oh no. I only have two sons."

"Is it all right if she calls you?"

"No. I don't think she'd better. I'll call her. I'm a psychiatric nurse and I'm on call all the time. My schedule is funny." They talked for a long time.

The next day the phone rang. "Is this Maria?"

"Yeah."

"This is Vivien Ortez."

I didn't say that I thought she was my mother. I just said that I thought she knew a lot about my past and I wanted to know if she could help me.

"I'll tell you whatever I can. I knew your mother, but I can't talk to you today because I have a funny schedule."

On Friday morning she called again and we decided to meet in front of a department store. I got there five minutes before her. She just started talking and she told me a big lie.

She said she was at the show one night and my mother was there. Vivien didn't have a ride, so she went up to a girl and asked her for a ride to her apartment behind a restaurant. The girl was about nineteen. They became good friends and later the girl moved in with her.

The girl had been living with Vivien for three weeks when she said she was pregnant. She had left her husband because he used to beat her all the time. She left with another man but that didn't work out so she came to Vivien's to hide out.

Vivien said she and my mother walked out of the hospital together and she handed me to Juan and Rita herself. They were waiting in the car. Vivien said that I was never legally adopted by Juan and Rita, that I was never legally adopted until Juan's mother got me.

We talked for three hours. I said, "I don't think I should talk to you any more if that's all you can tell me." I had six pages of questions to ask and she didn't have answers to any of them. She said she knew nothing about my father. She said she never had an affair with Juan.

Then I asked for her phone number.

She said, "But my sons don't know anything about this."

"So what?"

"Well, they're going to think how stupid I am for helping my best friend to do something like this. If I had known this would happen I never would have done it in the first place. I never would have gotten involved. I don't think it's legal."

I said, "If your sons find out, just tell them what you told me. That you helped your best friend give her baby up for adoption and that's it. You're not going to get in any trouble, so why can't you tell them?"

"They're going to think I'm stupid for doing this stupid thing."

Then she said something about doing an evil thing and didn't explain. Finally she said I could call her, but if one of her sons answered I should say I was a patient.

I wasn't going to call her because I knew she was lying and I figured she would go on lying. Then the next Monday she called again.

"You don't have to look any more. Give me a little time and I'll tell you who your mother is."

"Why can't you tell me now?"

"Give me some time. I need time."

She didn't call for three weeks, so finally I got impatient. I told her I wasn't going to wait for her to tell me anything, I was just going to go ahead and find out. She had said something about switching names with her "friend" and now I told her that she was lying and that I could press charges.

I was really mad at her. "How could that lady, your friend, go into the hospital and give your name and you walk out with the baby? The hospital's going to think you're kidnapping it. They're not going to say, 'That is the mother, but we'll give the baby to someone else.' They give babies to their mothers."

She was trying to give me some story and I told her that I was going to try and find out the truth anyway. I said that there were lawyers involved and the files were going to be opened.

Then I said, "I don't want to get anyone in trouble, I just want to find out the truth."

"Why do you want to know your mother?"

"Because all my life people have pushed me around and lied to me, and now I just want to know the truth."

"I have an appointment. I'll be back at one o'clock and I'll call you."

An hour later she called. I asked, "Where are you?"

She said, "At a friend's house."

"Aren't you afraid that your friend will find out what you did?" I still couldn't get over my anger over her secrecy.

She said, "My friend doesn't understand English."

"How come you couldn't come over and tell me in person?"

"I just couldn't do that right now. I couldn't handle it."

The reason she lied about my mother, she said, was that she wanted to find out what kind of person I was, to know I wasn't going to get all hysterical and start to cry.

Before I was conceived, she lived with my father, who was married to her, and my older brother. They were really happy for a year and a half after my brother was born, then my father met another woman and went to live with her. He started pimping her and making his living from her. Then the cops caught her and put her in jail for thirty days for prostitution. During those thirty days he came back and got Vivien pregnant. When his girlfriend's time was up, he went back to her.

"Did you tell him you were pregnant?"

"Yes, but she convinced him that the baby wasn't his, I guess. I guess he just wanted her more."

Vivien had nowhere to go. A lady took her in and looked after her. That's where she got the idea for her first story. She hasn't seen that lady since.

On May 13 I met my brothers. On the fifteenth one of my brothers, Chris—the one who was called Richie—went to see one of my father's ex-wives to find out where he was. In all he was married five times. She said he had moved to Texas. She gave us the address she had and my brother lost it. So then I called information in Texas and found him.

Chris tried to call and couldn't reach him. Then he wrote a letter and got no answer. Chris hadn't seen our father in eleven years. Finally we spoke to him over the phone. He said he got the letter but didn't know anything about me. Chris said, "It was during your time," but he still said he wasn't my father. The last thing he said to Chris was, "Ask your mother."

The whole story is still confusing. My husband insisted that the best way to find out the truth was to get Vivien and Rita together. They would both tell their stories and they would argue and I might be able to figure out what really happened. Rita agreed and Vivien agreed, but at the last minute Rita had my cousin call to say that she had a heart condition and she couldn't come. Freddie thinks that she must be hiding something.

Vivien tells me that my grandmother, Juan's mother, threatened to hurt Chris if she didn't give me up for adoption. Why? What did she have to do with it?

One day Rita called me. It was my anniversary. We had gotten in an argument about a month before because I told her I would never call her again. I told her that I only called her to please her and because I didn't want to start any fights. So she was in town visiting Ella on my anniversary.

I was already stirred up. I wanted to let it out. I couldn't take any more.

"What are you going to do? Call me when I die?" she said.

I told her, "You can't even come over here to visit for a little while because your daughter will get mad at you. Do I owe it to you?"

"Yeah."

"Why?"

"Because I raised you."

That did it. "If you raised me, then how come I had to go with other people all the time? How come I had to go live with my grandmother if you raised me?"

"Because I took off with another man."

"See? So don't tell me you raised me, because you didn't."

"Well thanks a lot. God bless you!"

That kept up for forty-five minutes. I told her that I had found my natural mother. I told her the reason I threw her out of the hospital room was that she put me there. A whole lifetime came out on the telephone.

My brothers are like good friends. I separated from Freddie for a while in the beginning because Chris stayed with us for two weeks and I did everything with him. Freddie never had to share me before that and he couldn't handle it, but that didn't last long.

Vivien once had trouble sleeping too. Now neither one of us has nightmares. She used to wake up in the middle of the night all the time. She had dreams that I'd come up to her on the street and cuss her out. After she had me she worked in the delivery rooms of hospitals. The little boy babies didn't bother her, but when it came to the little girls she remembered me and had nightmares all the time. Every little girl that looked like me reminded her of me.

She calls me to ask me how I am, but I don't feel like I have much to tell her. She's just somebody I know. I'm glad that I have Freddie. He's good for me.

I can sleep at night. I don't have nightmares. I'm not as nervous as I used to be. I have finished school and become a real-estate broker. Even though I don't know exactly what happened I feel like I'm resting. My head is resting and my body is resting. Now I know I never forgot what Vivien looked like. I could have picked her out at that church just like that, so it didn't make any sense for her to pretend she wasn't my mother. She isn't the mother I always wanted, but I'm glad I found her.

I guess I have led an exciting life.

# An Intermediary
## —— Peter ——

*Many legislators and adoption professionals around the country favor
an intermediary approach to reunion. Under such a system, searches
would be initiated on behalf of the adoptee. Upon completion, a
discreet approach would be made to the natural mother who would
then have the option of refusing to meet her child. Some social
agencies, such as New York Foundling Hospital, have initiated
search programs.*

*But many argue that such an organization, with a massive foster
care program to administer and with employees' work loads already
heavy, should not stretch its resources even further. They claim
that the adoptee himself is best qualified to conduct this search;
taxpayers should not be expected to fund the correction of mistaken
policies when adoptees are willing to conduct searches themselves,
efficiently and tactfully as only people with a personal stake can. The
specter of a public body inquiring into the moral backgrounds of
thousands of women is considered to be truly frightening. In cases where
such disinterested intermediaries have made the first contact, natural
parents have often expressed alarm because their secrets were in the
hands of a third party.*

*Peter Walker waged a long fight with the welfare department of
his New Hampshire county. He finally persuaded a judge to grant an
intermediary the power to conduct a search for him. What he didn't
count on was the judge's choice of an intermediary—the adoption
worker who Peter felt had been trying to thwart his search for months.
That Peter himself found his mother is support for the contention that*

*an adoptee, with his own resources of time, imagination, and self-interest, is his own best searcher.*

When I was five, my folks told me I was adopted, but I recall having suspicions even before then. There have always been very real, practical reminders of it. I have always had coordination problems, difficulties with math, and a blindness to certain kinds of spatial relationships. My mother, a school nurse, told me I had brain damage. I was relinquished for adoption at eighteen months of age. When did the brain damage occur?

There have been other problems, less concrete, that have also bothered me. From the beginning, my father and I have had no rapport. Male images and examples are a total blank. My mother and I have gotten along better, but she is a devoted, church-going Protestant while I have always had strong psychic experiences and that kind of religion has never meant much to me. My intuitions, no matter how correct, have always met with little sympathy from my parents.

When I was eight years old, I told my mother that I thought I had lived in a city, and described a tenement neighborhood to her. We had lived in a small New Hampshire town as far back as I could remember. We had never traveled. I couldn't have seen a neighborhood like the one I described.

When I was eleven, I found a paper in a drawer with my birth name—James Michael Marshall—and some information about my medical history. The only extraordinary event listed was a bump on the head I received. It also said that my mother, who was seventeen at the time of my birth, had a child two years older than me. She had been married once. My father, eighteen at the time, came from a family of five children.

I showed the paper around school, then hid it in my pillow. The next afternoon the paper was gone. I assumed that my mother had found it.

All during adolescence I had problems in school. I developed all sorts of neurotic symptoms. They were compounded by the fact that my mother was the school nurse. The only place to send a student with such problems was the nurse's office, so I kept my tension bottled up inside.

When I was eighteen, my mother went with me to the county welfare office to try to find some information. In New Hampshire two agencies have a hand in adoptions, since adoptions are never permitted within the same county in order to ensure some distance between the families. As it turns out, that distance means nothing at all.

The case worker who had handled my adoption wasn't available, so I was given a case worker named Helen Dunmore. I explained to her that I felt my mother had always wanted to find me and needed to find me to relieve her feelings of guilt. I told her about all the empty spots in my own life and listed my problems.

While we talked, my mother started to cry, and the case worker used that as an excuse for cutting me off. "Look what you're doing to your mother," she said, laying the whole burden of guilt on me. I left and stayed away for a year.

I had overlaid my determination to find my natural mother with concern for the feelings of my adoptive parents. As a result, the first lost out to the second, and my daily life deteriorated. In 1973 it reached a crisis point. After going to night school for a while, I gave up and withdrew from everything. I turned lazy and undisciplined. I daydreamed all the time.

At the same time I resisted the idea of having counseling. I was convinced that my problems were genetic in origin, but every time I brought it up, people accused me of using my adoption as an excuse. I was sure that any counselor would tell me the same thing.

I returned to the welfare department the week after my twenty-first birthday. Helen Dunmore was my case worker again. She told me that the records were destroyed when the adoptee reached the age of twenty-one. "There's no chance to find anything out," she said.

I didn't believe her. In my dealings with her and another social worker and clerks and recordkeepers all along the line, I learned to be suspicious of everything they said. They never hesitated to tell a lie that might put me off. More often than not, they would fabricate laws and policies of which they were ignorant just to save themselves the trouble of finding out the truth.

I had researched the law on destruction of records. There are files in the county of birth, the county of adoption, and the state capital. Some records had to be available.

She consented to send to Concord, the capital, for the records, and in the meantime, for three months, I returned to her for some of her pseudo-counseling. She blamed my emotional problems and "resistance to life in general" on the fact that I couldn't deal with the fact of my adoption. It wasn't a mature attitude to take, she told me, implying that a mature attitude would be to forget all the factors that continued to remind me about it.

Besides, it was very destructive for my adoptive parents and would damage my natural parents, "if they are still alive."

When she said that, I pointed out that my parents would be in their late thirties, so unless they were killed in an accident or two accidents it wasn't likely that they were deceased. Furthermore, people who are born in New Hampshire don't move away that much. If my father had five brothers and sisters, some of them would still be around.

After three months of this I told her that I wouldn't come in again. I didn't need counseling, but I would check in to find out if the records had arrived.

When I called, she said that the records had arrived. The welfare workers proved to be very able liars. It seemed that every time I caught them in an apparent contradiction they had an excuse to let them off the hook. The reason my file (which should have been destroyed under the policy she had quoted earlier) still existed was that it had been placed with the file of my adopted sister who is six years younger than me.

All she told me was that my mother had been raised by an aunt. Otherwise, she said nothing that hadn't appeared on the paper I found when I was eleven. She told me that I could have no identifying information, even though I had been candid from the beginning in saying that was my goal. I had said over and over again that I had to settle this in my own way.

I didn't bother to see her for a long time. I knew she wasn't going anywhere, so I could see her at my own convenience. I knew she felt threatened, not only for the security of her job, but for the entire premise her job was founded on.

The files I needed were in her office. I could have walked off with them any time. I knew the people who worked there and they were accustomed to seeing me around. Her counseling had nothing officially to do with her job.

In the spring of 1975, I began my last push. I was with two friends, a married couple. We went over to Raymondville to a record store owned by Ernest's father. A woman who worked there asked me my astrological sign. I said, "Virgo."

She said, "What's your rising sign?"

"Virgo."

Pam said, "You don't know what your rising sign is because you don't know what time you were born."

The woman asked, "Why don't you know what time you were born?"

"I was adopted."

"Have you ever wanted to find your parents?"

"All my life."

She said, "I have a friend named Jack Petty who has been active in politics for years. He's gone right into state agencies and walked off with confidential files. I'm sure he'd do the same for you."

I said, "I'd appreciate it, but I'll wait until I've tried other ways myself."

I asked a number of lawyers and none had any advice, so I started a personal tour of different offices. The City Hall in Raymondville yielded nothing. In fact they were the first people to show open hostility. The social workers had been sweet. I don't know which was worse. Probably the sweetness, since I was trapped into returning and wasting a lot of time.

At the City Hall they told me that they weren't lawyers and couldn't be bothered to find out what I was entitled to know. I went to the public hospital. I told the receptionist that I wanted some information—just my birth name and the time I was born. She told me to go to the records department, but when I arrived the militia came out in the form of a huge head nurse. She took me to the director of the hospital.

He said, "I've only been here about a year, and I've never encountered this before. I worked in a big hospital in Chicago, and I never met anyone who was looking for his natural parents."

He was sympathetic, however, and told me that if I could get a court order from the Probate Court he would give me what I wanted.

Next I tried looking in microfilm records of birth announcements for the week of my birth, but my birth had been illegitimate, and illegitimate births weren't announced even if the mother requested it.

I went over to Probate Court and told the secretary what I wanted. She looked startled, and said, "I'm not sure you can do this." I asked for the head of personnel. She brought out a man who was built like a football lineman. Mr. Barnett gave me a long line of garbage. "Why do you want to ruin your parents' lives. . . ? Why are you dissatisfied. . . ? Why don't you cut your hair and get a job?"

"Why don't you just call City Hall and tell them to give me what I want?"

He said, "No need. We'll just go through the records ourselves."

I was naive enough to believe him. We looked in some files—the wrong ones, it turned out. He knew it but I didn't. "Are you sure you were born in this county?" he said.

"I'm certain, unless I wasn't adopted and that paper was planted in the drawer."

I went back to the record store and asked the woman to contact Jack Petty. She made a call, and half an hour later in came a very odd-looking fellow who said, "Who's the dude who wants to find his natural parents?"

We breezed across to the Probate Court and went straight to the judge's office. Jack said, "I've known the judge all my life. He's like a father to me." He proceeded to talk to the judge like a snotty son.

He took the judge by the sleeve and led him into the office. "Why don't you give the guy a break?" He began to criticize New Hampshire laws from top to bottom.

The judge looked at me differently this time. "Why do you want to know?" I told him again. "Don't you think it's harmful?"

Jack said, "Cut the crap. This isn't a psychological interrogation. You don't have any right to ask him these things. This is a human being. This human being wants to know. Stop playing games."

The judge called City Hall and asked for verification of an adoption. The record was there, but they couldn't release it without a court order. The judge looked up the law and said that the court order would have to come from the Probate Court in my county of adoption. Access to my records had recently been further restricted by a New Hampshire "right-to-know" law that had gone into effect that year. It gives students access to their school records and workers access to their work records, but tightens the lid on adoption records.

At Jack's urging, the judge promised to write a letter to my home county probate judge, but I doubt if he ever did it.

We went to the Bureau of Vital Statistics to look up birth records, but they were listed by number and I didn't know my number. Finally, Jack gave me the name of a lawyer and said to tell him that he had referred me.

Jack Petty's assistance didn't come to anything, but it did serve to fire me up even more, and I also admired the way he just cut through red tape with his determination and self-confidence.

The lawyer he told me about accepted the case, then dropped it with the explanation that a big case had come up which would occupy him for two years.

I took a summer job working with gifted adolescents at a college. I met a girl whose brother had been adopted before she was born. She lived near Raymondville, conveniently enough, so I could stay at her home while I was knocking on doors over there. We decided to help one another in finding our relatives.

I decided that the next step had to be through the Probate Court. The judge set August 19, 1975, for a hearing. When that day arrived the regular judge was on vacation, and the replacement, who came from another county, said, "I cannot act on this matter because I'm not the regular judge."

Then he began with the standard questions. "What's wrong? Why do you want to bring guilt into the life of your mother? Maybe she has forgotten this."

"Why don't you ask her and see?" He told me to come back in an hour. At the end of the hour, I went back and had to repeat the whole thing. "Come back in another hour." I ended up back in his courtroom four times.

"I'm sorry," he said at 4:00 PM. "I didn't want to make a decision in this. But at your insistence I have made a negative decision."

I went through half an hour of moaning and complaining and breaking down. I told him the procedure was a farce and the laws absurd. I said that no lawyer would help me.

"Lawyer or no lawyer, I wanted to hear you make a case for yourself. You didn't do very well. I don't think you are mature enough to be entrusted with this information."

"I'm twenty-three. How old do you think I'll have to be? Sixty? All my relatives will be dead then."

"No, not that long. Don't get upset."

"Why shouldn't I get upset? You're playing with my life and the lives of my natural parents."

"Aren't you playing with their lives?" he asked.

"No," I said. "I'm willing to go along with the idea of an intermediary, whom I trust, to locate my natural parents and ask them if they will see me. If they say no, I'll back out of this completely."

He left the room and spoke with his secretary. The secretary, Carolyn, is my adoptive father's first cousin. Small world, New Hampshire.

He refused my request.

I was feeling desperate. My mother suggested that I go talk to a friend of hers—Terry Arnold, the head of the county family health services.

"I'm not going for counseling," I said. "I don't think I'm neurotic for wanting to do this. For other reasons, yes, but to me this is the most normal thing in the world."

"No," she said. "I think he might be able to help you search."

I went over to see Terry Arnold. He didn't give me any useful suggestions, but he was the first person in any position of authority to listen to the whole story start to finish who believed everything I said.

He said, "I think this is a need and that you should do it. I don't think you are neurotic. You're intelligent and well prepared."

He suggested the lawyer who had accepted the case and then

rejected it. He named another lawyer who might be able to help, and volunteered to contact him.

Ernest and Pam had planned to drive out to Oregon. I decided that I needed to get away. The search had made me so frustrated. Terry Arnold said he would do what he could in my absence.

Two months later I returned to New Hampshire briefly, then went to live with friends in Maine. I had no money left. I went home to confer with the second lawyer Terry Arnold had mentioned, but he painted a bleak, expensive picture of my prospects. The state could change lawyers and judges on me so often that I could end up spending thousands of dollars with no results.

I had no money. My family was in a mess. I moved back in with them. I tried to find Jack Petty, but he had moved to California without leaving a forwarding address. My mother was really worried about me. She went to talk with Helen Dunmore, who had become the head of the welfare department.

"You've come to the right place," Helen told her. "We think he needs to be helped. Send him in and we'll assign a case worker." Now that she was the boss, Helen didn't have the challenge of dealing with me directly anymore.

As head of the school nurse program for the district we live in, my mother is a public figure of a kind. She didn't want to ruffle any feathers, so she was careful not to stress what it was that I wanted. She also had doubts of her own.

I said to my mother, "I told you that's what they would do, shuffle me off to a mediocre caseworker."

"Aren't you being negative?"

"I'll give it a go."

My first impression of Evelyn Brown was that she looked like a white raisin. She was probably just under sixty-five. She began with the familiar questions—who? where? what? why? A whole psychological profile in one fell swoop. I went along with it, stressing that this was the last straw, and I intended to find out the names. I wouldn't submit to any counseling.

I thought that an intermediary would be the most neutral way of dealing with it. I thought that Evelyn would just go to court and speak in my behalf, but I didn't think the court would appoint her.

At first she led me to believe that she could do nothing, let alone present my point of view to the court. She said she was the only one in the county who dealt with adoption. She said she had never met anyone interested in learning about a missing relative, except for the mother of an underage child who only asked for some information about the family that adopted her child and assurance that the child was well. They gave her very little, and Evelyn excused that on the grounds that the woman was from out of state.

We met three times before she agreed to go to Probate Court. She set a date at the beginning of May. As the date passed I went to see her. She greeted me very sweetly and invited me to sit down.

"What happened in court?" I asked.

"I didn't go to court." In a few minutes she told me three different reasons why she hadn't gone to court. Too much paperwork. Emergency adoption situation. She went to court and the judge wasn't there.

That was the hardest one to swallow because I knew that he stays from nine until four and, while he may take two hours for lunch, so does Evelyn. I knew a lot about Evelyn's work habits. She frequently slips out and goes home early. There are qualified people lining up for her job, but she's got money and contacts in addition to seniority and won't give up that job until she has to.

I couldn't believe her excuses. "You told me you were going up there. I knew this would happen."

"You're very distrustful, aren't you?" By now I had seen people make these specious judgments enough so that I had learned to control my temper. I knew that if I lost my cool then she could use it as ammunition against me. I went back to playing her sweet little game.

She said, "I'll see the judge on the eighteenth."

I went home feeling dismal. I knew her game. Probate Court meets only twice a month and once a month during the summer. If she played it right, between her vacation and the judge's vacation, she wouldn't have to deal with it until October.

I explained this to my mother. "What did you expect? A miracle? You expect all public employees to be as honest as you are. I'm not going to get anything unless I beat them over the head."

"You might not like what you get."

"That's not important. Knowing would be better than wondering. There are things I must ask my mother."

Evelyn made an appointment for me for the nineteenth, the day after she saw the judge. I told her that I would call her the same afternoon instead. I didn't want her to feel she could always set the conditions for our meeting and dictate my movements. I live ten miles from town and don't have a car. I didn't want to have to ask anyone to drive me or hitch into town for any more disappointments.

She led me to believe that she had been to court that day, but her story sounded contradictory, so I think she probably just saw the judge at some other time and happened to bring this matter up.

She had been granted permission to act as an intermediary and find my mother.

I said, "Well, you must have the names and the rest of the information."

"No, I didn't go up there this afternoon."

"You just told me you went up there. All you had to do once the judge gave his approval was to go next door and get the files."

"They'll arrive by mail in a few days."

"Can't you just walk over there in your lunch hour?"

"I'll get it by mail."

That was hopeless, so I changed my line. "When will you begin looking for her?"

"Next week."

"Monday?"

"Monday or Tuesday. Whenever I get around to it."

For the next two months at the beginning of each week I would call her and she would say, "I haven't had time. . . . I don't have any time this week. . . . I'll try to get to it next week."

I made some helpful suggestions like, "You have a phone. Why don't you make a few calls? At least call the hospital."

All she had was a name, she said. I told her I thought that, since she was a welfare worker, she would have access to welfare records in Raymondville. There must be reciprocity, I said, but she went on insisting that such things couldn't be done. She talked about how she would have to present her credentials and have them verified. What she didn't say was why, if it was really so complicated, she hadn't taken such steps early on. She did not want to do it.

A friend gave me an article recounting a similar experience an adoptee had with a social worker including the line, "Have you ever considered counseling?" I took the article to her office, and when she said, "Have you ever considered counseling?" I handed it to her.

I laced into her. "This isn't personal anger," I said. "This anger comes from the fact that you have conditioned yourself into being unthinking. Being taken over by your job and becoming nothing, not even a person. You don't think. You don't reason one iota when I talk about this. You're a wall. Everything I say bounces back in my face."

She didn't respond. She was probably trying to think of some way she could use my anger against me, but to do so would have meant exposure of her delay.

· I asked her if she would give my mother a letter when she found her. Of course not, she said. We didn't even know my mother's attitude.

"We don't know what you'd put in the letter. We'd have to read it."

"I don't care if you read it or not. I'm going to put my name and address and the reasons why it is important for me to find her."

"Well, we can't take the risk of your upsetting her and ruining the life she has now."

"You're not going to do anything about this, are you? I bet you have the records right here in this office and you've had them from the beginning. If you did a little bit of research you would find her."

Two months had passed since we began our shenanigans and all she had was the name of a teenage girl and a birthdate. I asked her for the birthdate. "No technical information," she said.

Then I started to look for outside help. I called the ACLU in Concord and a lawyer there began to call Evelyn, throwing all sorts of legal technicalities at her. I called New Hampshire Senator John Durkin's Hotline Committee in Washington and they called her. The Bureau of Vital Statistics called her. The hospital called her.

A secretary (not my father's cousin) from the Probate Court told me that the judge and Evelyn had gone over the files. There wasn't much there. The secretary hinted that if I could get Evelyn into court for a hearing, I wouldn't have much trouble. She suggested that I get the judge to issue a subpoena.

On July 7, I appeared before the judge. He said, "I'm sorry, Mr. Walker, I can't say anything one way or the other. I can't act on this until Evelyn comes in and gives a progress report."

"You're not getting a progress report because she hasn't made any progress. She's not doing anything at all. She was going to go to do research. Now she's not even going to do that. She's checking with the Bureau of Vital Statistics and the Motor Vehicles Bureau under my mother's teenage name. She probably didn't even drive when she had me. In any case I'm sure she's married at least once. And Evelyn put an ad in the paper. How's that for protecting my mother's privacy?"

Then I started reeling off a list of the organizations I had contacted. As soon as I did that, he called his secretary in and started to dictate to her. He made a mistake. He began, "Mr. Walker has informed me that you have made no attempt to contact his mother." I could see myself going up on perjury or slander charges. I didn't say "no attempt."

In any case, the subpoena and three phone calls from outside organizations arrived on the same day. When I went in to see her she was visibly shaken. "I'm not stupid, Evelyn, and I'm not fooling around. I want this information and I'm going to get it one way or the other, and if you stand in the way, the law's going to catch up with you."

She started spitting out little bits of information. "Your mother was married before and you have a half-sister. Your mother had a terrible life. Someone, I think it was her husband, tried to kill her."

I asked how she knew this if the records were not in the office.

"Your mother was born in 1935."

"I know she was born in 1935. I read it when I was eleven years old. I can add."

Then I tried to be a little nicer. I said, "I'm interested in astrology. What month was her birthday?"

"March."

"What day?"

"The fourteenth or fifteenth. I'll look it up." She left the room. The records weren't there but she could go and look up my mother's date of birth.

When she told me it was March 28, I thought, "This is a small state. All I have to do is look it up."

"Is she a native of New Hampshire?"

"I'm not free to tell you," she said. "Now what does the birth-date tell you about her astrologically?"

"She's an Aries."

"Is that a good sign for you to get along with?"

"No. Not particularly." I waited to see if Evelyn was going to try to use astrology to dissuade me from seeking my mother. It would have been more scientific than anything she had tried so far.

Instead she asked, "What sign do you think I am?"

"You're a Taurus because you're very stubborn."

"I am a Taurus. What are you?"

"Virgo."

"Do they get along well?"

"Oh yes. Tauruses and Virgoes get along just fine."

"So much for the stars, buddy." As I was leaving she said, "I've never met anyone so persistent in all my life."

"I haven't finished yet."

Now she couldn't wriggle out of going to court, but instead of waiting for the hearing, which might lead to more delays if Evelyn could think up some way to discredit my complaints, I decided to go on looking for clues. With a friend I went to the Raymondville library to look up the names of all women who had had children the same week I was born, on the theory that someone might remember my mother. We looked up both those who had been at the Catholic hospital and those who were at the public hospital, although I was pretty sure I hadn't been born at the Catholic hospital since I was placed with a Protestant family.

Luckily all but one of the women listed still lived in Raymond-ville, according to a phone directory. I called the mother of a girl who was born on the same day.

I said, "I would like to know if you can remember a sixteen- or seventeen-year-old girl who was pregnant at the same time you were and had a child the same day."

At first she was silent and I thought I might have put her off. Then she said, "Who are you?" I explained. She said, "I'd like to help you, but at the time I was so heavily sedated and it was such a hard birth, I don't even remember the room. But I had a child a few years later and I remember everyone was talking about a seventeen-year-old girl who was having a second child out of wedlock."

I got excited. "Do you think you could have transposed the dates?"

"I could have, but I didn't meet her. I only heard about her."

She gave me the names of some attending physicians and promised to ask around. It turned out that she gave me the name of the right physician, but he had died. She also lived in the same town where my natural mother lives.

I looked up the name of principals and school nurses who, I thought, would remember young girls who dropped out of eighth grade to have children. Small town principals have long memories for things like that. But I got cold feet before I visited my first house. It had taken a lot of nerve to call that woman, nerve which I had lost again. So I sat on the information I had until the court date rolled around.

On the morning of the court date, something happened which convinced my adoptive mother to go with me and to speak on my behalf. She went to clean out some old furniture and found some bits of paper in a drawer. She taped them together and it turned out to be the same piece of paper that I had put in my pillow all those years before. She had washed the pillow case, found the paper, and put it away without reading it. She interpreted this as a sign that she should actively help me.

I felt now that I couldn't lose, whereas before I wasn't confident at all. On our way into the judge's chamber, the secretary assured me there would be no trouble, because the judge was annoyed with Evelyn's delays. Two friends came with me for moral support.

The appointment was for eleven, and at eleven neither the judge nor Evelyn was there. I went to call the welfare office to remind Evelyn and she walked in. She greeted me in her sweetest voice. She sat alone in a corner. When the judge entered and sat down, he asked her what she thought of the notion that I be given identifying information directly.

"Well, I guess the welfare department supports the idea that he should have the information." Maybe she did this out of sympathy for my adoptive mother, who she felt was having a breakdown. Of course, to her, I was neurotic to begin with.

He was very blasé about the whole thing. He listened to my mother's statement. She said that it was crucial to my emotional well-being.

He looked me in the face for the first time. "You will be granted the name of your mother and her address as of July 1953 and no other information. You will have no direct access to the records so that no state law will be broken and no precedent set."

I surprised myself at that point. I had never had any feelings about my natural father, but I spoke right out and asked for his name too. The judge asked Evelyn how she felt about it.

She said, "He was no help. He was only an alleged father anyway. We couldn't get in touch with him and we don't know where he is."

I said, "I don't care if he is an alleged father or not. Chances are that he is my father and I don't want to be penalized for the welfare department's inadequate procedures."

It was granted.

Carolyn, my father's cousin, was in a petulant mood and told me she was too busy to type the information right away. I returned at three and she gave me a name—Genevieve Martine Marshall, Raymondville, New Hampshire. She didn't have my father's name.

I went to the welfare office. Evelyn had just gone out the back door. I left a note telling what I wanted. When I returned she greeted me as if it were a social call and led me into a conference room.

"I want my alleged father's name and address."

"I can't give you any more information."

"Of course you can. You were told to by the judge."

She went and got the file. "Frank Ratelle is the alleged father. We don't have anything else."

"I want verification of my mother's date of birth, in writing."

She pulled out a sheet of paper that had been in the office for months. It said, "Genevieve Martine Marshall/Parents James

Edwin Marshall, Emily R. Morris Marshall/Alleged father Frank Ratelle/Birthdate of mother 3/28/35. Baby James Michael Marshall. Mother also known as Genevieve Marais.

Ernest drove me to Raymondville. There were so many Ratelles in the phone book that I decided to call every family named Marais first, since Genevieve Marais was definitely my mother, and my grandfather was definitely James Edwin Marshall. I thought that I must have got my first name—James—from my grandfather.

In the phone book I found a Gerald Marais. I followed it back in the city directories to the 1930s. I went to Dickens Street, found the house and rang the bell. A woman dressed like a gypsy came to the door. I said, "I'm looking for someone who might have been married into your family at some point."

"Who?"

"Genevieve Martine Marshall. She was also known as Genevieve Marais."

"Wait, let me get my husband."

I thought for a minute that I didn't want to be related to them, but I wasn't in a position to choose.

We went in and beat around the bush for a while. Finally I mentioned Genevieve's name again. He said, "I'm sure you're Genevieve's son."

"I'm Genevieve's son, all right, but I don't know if it's the same Genevieve you are talking about." Their son came out and listened to our conversation.

He was a big help. "You don't want to be related to this family," he said. "Half of them are in mental institutions, and they're all crazy."

Mrs. Marais said, "Ignore him. He's a cynic." I had the feeling he was telling the truth.

I remembered a conversation with Evelyn in which she painted a bleak picture of my mother's life. She married a much older man, who then tried to kill her, and the marriage was annulled by the state. I thought that if the guy had tried to kill Genevieve he might have ended up in an institution and the Marais's son had just told me that half their relatives were institutionalized. I figured my mother had needed a shoulder to cry on and that my father had come along to provide it.

They gave us the names of some people to look up. The people weren't home, but we ended up in a section of the city where I had been before. It can only be described as a slum, and it was the slum that I described to my mother when I was eight years old. I even recognized the building where I had lived in the first year and a half of my life.

The next day I went into Evelyn's office and feigned defeat and despair. "I can't go on with this, Evelyn. I feel like I'm so close and yet it's still a needle in a haystack. I can't think of the next step." Then I said, "I know that you wrote back in July to a woman who once lived with my mother, and the letter came back. If you would give me her name I could find her in twenty-four hours."

"I can't give you that name. The court didn't authorize it."

I went into a funk, and once she thought she had me down, she said, "I'll give you the name, but if you ever tell anyone, I'll get in big trouble and be fired."

"I'll never tell anyone."

She got the letter. Mrs. Charles Cardone, 16 Ferris Street, Hartfield, New Hampshire. I had been concentrating on Raymondville, but there are a million little towns nearby. I went to the Raymondville phone book. There were no Cardones, but I looked up Ratelle. There were no Franks, but a whole slew of others, and they lived on Ferris Street in Hartfield. My mother lived there and my father lived there. They met and became involved.

I knew someone who had lived in Hartfield. She's a terrific gossip. If I played my cards right she would tell me something I needed to know. We chatted for a few minutes. Then I asked, "Amy, do you know anyone from Hartfield?"

"Sure. I went to a Catholic school nearby and I know all kinds of people."

"Anyone named Ratelle?"

"I know Christine Ratelle."

"Who's she?"

"Her father runs an automobile dealership. Name's Leonard. Why?"

"Just tell me a little about her."

"She had plenty of trouble growing up. She was the last of a lot of children. A mistake, I guess. Her parents are much older than she is."

I knew from the paper that my father was one of five children. "How many brothers and sisters are there?"

"Six, including her." Too many.

"When was she born?"

"1953." I was born in 1952. That meant that Christine Ratelle hadn't been born yet. It fit. Leonard Ratelle was probably my grandfather.

"What are they like?"

"Very rich."

I blurted out, "I think Christine Ratelle is my aunt."

"You're related to Christine Ratelle?" She mulled it over. "Yes, it fits. Christine is very weird and you are very weird." Then she changed the subject.

I left and bumped into Ernest. I told him everything that had happened. He seemed very impressed by my detective work. We drove over to Hartfield and found the automobile dealership. A Cadillac drove up. A tall man got out. "Can I help you?"

"Yes," I said. "I'm looking for someone named Frank Ratelle."

"I have a cousin named Frank Ratelle. He's about forty-one. Is the guy you're looking for that age?"

"Yes."

"I don't have his address, but I'll give you his mother's phone number and address and you can check with her." While I stood there, he described Frank Ratelle as very tall, six-feet-four, with blond hair. That didn't sound like me. I'm five-feet-eight and dark.

We found my grandmother's house. I went up to the door. A very French-looking lady came out. I asked for Frank Ratelle's address.

"Come in," she said. It was obvious she knew who I was. "I've been expecting you for a long time. Frank lives in Florida now. Have you ever considered going to Florida?"

I said, "I don't like Florida, but I may go down there if there's anything worth seeing."

We talked for a long time, going round and round, but never mentioning the relationship. She showed me a picture of her son—

my father. I couldn't see much resemblance except for the jaw. That was a disappointment, but it was taken when Frank was in the service, so that's what he looked like when I was born.

Frank is married and has seven children, so that made seven half-brothers and half-sisters. It was obvious that my grandmother had kept track of me all those years. I don't know how. I mentioned that I was going to college. She said that she had a nephew who went to the same college I did, but I hadn't told her the name. She just knew it already.

When I left she said, "Mr. Walker, I think you should go to Florida. I know Frank will be happy to see you."

I decided to go back to the house of David Marais who hadn't been at home when we called the first time.

He answered the door. I said, "I'm looking for a relative you might have known at one time. Her name is Genevieve Marshall."

"Never heard of her."

"How about Genevieve Marais?"

"Oh sure, I know Genevieve. She used to be married to my cousin Willie. She lives over in Hemphill, New Hampshire. Her last name is Wagner now. I haven't seen her for years. Tweed Road." We thanked him and drove to Hemphill. Hemphill is a rich country town. The neighborhoods seem to be grouped according to status, starting with the very well off. It didn't seem likely that the woman in that sordid picture could be living there. We drove up and down Tweed Road and didn't find any Wagners. The only name that began with W was Walton. We quit and went home.

Then a few days later we went back over to see David Marais. He said, "Couldn't you find the house?"

"We couldn't find anyone named Wagner around there."

He looked puzzled. "I'm sure she lives in Hemphill. We'd better go talk to Willie."

"Who's this Willie?"

"Her ex-husband, Willie Marais. Maybe Susie will be there."

"Who's Susie?"

"Susie's your sister."

"Yeah, sure." I was nonchalant about it. He knew. I hadn't told him but he knew. "What does Susie look like?"

"Dark hair, dark eyes. I knew you were related to Genevieve the other day. You look like her."

"No kidding?"

Willie Marais drove up as we were standing outside his house. He got out of his car and looked at David as if he didn't recognize him.

"I'm your cousin David, remember?"

"Oh yeah, haven't seen you for years. How you been? Let's go have a drink tonight and catch up on things."

David asked, "Have you seen Genevieve?"

"Not for years, but she still lives in Hemphill. Her name is Walton now." So David had made a mistake. Willie looked at me. "Who's this?"

"Do you remember Genevieve had a kid she put up for adoption?"

"Yeah, he was gone years before I married her." To me he said, "Are you that kid?"

I said yes. I thanked them both and we went back to Hemphill.

I stood at the front door and rang the bell. A big plodding fellow came out. "Is Mrs. Walton here?"

"I'm Mr. Walton."

"No, *Mrs*. Walton."

He called back into the house. "There's someone here to see you."

A black-haired woman, about five-feet-four, came out. Oh God, it was like looking into a mirror. She looked exactly like me except for her jaw.

"May I help you?" she asked.

"I think you already have." I asked if I could sit down. All I could think of to say once I was seated was, "Are you forty-one years old?"

She burst into tears. "Are you who I think you are? I thought they were never going to tell you you were adopted. I thought you would be unhappy if you knew."

"I've wanted to find you since I was five years old. I'm so unhappy and so neurotic that now I'm not even sure if I'll stop looking."

She called her husband in and said, "Remember I told you I had a son and put him up for adoption? This is him." He came over and shook my hand and walked out again.

She said, "I judge horse shows around here. I thought you were someone who thought I had given you wrong points in a show and wanted revenge. Then when I got a closer look I saw a resemblance to my uncles. I thought you might be related. I guess I was right."

There were four teenage girls running around the house, two blondes and two brunettes. "The brunettes are your sisters. The blondes are your cousins."

She showed me pictures of all her other children. I had still another sister named Joann who was married and had a son. I remembered then that Ernest was still in the car. We invited him in.

He said to me, "You life is so weird, I just know there will be more twists to the plot." Ernest's wife's mother had died in childbirth, and she was raised by a woman named Millie Baxter. When he looked at the photograph of Joann, he said, "She looks familiar."

He asked Genevieve what Joann's name was now. Baxter.

"I know Joann," he said. "She's married to the son of the woman who raised my wife. Peter, you met Joann at a party last summer."

When Genevieve heard that, she insisted on taking us to meet Joann. We spotted her car at a bowling alley. Genevieve went in to get her.

"What's this all about?" Joann asked. "Who are those long-haired guys in the car?"

"That's your brother Jimmy."

"What? He looks just like me." She brought her son over and introduced me as Uncle Jimmy. It took a long time to get them straight on the name. I was raised as Peter and wanted to be called Peter.

Genevieve looked very pained as Joann went back into the bowling alley. "I think I'd better tell you something," she said. "Joann is not your half-sister, but your full sister. Frank Ratelle got me pregnant when I was fourteen. I had Joann and never told anyone who her father was. Joann doesn't know. The family arranged a marriage to a man of twenty-four and Joann was born with his name. The marriage was annulled because we never slept together. When I married Willie Marais, he adopted her. I told Joann that her father was someone from out of state. I named someone I knew had died."

Later Joann took Genevieve aside and said, "You'd better tell me the truth. He looks a lot like me. Is he my full brother?"

"Yes."

She thought she was protecting Joann, but of course she wasn't. She was an ignorant kid when she had Joann, and now Joann, twenty-five years old, unhappily married, a mother, had just found out the truth of her birth. I knew then that being raised by Genevieve wouldn't have guaranteed me any happiness.

Genevieve is half-Irish and half-Cherokee Indian. Her father died in one of the last battles of World War II. Her mother married a terrible man who once tried to kill Genevieve. He threw a knife at her. Rather than leave her second husband, Genevieve's mother sent her to live with another couple. Genevieve has a full sister whom she has met once and a half-sister she sees fairly often, but she never visits her mother because of her stepfather.

Genevieve asked me if I was psychic. I said that I had always been psychic. I had always had very strong intuitions about things. I was sure for years that she needed to see me. I knew that I had to find her for her sake as well as my own.

She said she was psychic too, and there was a strong tendency to be psychic in the Cherokee side of the family. In fact one ancestor was run out of the town she lived in because she was suspected of being a witch.

While she was pregnant, Genevieve heard voices that told her I was not her child and she should not try to raise me. When the voices started she had no intention of giving me up for adoption. She didn't feel any stigma, since she was already raising a child of unknown paternity.

Frank's father tried to force Frank to marry her, but Genevieve got into an argument with Frank's mother at the courthouse and by the time Genevieve stopped yelling, the wedding was off. Frank's mother kicked him out of the house and he joined the army.

She developed general toxemia during her pregnancy. Her family was inclined toward kidney trouble. At three months she tried to commit suicide by gassing herself. The voices kept reminding her that she should not raise her child.

She went into labor prematurely, which the doctor later described as a good thing since even with my premature birth, by Caesarian, I weighed six pounds eight ounces. At first she didn't believe it could be labor. She was alone in her apartment.

At five days, I was put into a boarding home. Joann was being kept in another home. When Genevieve came to visit one day, she found the son of the couple who were caring for me trying to plant me in the garden. He dropped me on my head and it knocked me out. They rushed me to hospital where I was pronounced fit, but I began to get ear infections on the side of my head that had hit the ground. I still have trouble with that ear. That was where the brain damage that blocked my math and other abilities came from.

Genevieve kept changing her mind about giving me up. Finally, after months of resistance, she yielded to the voices in her head and to the welfare department.

Later on she described my health problems to a friend. The friend told her it sounded like I had birth defects, and claimed that children with birth defects were put in institutions, not adopted. Genevieve went to the welfare department in a panic, but they convinced her that I had been adopted.

They told her a false story about my family, but she believed them. She had to believe them. Still, believing didn't stop the guilt.

The welfare department kept track of her for five years—no one had ever mentioned this to me, nor have I ever heard an explanation of why it was done. Frank saw her twice. The first time he was already the father of three more children. That's when she told him about their son. He asked her to marry him. The second time they met he had five children.

After Genevieve's sixth child was born, and she was on her third marriage, she went to the hospital and was given a hysterectomy without knowing it. After that, her psychic abilities were curtailed.

She is getting divorced now. She was adamant that I should not blame myself for this. Her husband was a terrible man, a mean man. He wouldn't let her go to school or work. She started running horse shows so that she would have something to do with kids. Her husband wouldn't let her have a social life, and her other children are very cold to her.

She said, "You have reminded me of everything I kept hidden."

We are very close, but I also know that there is a big difference between the kind of love she feels for me and the kind of love my adoptive mother feels. My adoptive mother's is a more mature love. I'm grateful for that now. If I had been raised by Genevieve, I would have had two miserable stepfathers.

Frank Ratelle was glad to hear from me, although it took him a few minutes to warm up. He has invited both Joann and me to come down to meet him. I'm more inclined to do it than she is.

After it was over, I went to see Evelyn Brown again. She said that my experience had changed her mind about the whole business. She says she will be more helpful to other adoptees now that she has seen how my case turned out. She said, "You weren't the first and you won't be the last."

If I wasn't the first, it means she lied from the very beginning.

# Adoptive Parents
## —— An Interview ——

*Many adoptive parents feel that adoption procedures can be unfair —or at least inadequate. The adopting couple are often left to imagine for themselves what all the interviews and discussions represent. They know they are being judged and tested, but they are seldom told what criteria they must fulfill, and they are offered little information about some of the unique problems faced by adoptive parents. Some potential adoptive parents will of course demand answers for their many questions, just as some agencies will readily provide them with information. But many will never do or say anything that might cause them to lose a chance to adopt.*

*Tom and Molly Anne Green are, like many, extremely conscientious adoptive parents. They adopted a baby girl from a reputable agency only a few years ago. They have made certain that their daughter will never suffer from not knowing about her own heredity if she should reveal a desire for such information. This story of the Greens' experience reveals some of the common weaknesses of agency procedure and shows an admirable way of coping with some of the common problems of adoptive parents.*

*Molly Anne:* After about three years of marriage it began to look like I would never bear a child. We were in Europe when Tom was in the service, and I had just had a second miscarriage when I began to think seriously about an adoption. I wanted very much to be a mother. I felt I was missing something. I thought that having a child was something I should be able to do, it was something I wanted to do, and other people seemed to be able to do it so easily. It got so that when I heard about people having their fourth or fifth child I would get angry. When I heard about people having illegitimate children I would start to think, "Why them and not me?" In the beginning it wasn't even a medical thing; it was a question of what was fair.

*Tom:* I don't think I ever had a feeling of failure the way Molly did. It wasn't hurting me to the point it was hurting her. It bothered me too. I'm not saying that I wasn't affected, but I think it did affect her more than it did me.

Adoption has always had a spot in my mind. I have two uncles, each of whom adopted three children. It was a completely accepted thing when I was growing up. As far as I knew then, the adoptees were treated no differently than the others, although as an adult I have found that one aunt had been careful all along to draw distinctions between us.

We've never had any tests, but I'm sure part of the reason we didn't have a child sooner was that I had a low sperm count. My brother did and two of my blood-related uncles did, so it would logically follow that I did too.

*Molly Anne:* We wanted two children, a boy and a girl. We started looking into adoption formally when I was pregnant with Ned, because we knew that whether it was a live birth or not, it would be my last pregnancy.

We were on lists all over the country and internationally. Whenever we heard about a child who was adopted, we contacted the parents to find out which channels they had gone through.

We believe in destiny. We knew that the child meant for us would come from somewhere, we just didn't know where. We opened up every door we could and it took three years. One year, as part of our Christmas letter to 122 people, we sent out an appeal saying that we were looking for a daughter to adopt. If any of them knew anyone who had a daughter they could not care for, they should contact us.

We were open on national and racial origins. We had certain limits and we did want a healthy baby. That was our last massive effort and it didn't yield any results.

We called the Child Shelter Association (CSA) early on and they said that they were not accepting applications. The reception-ist had memorized a speech, "I'm sorry, we're not accepting applications. Please feel free to check back in six months." Every time I heard that, I would mark my calendar for six months ahead.

It was July 1973, and I was thinking about adoption, writing letters about it to friends and to anyone else I knew who had any connections with the social work field. I had a strong compulsion to call CSA. I thought, "It's not time." I picked up the phone and started to dial, then hung up. I even went to the calendar and checked. September was the next time. I went back to my letters, but I couldn't concentrate.

So finally I decided to call. I thought, I'll hear the recording and it will put my mind at ease. I told the receptionist, "We want to adopt and I wanted to know if you were accepting applications."

She said, "We just opened our applications yesterday, so feel free to apply."

I was flabbergasted. We put our names on the list. They sent forms to fill out and a list of requirements. They urged us to broaden our acceptance limits to increase our chances of being accepted. If you were boxing yourself in for a normal, healthy infant, your chances were very slim. We decided that we would take a healthy girl up to three years of age, since that's how old Ned was. We sent in the application and were notified that we had been accepted for an interview.

At the interview, the first thing we heard was, "Don't expect a blond, curly-headed, blue-eyed child. We don't make those any more."

Our social worker tried to find out all the reasons we should not adopt. That's all she tried to do. Finally she found the right reason. Ned wasn't old enough. There was a rule as to how many months there should be between the children. By doing instan-taneous head calculations, the social worker came up with the idea that Ned would be too young for us to qualify to adopt.

They had said that it would probably take a year and a half before we would get our daughter. Tom is very good at math and he came back with his own figures. "You're wrong," he said.

"There is enough time."

"No, I'm not," she said. "I'm sorry. Thanks for coming in. Do check back with us."

My eyes filled with tears. They were sending us away, the only time we had actually gotten in to talk with an agency.

My husband said, "Look, we are fantastic parents. We are the best-qualified parents we know. We deserve to have a child and if you are not going to interview us, we'll interview ourselves, but we're not leaving." And he started telling all the marvelous qualities he had as a father. When he finished he turned to me and said, "It's your turn," so I started telling about how wonderful I was as a mother, about all the hopes and plans and dreams we had for ourselves and our children, regardless of the fact that one came from a different place than another.

When I finished, Tom said to her, "I know that when you re-calculate, you'll find that the age span is right and we'll hear from you in two weeks in a positive way."

She said, "I'll have to contact the director and make special arrangements to take you on because my arithmetic is correct." But two weeks later we got a letter that said that we had in fact been accepted, "with special exceptions to the rules."

In August we began our group meetings with other parents and had two visits to our home. We found out that applications were closed, so if I had not had my intuitions we would have been out of luck.

The personal visits were frightening to me. We always feared that the smallest thing out of place would disqualify us. I never cleaned so hard in my life as when I was getting ready for the social worker. I wanted Ned's shirt to be absolutely spotless. "Don't drool, kid," I was thinking. "You have to look clean."

I was scared that he might ask for something he couldn't possibly have, like a hamburger in the middle of the afternoon. If I said no it might look bad, and if I said yes it might look bad, depending on her standards. But it came off beautifully. He just clambered around like a two-year-old, chattering and asking questions. The social worker didn't try to interview him at all, but just observed how he related to his Mom and Dad. I never stopped worrying. When he would fall, I would scoop him up and kiss him and reassure him. Would I overdo it? Would I not do it enough?

*Tom:* Our adoption group had six couples. We got together once a month and discussed different aspects of adoption. When you're going through it, it's a game. There's no other way to put it. In order to determine which terminology to use, you have to make a judgment as to what they want to hear and play it their way. At least that's the way it seems.

In the first meeting no one knew if they were going to get a child or not. The whole group felt that one couple would get a child and the rest would be eliminated. It became a game. The social worker would throw out an idea and someone would make a comment. You'd have to say quickly in your mind whether it was right or wrong, and if it was wrong, wrong according to the way you thought the social worker thought, you'd quickly try to shoot it down.

Figuring out her point of view wasn't easy. Our social worker had the best poker face I'd ever seen. If she went to Las Vegas to play cards, God wouldn't have been able to tell by looking at her if she had a pat hand.

*Molly Anne:* The competition was so fierce you wouldn't believe it. The social worker once asked, "Do you feel the child should be told he was adopted?" We sat there with five other couples thinking that the way we answered the question would determine whether we got a child or not. Our minds would be racing to find the best answer; at the same time we tried to figure out her answer, but not in terms of sharing our feelings and coming up with a consensus of the best way to do it, just trying to outdo the others.

If you didn't say anything you looked dumb, so you had to speak. I tried to let someone else answer first. Then if they were wrong, I would challenge them, and if they were right I would try to top it with something I had read. At that point I was reading a lot of adoption books and had plenty of information I could use.

*Tom:* After our second meeting someone suggested that we go for a pizza, just the couples, not the social worker. We decided to pin down the social worker and try to find out what we were doing in the group. At the third meeting we asked directly, "What are we doing? Is only one couple going to get a child or does everyone have a chance?"

She told us that once you are accepted for that group, the only way you don't get a child is if you make some really bizarre statements. Or you may decide that you can't take it and drop out. Otherwise, all you have to do is participate reasonably in the discussion. It's automatic, just a matter of time, but prior to that we had no hint.

After that it came out that all five couples resented us because we already had a child. In fact, several still do.

*Molly Anne:* It wasn't healthy at all. We would be in knots after the meetings. We were the only ones who had done any homework when we started. I read up on child rearing all the time, as I had been doing for years. Tom couldn't read as many books as I could because of his business, but I would review them for him and tell him if there was anything in a book that he didn't know already. We took one class at the Red Cross, and another offered by the county.

We brought in a reading list and spoke on various books. Some rushed out and bought the books, but some didn't. We told about the Red Cross course and two couples took that, but the social worker didn't even know that it was offered. All her notes and handouts were on adoption, not on parenthood.

*Tom:* There was nothing on how to raise a child. It wouldn't have come up at all if we hadn't mentioned it. If some question on raising a child did come up, the social worker had little or no comment on it. It was just as if my wife and I were conducting our own discussion group at times. You wouldn't believe that people who were so ill-prepared would be approved for adoption. I kept thinking, these are the cream of the five hundred or so who applied. These are the ones who made it past the interview.

*Molly Anne:* It's as if having babies and raising them should come naturally, and if giving birth doesn't come naturally, then at least you hold on to the instinct for raising them. You don't fog up that naturalness by reading anything.

We ended up getting the first baby of any couple in the group. We were discussing hypothetical combinations of ethnic origins. Black, Oriental, Spanish, Indian. The social worker would say, "What would you think about someone whose parents were . . . ?" and she would name two or more ethnic groups. There wasn't anything to tip us off, but at one point she said, "What would you say to a child whose mother was Caucasian and whose father was Filipino?" There was something about the way she said it. I knew she was talking about a real child.

I said, "If it's a girl, I'll take it."

She looked at me and asked, "How do you know?"

"I just had this feeling."

*Tom:* We talked for a time about what the child would look like. It could have been Spanish or aboriginal or even the grandchild of an American serviceman. Nobody had a clear picture of what a Filipino looked like. We settled on a dark Spanish type with almond eyes. Molly didn't hesitate, while all the others had doubts.

*Molly Anne:* One man said, "I could accept it, but the grandmother couldn't accept dark skin or almond eyes." I said, "If grandmother can't accept it, then find a new grandmother."

"You're kidding," he said.

"Absolutely not. When our baby comes to us it's going to be the child we're supposed to have and if any aunts or grandmothers can't accept her, we'll replace them, not the child. There are lots of elderly people in nursing homes or church groups who don't have grandchildren or even children to visit them. We'll adopt everyone we need to get the family we want."

*Tom:* The social worker asked me. I said, "I'm willing to accept a darker skinned child, but I'm enough of a realist to know that I'm not prepared to go through raising a black child in a white family. I'm equipped to handle a lot, but I know what that does to people, and if the child was very dark, I couldn't take the pressure. A dark tan or a light brown wouldn't bother me, but my wife and son are very fair. It wouldn't work. In Molly's first teaching assignment she taught the first black in town, a child with a white mother and a black father, and we saw what all three of them went through. I just know I'm not ready for that."

It turned out that the baby was born on Monday, March 13. This discussion took place Tuesday, the fourteenth. The social worker had seen her, knew the skin color. This was the first available child and our reaction determined the parents.

*Molly Anne:* We had known since January that we would be getting a child. We were eating lunch when the mail came with a letter saying that as soon as a child whose needs we met came along we would be notified. I liked the way they put it. They didn't say a child who met our needs, but the opposite. We burst into tears. We had waited so long and now it was just a matter of time. Ned was concerned because we were crying. We explained that our tears were tears of joy, that he would have a sister.

He made the classic statement, "You promised me a kitten. I'd rather have a kitten." We said he could have both.

It became a problem of preparing for a daughter of indeterminate age. We decorated the room with pink. We had to explain to Ned that his sister might be walking or talking, but she might not talk or even walk yet.

One day in April I had been out since 8:30 AM. Ned was at the sitter's. I got home at 3:55 PM. Ned was due home at 4:00. Absolutely nothing had been done to the house. It was a dreadful upside down cake. I thought, "At least I'll make the beds."

The phone rang. The voice sounded slightly annoyed. "Where have you been? I've been trying to reach you all day."

That made me angry. I was rushing around trying to get done what I should have done that morning. And here was this voice accusing me.

"Who is this?"

"This is your social worker."

I thought "Oh, wow, now I've blown it." You get the feeling after months of this that if anything goes wrong, it's all over.

"I've got some marvelous news. We have your little girl for you."

"I'll be right down."

"Oh no. Don't do that. Come tomorrow."

"I can't wait until tomorrow."

"You've got to."

"Well then, tell me about her."

She briefly described her. "She's just perfect," I said. Ironically, she turned out to be a blue-eyed blonde. Then I realized I didn't know how old she was.

"When is her birthday?"

"March."

"Which year?"

"This year." That meant my new daughter was a month old. I was told to come in at 9:30 the next morning.

I called Tom. He wasn't at the office. I had to call several times before I reached him. He came right home. We danced around the house. We were so happy. I called a friend who had been waiting very anxiously for this information. I told her how the social worker had described her and how old she was.

We had so little time to get ready. We now knew we could use the cradle. At seven that night my friend came in and dumped four bags of baby clothes on the floor. She had gone from one friend to the next to collect them. The stuff I had left over from Ned was pretty asexual. I had saved all the blue things that didn't have baseball bats embroidered on them and given the rest away. We spent the whole night doing laundry.

At CSA you are supposed to go in once to look at the child, then wait for twenty-four hours. We told them from the very beginning that that would not be possible because we knew whatever child was offered to us was our child and we wouldn't think about it. We left Ned at the sitter's. We felt that this should be a private time for parents and child—the way it would be at a hospital. He knew we would return with his sister.

We took a blanket and an infant seat with us. Our social worker had not arrived yet. We were welcomed by another social worker. "You look like you've come prepared," she said. She took us into her office and told us about our child. She asked if we had any questions.

We were not prepared to ask questions. We thought she would talk to us. Our minds were blank. Nothing seemed important except holding her. We asked a few things about her parents' ages, heights, weights, and interests. We tried to remember it all so that we would be able to tell her some day. We ended up going back several times. That day it seemed unimportant.

What was important was that she was there, a reality. We were shown two Polaroid photographs of our little girl, one taken at a week and the other at two weeks. The social worker said that she was indeed an adorable child and that our worker would be there at any moment.

She showed us to a waiting room, and I reached to collect the photographs. The social worker said, "What are you doing?"

"I'm taking the pictures of my girl," I said.

"You're determined, aren't you?"

"Yes, I am."

"But you haven't even seen her yet."

"I don't have to see her," I said.

We waited in a little room, very light, decorated with yellow and white wicker. We heard the social worker's footsteps fade down the hall. Then we heard other steps getting louder and louder until they stopped. We looked up and there was our social worker with our girl in her arms. She wore a precious pink dress and hand-knitted booties. Our worker offered her to us and waited until we were ready. Then there was a scramble to reach the door first. I won. The social worker left us alone. I held her. Tom held her. We cried. We looked at her. Our long wait was over.

There was a form on the table. We had to decide on a name, and we thought we couldn't leave until it was done, so we sat for a long time and talked it over. We had made up our minds, but now we had second thoughts. Finally we decided on a name, the social worker countersigned, and we left. The social worker had tears in her eyes as we left. She said, "Bless you and have a wonderful life together."

That surprised us because we figured that she had placed so many hundreds of babies, one more wouldn't matter, but she was genuinely moved.

When we got back to the baby-sitter's home, Ned came running up and said, "Oh, she's very nice." He poked his head in at her and she punched him in the nose. Then on our way home he pointed out that we had no diapers in the house. In all the excitement we had forgotten about them.

*Tom:* My wife always felt that an adopted child had a right to know who his parents were. Until we considered adoption I never even thought about it. Like everything else we do, we wanted to study, investigate, and find out how we actually felt about it before we took any steps.

In the beginning I wasn't even sure whether I could accept an adopted child on an equal basis. Ned was here and I loved him as much as I could. I can't say the doubts were any more than a nagging thought in the back of my head. We began to discuss it while we looked for a daughter to adopt. That gave us plenty of time. It turned out to be no problem at all.

I think our decisions about Diane are based on whether any individual should have the right to know everything about himself. Looking at it from that standpoint, I just couldn't conceive of not letting her know at some point in her life what every person has a birthright to know.

Molly and I have very open, floating discussions about most things. We've expressed doubts, enumerated why and why not, but I don't recall her ever having the same doubts I did. I thought about the effects on people's lives of a person walking into their lives after eighteen years and reminding them of an act of haste or a mistake. I had to keep eliminating each argument and running new ones through my mind.

What made the final balance on the scale for me was the fact that at the time of the adoption, the only person who doesn't have a choice is the child.

*Molly Anne:* We didn't bring this up in our group because we didn't know how others felt about it, especially the social worker. The only time we came close to mentioning it before the adoption was when the social worker asked if any of us had heard about the adoptees' rights movement. We said we had heard about it, but we didn't say that we agreed with the aims of the movement. The discussion went no further that night.

In meetings with our group after our adoptions were complete, the subject came up and the convictions were the opposite of ours, at least in the beginning. We feel that if after eighteen years our relationship is so shallow with our little girl that it can't survive contact with an outsider, then we haven't done anything right all along. It's not going to be a birth mother who breaks things up, but a boyfriend or a girlfriend. It's a circle and if our circle is solid, we can open it up and admit one or two more people. To feel differently is to say that when she gets married she's going to love her husband more than us. It's just a different kind of love, that's all.

Our friends feel very threatened by it. One woman said that if her child asks any questions about her background, she will feel she has failed as a mother. Her husband says that the child should never ask questions about his "real parents"—that's the term they use. They have three adopted children. We asked them to read up on it. We told them that when their children are of age they can come to us for help. Several of our friends have come around to our way of thinking.

I think it comes from a feeling of possessiveness about your children. Most people who have adopted have a let-down feeling. There's something in our society that says, if you're a real man you can father a baby, if you're a real woman you can give birth. And so the underlying message is that if you adopt there's something wrong with you, unless you do it as an act of kindness.

Most of our friends wouldn't even say which one of them had the problem. We found out much later that it was usually the male. At the beginning they used to say we don't know which one of us can't, yet it was an established fact that the sperm counts were low. Not that we had to know, but we had been discussing it.

I think that when you feel that way about yourself, if you don't feel secure, then a child has to affirm your identity for you, whether masculine or feminine. In that case, of course, you feel threatened by those people out there who were capable of the thing you couldn't do.

My child's birth parents will have a special place in her life but no more special than ours. It will be a different place, but we've got the envious position because we get to see her all the way through. Our friends who think that any questions will mean failure as parents want to be their children's total existence. They have staked their self-esteem on that one consideration. They could not identify at all with the need to know and we could not explain it except on an intuitive level. They would not read any books we suggested. From what we've heard, most people blame it on the adoptive parents if the adoptee wants to know. As far as we are concerned, the adoptive home, happy or unhappy, is irrelevant.

*Tom:* We have three sets of records in three safe deposit boxes containing the information Diane will need to find her birth parents. We acquired it in different ways. The first thing we did was to retain an attorney to represent us in the adoption—a man who could be trusted to get the information for us. To be sure of his intentions, we retained a lawyer who was new to adoption, one who had no stake in sealed records and who could be persuaded to think as we did. We met with the judge in chambers and he sent us with the files to the clerk. The judge didn't call down to say when we would arrive. We could have gone off into a corner and taken whatever we wanted. As it was, I was able to get a good deal of information from reading upside down and sideways while the clerk had the record open on his desk. This was a precaution against the attorney's changing his mind. We were lucky that the father signed a relinquishment so that we were able to get his name. We thought the social worker would be some help since she liked us and was nearing retirement and might allow personal feelings to override the rules, but while she sympathized, she wouldn't give any identifying information. The little she did give us helped with verification. Then we turned over what we had to a genealogist for further research.

We had a great deal of difficulty turning our opinions into a workable system for ourselves and for our children. There are the terminology differences. You can't just mix it all together and say she has two mothers and two fathers. It would be too complicated and cause too much unrest for the child. I think it would be too painful to try to cope with the idea that a mother gave her away. We use "the lady who gave you birth and the man who was with her." We try to leave them anonymous whenever possible, rather than label them. It's hard enough for an adopted person to go through life full of questions when one of them is "How could a mother give up a child?"

I feel that when the time comes for Diane to ask, we're going to have to work hard with her. I think the way we're approaching it will make it easier. Whatever age it is, ten or twelve, it's going to take a lot of the child out of her.

*Molly Anne:* I dislike the term "real parents" very much. It's ridiculous to get into who's real and who's not real. I don't like the term "natural parents" either because it implies there's something unnatural as well. I don't think there's anything unnatural about my relationship with Diane. To me it's perfectly logical, since the people who gave her birth were unable to care for her and we were, that we should do so.

There are adoptive parents who are so sensitive. They feel that after eighteen years of love, if a child isn't bound to them, they have done it all wrong. What they need to know is that there are many parent–child relationships that explode when the child becomes an adult. Our parents were not on the best terms with us when we reached adulthood. In fact, I think it's healthy to make that separation. We have to say, "I'm on my own two feet and I make my own decisions." But many adoptive parents panic when their children start living on their own. "Oh gosh. There it goes. I knew it. I wasn't the real one. If I were, she'd stay with me."

We have many warm feelings about our agency and about our social worker, but they failed in many ways. Not only did they neglect dealing with the parents' feelings for the long term, but the short term as well. They don't discuss how the child affects the husband–wife relationship, for example, something that all parents have to face. A child changes the whole ratio of the household and the schedule of your day.

All parents feel anger at some point toward their children for demanding so much time, separating them from one another and from their friends. If you want to go someplace and the child gets a sore throat, you have to care for it. Adoptive parents, I think, tend to feel more guilty about that anger because they were singled out from so many others to be parents. The agency omitted all discussion of parenting, including discipline. It isn't easy to discipline a child who was so difficult to adopt.

Another problem we had that no one seems to think of as a

problem is what to tell neighbors on the first day. Everyone wants to know about your child's background. On the first day many adoptive parents are very open about sharing that information. We discussed it well in advance and decided her heritage was not ours to hand out. To those who asked, we said, "Diane will share it with you when she's ready."

I don't know very much about Diane's birth mother. I don't ever want to have to lie to my children and I purposely avoided learning too much. We want her to have whatever she wants when she comes of age, when she's an adult and she is sure she can handle it. She may not go and get it right away, but when she does, it will be there.

We are keeping an album of photographs for her birth mother so that she can see Diane growing up. We have left word in writing at the agency that they should give her birth parents information about us if they inquire and that the agency is free to call us to keep the file up to date.

One day recently I went on a shopping trip with the other mothers in our adoption group. One of the mothers remarked that she felt sad for her child's birth mother on the child's birthday. I felt that way too on Diane's birthday and I was glad to hear her say it. Two others felt no sympathy at all. Their attitude was, "There's no reason to feel sorry for her. She gave her up." We just hope that those young women have someone to turn to on their children's birthdays.

Tom's and my fantasy is that some day there will be a Christmas dinner and all of us, both birth parents, their families and our family will get together.

*Tom:* All this suppression is based on fear, fear of being diminished because the adoptee would want to find his birth parents, fear that it will upset the lives of others. I would love to be able to sit down and shake their hands and say, "Thank you. Look what you've given us. Look at the pleasure you've given us."

# Natural Parents
## —— An Epilogue ——

The issue of adoptees' rights has grown from the lonely quests of a few isolated individuals into a national debate. By now, even many opponents of open records do admit that some adoptees have a genuine need to search, although they tend to demean searchers' motives by labeling them neurotic or pathological.

The major point of contention is now over whether the adoptee's pursuit of identity constitutes a threat to his natural parents' privacy. My feeling is that the adoptee's personal history is basic to his humanity while the secrecy of sealed records is a mistaken legal invention. Opponents of open records defend the interests of a group of people whom they know almost nothing about. The conflict over rights will have to be resolved in the federal courts, but in the meantime it is important that we learn as much as we can about natural parents and how they feel about open records.

Natural mothers and many natural fathers are profoundly affected throughout their lives by having given up their children for adoption. Each birthday of the relinquished child may recall the circumstances of adoption, the emotions that accompanied the decision, or, in many cases, the relentless pressures that led to signing away a child they really thought they could care for themselves. Doubts, guilt, and wonder may be suppressed in later years, but they do not disappear. It is no surprise, therefore, when the release that comes when parent and child finally meet turns out to be as rewarding for the natural parents as for the adoptee.

Since natural mothers are more often deeply affected by adoption *than are natural fathers, this epilogue deals primarily with the experiences of a few natural mothers as it attempts to examine the need for open adoption records for adults.*

No matter how compelling were her reasons for deciding to relinquish her child, the natural mother asks the same questions again and again over the years: Did I make the right decision? Is my child happy? Does he know he is adopted? Does he blame me? Could I have made it on my own? These natural doubts have long been a private source of pain. Only recently have natural mothers begun to reach out to one another to share their problems, and with this contact has come some relief.

The following is a letter from a young mother to the coordinator of an ALMA chapter.

I was wondering if you have any concern or respect for the natural parents. I will explain my situation. I am twenty-two years old and will be twenty-three in December. I gave up my daughter when I was seventeen. My parents left the decision up to me. They wanted me to keep her. I fed her all the time I was in the hospital. I must admit it was a tough decision. I felt that at that age it wouldn't be fair to a baby to be brought up without a father or be brought up in the company of a baby-sitter while I worked. I knew that I could spare my feelings by keeping her, but she would suffer with one parent. I knew that if I gave her up I would suffer, but if she needed a new pair of shoes she would have them. There are many wonderful people who are willing to accept another person's children and love them as their own. I knew she should have a chance for a college education if she wanted one. I knew I could not give her this. I suffered a severe depression for a year and a half after giving my child up. I do not feel that it is fair for a woman to knock on my door fifteen years from now telling me she is my daughter. I do not feel it would be fair to my husband or children either. Mentally I do not think I could handle this. I forfeited everything to give this child a loving home and a fair chance and now people like you start movements like this. Why? No child has its full birthright unless it is born gleefully wanted by both parents. Would you do me a favor and show this letter at your next meeting to those who are seeking their natural parents? I am now in tears. I will never live a comfortable life without being full of fear that the adoption records will be obtainable.

The task of responding to this earnest letter was given to an ALMA volunteer named Marilyn Springer, who is particularly interested in the problems of natural mothers. Marilyn believes that for thousands of natural mothers, the responsibilities of maternity do not end with adoption. If relinquishing a child is truly an act of love, it should follow that concern for the child's well-being does not end with relinquishment. All too often a natural mother replaces her own feelings with reasoning provided by an adoption agency.

Marilyn Springer gave birth to her own son when she was twenty-two. The child's father, whom she thought of as her fiancé, was in trouble with his Selective Service Board. When she was five months pregnant, he told her he would not marry her. Her family was shocked. When they found out that she would not be getting married, they tried to send her away to have the baby and spare them the shame. Marilyn's reply to the letter of the other young mother conveyed her own story.

I moved in with married friends who had two small children and a very tiny home. I slept on a couch behind a curtain and helped with baby-sitting and housework. Although my boyfriend didn't physically desert me, what he did was much worse—he withdrew all love and looked at me with my expanding figure and pitiful need as if I were loathsome. He spoke of the child as if it were an abstraction. He paid the bills but didn't seem to care what happened to me or the baby.

When I moved, my first action was to get medical care. I chose a hospital where they didn't require any money in advance. This was my first step toward losing my child. After attending a prenatal clinic I was referred to the psychological clinic because I was "upset."

When I asked for help in preparing to care for my child—

adoption had not occurred to me at that point—I was referred to the State Bureau of Children's Services. All counseling I received pointed to adoption as the only "good and reasonable" choice for an unwed mother. Stressing the benefits of adoptive homes, they treated me as someone who existed only as a collection of statistics and sociological clichés.

The night of the delivery, my boyfriend picked me up and drove me to the hospital. His behavior was so remote, I thought, "This is the way people treat their senile relatives." Years later I learned he spent the night smoking cigarettes and drinking coffee and worrying about me and our son.

I spent the night in terror and pain as I had been in no way prepared for labor and delivery, and didn't know what was happening or when the pain would end. I was alone in a cold room and could hear women screaming as I screamed.

They brought my son to me twice to allow me to feed him. Then they transferred me to the psychiatric ward for "observation" and forbade me to see my child. I later learned that, even before I was admitted, a doctor from the clinic had instructed them to make this move twenty-four hours after the birth.

When I asked to see my child, a doctor threatened to have me transferred to the state mental hospital. My boyfriend sent me flowers with a card that said only "take care." He wouldn't use the word love even then. He saw his son once through the glass in the nursery. His new girlfriend was with him.

After the usual five days, I was released and returned to my friends' house. My son went into a foster home. I had to return to the agency to see him. I never complained or asked about anything. I felt I had no rights. I let myself become a victim and lost my son.

During the following year I lost what self-respect I still had. I moved in with my parents and started seeing a psychiatrist who filled me with drugs and ignored my emotional needs. I suffered from post-partum depression, which nobody attributed to separation from my child. My milk kept coming in for several months after the birth, and the doctors just gave me shots to dry it up. After losing my lover and child, I was treated like an ordinary college girl who suddenly became depressed.

The agency told me again and again that I was selfishly denying my son a normal home. They told me the older he got, the less desirable he became to potential adoptive parents. They told me I would be wasting my talents by raising a child. Their version of being a single mother was all bleak, and the alternative they gave me was rosy, with no mention of the problems adoptees often face or the grief of mothers who relinquish their children. My son was over a year old, quickly becoming "unadoptable." They ignored my virtues and stressed my weaknesses. As a single mother, I'd never make it. I gave up.

I stood in front of the judge, crying, and gave away my son. Nobody threatened me or forced my hand. I did it of my own free will, believing I had no options. I hoped my son would have a good life, a good home. I felt my own life was worthless. The agency, which had constantly appeared so concerned, never contacted me again. They gave me no birth control advice, but the psychiatrist encouraged me to go out with men. However, I couldn't forget my son's father. I suppose the psychiatrist wanted me to become more worldly, since my son's father was the first man I ever loved. He didn't concern himself with the possibility of another pregnancy. At my most cynical, I think, "Unwanted pregnancies mean more business for adoption agencies."

I got involved with a drinking, drug-taking crowd. I never enjoyed it, but I went along with whatever people wanted me to do. I felt that after giving up a child, I wasn't good enough to refuse anybody anything. When I had my second child and kept him, I proved to myself that I could be a good mother.

Now I am happily married. I have my "new life." It isn't the new life they described. My husband accepts my second son as his own, and he fully supports my efforts to be available for my first son, whom I think about every day.

Now Marilyn Springer's parents have changed their minds too. They feel guilt of their own for not assisting when she had her first child. The child's father has joined her in writing a full account of his life and an invitation to the child to meet him, for inclusion in the adoption records.

The honesty of women like Marilyn Springer has enabled many natural mothers to vent feelings once buried under shame. When the young mother read Marilyn's letter, she wrote in reply:

> You have shown me a side I never realized before. You are right. You stated that I should not be ashamed. My friends know all about her, but I am ashamed in front of older people. My grandfather never stepped in my house again or allowed me in his. I loved him. He is dead now. I often have dreams of seeing him and calling him, but he does not hear. It has been nearly six years since the birth of my child. In those six years I have never been able to look my father straight in the eye. I try. It's hard. I fail and cry. My mother still condemns me. I would like my daughter to find me. Your letter has opened my eyes. Would you please share this with your group again?

Mothers who have given up their children—sometimes quite willingly, other times under duress—are presumed to have the most to lose if adoptees gain full access to their birth records. But the adoptees' movement is not only for adoptees. One natural mother who has met her grown daughter through a search conducted with the help of adoptees said: "Society has not made us responsible by allowing adoption. Now we must be available for whatever the child wishes the relationship to be. We must help other mothers and fathers accept this final act of acknowledgment. It is this that releases guilt. I know. I have been there."

Such words tell us much about what is wrong with the perennial attempt to justify sealed adoption records. A familiar pattern of refusal by social workers, judges, and clerks confronts almost every searcher. They claim that the search, if pursued, will hurt someone who is not present to speak for herself.

The adoptees are the first corner of the adoption triangle. When the first searchers began to make their demands for openness known, they were told by authorities that they were mentally ill, that sane, happy adoptees do not have any reason to search.

As more adoptees began to request information, the argument for sealed records stressed the interests of loving adoptive parents. These people, the second corner of the adoption triangle, were being slighted and made to suffer. Searchers were considered not only sick, but ungrateful to the people who had been so kind. Today many adoptees search for their natural parents with the active encouragement of their adoptive parents. These adoptive parents do not consider their children ungrateful.

So now natural parents, the last corner of the adoption triangle, are being used as the excuse to keep records sealed. If you walk into the lives of your natural parents you may destroy them. Are natural parents hurt by the search?

Most natural parents acknowledge their responsibilities in some way, whether with joy, as we saw in Mimi's story, or with detachment, as in Hannah's case. Hannah's mother's curiosity was no less intense than Hannah's. Of course there are natural parents who want no contact at all, but for obvious reasons they are difficult to meet and interview. In listening to a number of stories of such rejection, however, it is possible to gain some insight into this reluctance.

An adoptee in California told me that in the process of her search she had found her natural mother's high school yearbook. Her mother's picture carried the caption "Wants a cottage in Portland with Sam." Marriage with Sam eventually occurred, but Sam was not the adoptee's father. In the one phone conversation she had with her daughter, this natural mother claimed not to know any more about the natural father than that he was from "somewhere back East." No name or place. She had given birth during her senior year. Sam apparently married her anyway. This natural mother may, understandably, feel shame, but the adoptee is no closer to learning about her origin than she was before.

An older single woman living alone was contacted by a social worker and told that her daughter wanted to meet her. Even with no family to embarrass, the lonely woman refused. The birth had been the result of a desperate fling after the mother passed for She prefers to live out her life without a reminder of that unhappy episode.

A natural mother, quoted in *The Changing Face of Adoption*, a pamphlet published in 1976 by the Children's Home Society, said: "I gave up responsibility for my child. He was mine for only three days. Would open records mean that eighteen years later he would be mine again? I just don't like the idea that the child can go to somebody and demand to see the papers."

It depends on what we mean by "responsibility." Responsibility toward an eighteen-year-old would be entirely different from responsibility toward a four-day-old. Her responsibility would be moral and cultural, not legal or financial. Should support of a human being—particularly one's offspring—be defined narrowly?

Above all, natural parents should realize that adoptees who may be searching for them have had a full share of human experience since the day they were adopted. They are no longer dependent children and do not expect to be treated as such. Even natural parents who welcome their children may do so without understanding this. Of course, natural parents who reject their children out of hand understand it even less.

Natural fathers have special problems. Many fathers never learn of the pregnancy they caused until they meet their child. Their confusion can be very deep, particularly if the sexual contact had been casual. They did not have nine months of reflection to form an image of an infant, much less of a fully grown son or daughter. Men also tend to be more aware of their material status, more wary of potential claims on their wealth.

Several adoptees have told me that, upon meeting their natural fathers, they felt they were thought of as living testimony to wildness and virility before marriage. The embarrassment can be even deeper if the adoptee is an attractive young woman. The father knows the young woman is his daughter, but he may also see her as a beautiful stranger, an incarnation of a former lover who never aged, vulnerable to the advances of a father figure.

For every father who is confused by his role there are others who are sincerely moved and gratified upon being found. I have spoken with men whose greatest regret is that they had been shut off from any chance of helping their infant offspring. They were not required to sign waivers of rights to custody for their children born out of wedlock, as men are today before adoption can occur, but they did submit to pressure and disappeared from the lives of their children. Widowers too, like unwed mothers, were often pressed to give up their children. If a man subsequently has no other children, the appearance of a grown adoptee can become the greatest joy of his life.

While some adoptees pursue their searches with the hope of experiencing some uncritical love, natural parents reunited with a lost child cannot expect to receive unquestioning love and respect. An adult adoptee may have searched for a long time, and he has a life separate from the search. He has mature attitudes and responsi-bilities, tastes and critical standards, and wants to be treated as an adult. The search is an accelerated growth process and the adjust-ments after reunion are accelerated as well. If a natural mother persists in treating the adoptee as the infant she remembers, the adoptee may decide that the friendship isn't worth the effort.

Another difficulty commonly encountered after a reunion stems from the tendency of some natural parents to stubbornly hide the adoptee's identity from their present families. It is insulting to have a parent introduce an adoptee as a distant relative or friend. Adoptees have lived their entire lives with the facts about their origins hidden away. No one who is serious about his personal freedom wants to end up in another closet after working so hard to get out of the first one. A reasonable period of adjustment is under-standable, but not a new and permanent set of secrets.

Natural mothers who have impressed me deeply feel varying amounts of guilt and anxiety over having given up their children. Pat, an ambitious actress I met by chance, gave up her child three years ago. Like Marilyn Springer, she underwent a prolonged period of self-degradation, but her guilt and anxiety culminated when the child was born, rather than afterwards as in Marilyn's case.

Pat described herself as having been promiscuous and self-destructive long before she became pregnant. She was not the

naive girl of so many novels who gets pregnant by her first lo,
and expects marriage or some miracle to rescue her. Pat had been
going with the same man for four years, yet dated everyone who
interested her, often without learning their full names. When she
neglected to take her contraceptive pills for three weeks, Pat
became pregnant. She is forthright in admitting that her careless-
ness was part of an effort to prove something to herself. Her boyfriend did not volunteer to marry her. The child was not his, but
this was proved only after delivery. The pregnancy was too far
advanced for an abortion when she was forced to make a decision.
Pat immediately began to investigate the possibility of adoption.

She attended public clinics for prenatal care. When doctors at
the clinics heard that the child would be given up, they flocked to
Pat with offers to place the child, all expenses paid and other
gratuities. But she had already chosen an agency.

Once the child was born, a social worker read Pat a letter from
the adoptive parents, who thanked her for the baby and promised
to do their best. Agency policy did not permit direct communication of such sentiments, and the letter had to be addressed to the
social worker and read to the mother.

Pat feels today that the way she lived before the birth of her child
had been destroying her and that to some extent she had been
trying to defy her own mother, who wanted Pat to keep the baby.
Having the child and placing it for adoption was for Pat a symbolic
purging of her old self-destructive ways and a rejection of her
mother's beliefs. Since giving up the child, she has been more
disciplined than she had ever been. She feels that the child would
have interfered with her ambitions. She does not worry that the
child may show up one day to "ruin" her life. If the child does
come along, she will not see the reunion as a threat. Pat now
understands the reasons she became pregnant, the reasons she
gave up her child. She knows that her daughter will have reasons
of her own for searching.

As with every other person I have met in connection with
adoption, Pat had a great need to talk about her experience.
Every adoptee, natural parent, and adoptive parent seems to have
thoughts that demand expression. In Pat's case, her reasons for
giving up her daughter were very clear at the time, but she has

second thoughts now and will continue to have them for years. The natural mothers who are prone to painful reunions are those who have no outlet.

After listening to hundreds of these stories, I have concluded that the more a woman values the concept of her virginity, the more difficult it is to acknowledge the child she has given up. One woman had a meeting with her daughter and now corresponds with her, but she will not reveal the identity of the child to her present family although they have all met her. The mother clings to the false story that she had been married when the child was born. The adult adoptee doesn't bother to argue, but feels a kind of scorn for her natural mother's childishness.

Obviously, natural mothers suffer in many different ways. Years ago Bill Michaels' mother tried to commit suicide. Ellen loved Claude but she wouldn't marry him for ten years because he wouldn't marry her when she needed him. Sarah effectively blocked her troubles, but she had plenty of other problems to occupy her. She did something very important before she put her concerns aside: she thought through her reasons for giving away her child. Sarah told her husband about her actions to test him and she did not hide her emotions. When her son returned to her life unexpectedly, she was able to accept him as a person whose needs paralleled her own. Mother and child were able to ask and answer important questions.

As Marilyn Springer found out, sleeping around does not fill the void left by surrender of a first child. Nor does a series of bad marriages. Peter Walker's mother is a case in point. She went through three marriages to men Peter wouldn't have wanted as fathers. Peter's search spurred her divorce, not because he changed the relationship between her and her husband, but because he stirred ambitions she had sacrificed for the sake of her marriage.

There are marriages that cannot stand the revelation of a grown adoptee, so the searcher must exercise sensitivity. An unhappy marriage is, perhaps, just a legal contract, and in that respect it is no different from an adoption. If, after assessing all the particulars of their circumstances, natural parents decide they cannot accept a relationship with the adoptee, I feel they should at least show enough concern for their child to present him or her with a full accounting.

It is important to remember that most natural mothers bear a double measure of guilt. Natural mothers have not only had to hide from the stigma of immorality for having conceived, but also from the heartless act—as many see it—of having given a child away. These mothers have felt the pressure of society, beginning with the shame and rejection expressed by their own parents and continuing through delivery and postnatal care.

The guilt of natural parents very often persists to interfere with their subsequent family life. Hundreds of mothers recognize this and are placing waivers of privacy with adoption agencies and courts all over the United States. If less shame is attached now to unmarried motherhood for young women, the same cleansing freedom may extend to women who suffered in earlier times. Adoption records will not be opened tomorrow, so mothers who care must speak out. For the mother whose letter began this epilogue, all it took to ease the pain she had felt for five years was communication with an understanding woman whose experience was similar to her own.

Some mothers have found their children and observed them from a distance, without approaching to identify themselves. They say that the relief it brings to know their children are well is a boon to their spirits and their relations with their other children. Troubled by the uncertainties surrounding the act of relinquishing their children, and concerned that some adoptees live in unhappy homes, a natural mother is helped by knowing that her own child has not been damaged.

The strains of maintaining the legal fiction that life for an adopted child begins with adoption, not with birth, have obscured the true benefits of adoption. The feelings of rivalry between some adoptive parents and what one adoptive mother called "the shadow of the other woman" have twisted love into obeisance. In growing up, adoptees and non-adoptees alike experience relief when they no longer see their parents as awesome figures. Once parents are seen as human, their virtues can be admired and emulated, their faults excused and overlooked.

More than anything else, I believe the search helps adoptees achieve this perspective. The natural parents are no longer mythic, the adoptive parents no longer a race apart. Secrecy prevents this necessary step from happening gently, privately, naturally. In the best interests of the adoptee, the adoptive parents, and the natural parents, secrecy must end.

The mystery of the adoptee remains constant, as we can see in literature from the Old Testament and classical mythology to the present. Isn't it time to adjust all adoption practice to the immutable fact that some people cannot be severed from their biological and cultural heritages without being hurt?